THE SUN MYSTERY

&

THE MYSTERY OF DEATH
AND RESURRECTION

Exoteric and Esoteric Christianity

RUDOLF STEINER (1923)

THE SUN MYSTERY
&
THE MYSTERY OF DEATH AND RESURRECTION

Exoteric and Esoteric Christianity

Twelve Lectures Held in Various Cities in 1922

Translated by Catherine E. Creeger

Introduction by Christopher Bamford

RUDOLF STEINER

SteinerBooks

CW 211

SteinerBooks
Anthroposophic Press

610 Main Street
Great Barrington, Massachusetts 01230
www.steinerbooks.org

Original translation from the German by Catherine E. Creeger

This book is volume 211 in the Collected Works (CW) of Rudolf Steiner, published by SteinerBooks, 2006. It is a translation of the German *Sonnenmysterium und das Mysterium von Tod und Auferstehung. Exoterisches und esoterisches Christentum,* published by Rudolf Steiner Verlag, Dornach, Switzerland, 1986.

Library of Congress Cataloging-in-Publication Data

Steiner, Rudolf, 1861-1925.
  [Sonnenmysterium und das Mysterium von Tod und Auferstehung. English]
  The sun mystery & the mystery of death and resurrection : exoteric and esoteric Christianity : twelve lectures held in various cities in 1922 / Rudolf Steiner ; translated by Catherine E. Creeger ; introduction by Christopher Bamford.
    p. cm. -- (Collected works of Rudolf Steiner ; v. 211)
  Includes bibliographical references (p.   ) and index.
  ISBN 0-88010-608-5
  1. Anthroposophy. I. Title. II. Title: Sun mystery and the mystery of death and resurrection. III. Series: Steiner, Rudolf, 1861-1925. Works. English. 2005 ; v. 211.

  BP595.S894S6613 2006
  299'.935--dc22

                    2006011305

Printed in the United States

CONTENTS

1.

The Life of the Human Soul in Sleeping, Waking, and Dreaming

BERNE, MARCH 21, 1922

Dream life: image content and dramatic sequence. Soul exercises to cultivate Imagination, Inspiration, and Intuition. Imagination: perception of the cosmic ether. Inspiration: perception of spiritual beings. Intuition: perception of the higher hierarchies and one's own karma. Form in animals comes about through the breathing process, in human beings through the word. Christ and Ahasuerus.

2.

The Three States of Night Consciousness

DORNACH, MARCH 24, 1922

The drama of dream life. The world of deep sleep. The world of dreamless sleep. Christ and Ahasuerus.

3.

The Transformation of Worldviews

DORNACH, MARCH 25, 1922

The evolution from earlier, unmediated perception of the soul-spiritual to the perception of the corpse of nature today. Ancient Indian exercises to achieve stronger self-feeling and thinking. The strengthening of the "I"-experience among the Greeks. The meaning of Greek tragedy. The form of Dionysus. The Mystery of Golgotha. Divinized nature today and reflection on the corpse of Jesus Christ. The "unchristianness" of contemporary theology. Necessity of an enchristening of social life.

4.

Historical Changes in the Experience of Breathing

DORNACH, MARCH 26, 1922

Breathing used to achieve "I"-experience in ancient times. Sophia (wisdom): the content of inbreathing reproduced through sense experience. Inbreathing: perception; outbreathing: action. Pistis (faith): the process of spiritual outbreathing. Science and faith today. "The Kingdom of the Heavens." The meaning of Earth for Heaven.

pages 40-50

5.

The Human Being as Portrayed in Greek Art

DORNACH, MARCH 31, 1922

The four members of the human being. The legend of Niobe. The task of Greek tragedy. Fear and compassion, Catharsis. Goethe's struggle for a worldview. Meeting with Herder, journey to Italy. The Niobe group and the Laocoön group. Lessing on Laocoön. Goethe and Shakespeare. Hamlet.

pages 51-61

6.

Investigating and Formulating the Cosmic Word in Inhalation and Exhalation

DORNACH, APRIL 1, 1922

Change in in- and out-breathing processes in recent times. The head as replica of the cosmos; the circling streams of the Earth in the chest organism. The working of the Earth forces in the limbs. The mystery of the AUM. Mauthner's "Critique of Language."

pages 62-69

7.

Exoteric and Esoteric Christianity

DORNACH, APRIL 2, 1922

The Risen One. In the earliest times there was no death; experience of death came with the development of the intellect. Ahriman as the bringer both of death and the intellect. The sending of Christ to constrain Ahriman's power. Ahriman's influence on human consciousness. The Mystery of Golgotha as the expression of a struggle among the Gods. The teachings of the Risen One to his disciples. Paul's Damascus experience.

pages 70-83

11.

The Threefold Sun and the Risen Christ

LONDON, APRIL 24, 1922

Present dangers of the Ahrimanic. Human development from the old Persian epoch to the Greeks: Zarathustra, Osiris, and Zeus. The Threefold Sun in Greek and Roman culture. Julian the Apostate. Through the Mystery of Golgotha, the Threefold Sun-Being came to Earth. Old mysteries: secrets of birth. The Risen Christ: secrets of death. The uniting of the Christ impulse with the "anti-spiritual" Roman sphere. Modern science as the foundation of freedom. Cardinal Newman, his spiritual background, life, and strivings. Overcoming Ahriman through setting free thinking from its bondage to the brain.

pages 125-136

12.

Anthroposophy as an Attempt to Enchristen the World

VIENNA, JULY 11, 1922

Esoteric character of the Anthroposophic Movement. Necessary dialog with science. Gap between esoteric and exoteric. Training of the human intellect. Ahrimanic powers in the being of nature. The coming age of light. The different kinds of elemental beings and their relationship to Lucifer and Ahriman. The Rosicrucian saying.

pages 137-154

A NOTE ON THIS EDITION

The translation of this collection of lectures is based on the second German edition. Both German editions were based on transcriptions of shorthand notes by various stenographers. (Helene Finckh of Dornach supplied stenographic notes of the first seven lectures.) The German editors made a few minor, logical corrections to these notes.

The German title of this volume did not originate with Rudolf Steiner, nor did the titles of the lectures, except for the two semi-public lectures given in London on April 14 and 15, 1922. The remaining lectures were those provided by Marie Steiner when the lectures were first published, either singley in pamphlet form or in the magazines *Das Goetheanum* or *Gegenwart*.

INTRODUCTION

CHRISTOPHER BAMFORD

THE year 1922, when these revelatory lectures were given, falls midway between the end of the Great War (1918) and Steiner's death (1925), a period marking both a turning point and a difficult time for Rudolf Steiner, now between his sixtieth and sixty-first year. Intrinsically interesting in themselves, the lectures will be of particular interest to anyone wanting to comprehend Rudolf Steiner's mature understanding of his mission. They also provide unexpected illumination into his deeper purpose in bringing Anthroposophy into the world.

As always, the substance as well as the form of the lectures must be considered in relation to the context of Steiner's life and work as a whole, specifically (and especially) in relation to their own particular context—in this case, the last phase of his life. Briefly stated, his last years were defined by a polarity: on the one hand, intense outer (exoteric) engagement with the world; on the other, an equal and increasing focus on the essentials of the inner life, especially as represented by the Anthroposophical Society, which increasingly became an area of constant concern as Steiner strove to make it adequate to the great task to which the spiritual world was calling it.

Mediating between these two poles—exoteric and esoteric—common to and uniting both in a single endeavor, flowed Steiner's own personal and constantly deepening relationship to the Christ, understood as the integral gift and presence of the spirit of freedom and love to all humanity beyond all religion, sect, or dogma.

Reading these lectures in the light of what came before and what would follow after, we are given a glimpse of Steiner's dedication and devotion to our human, earthly future.

Four years previously, the Great War ended, leaving Europe and particularly Germany, disoriented. Social, economic, and political

chaos reigned. No one knew where to turn. As in previous moments
of great uncertainty (one thinks of the seventeenth century, the Thirty
Years War, and the desperate clinging to Cartesian dualism and the
doctrine of "clear and distinct ideas" over against the more participa-
tory, complex, and holistic alternative offered by such as Giordano
Bruno and the Rosicrucians), people turned again to the apparent cer-
tainties provided by extreme ideologies and philosophies.
Fundamentalisms of the left and the right swept through the social
underbelly. Since the Revolution of 1917, Communism seemed to
promise a new, international program for universal social justice, while
apparently denying human freedom; Fascism, for its part—at least in
France, Italy, and (most perniciously) Germany—seemed on the other
hand to offer a viable alternative to safeguard and enhance the old values of blood and soil (family, nation, and the traditional ways of life).

Perspicacious observers sensed with foreboding that the Great War
had revealed more than the criminal foolishness of all-too-human
statesmen and national ambitions. Among those who could see more
deeply and read the signs of the times with greater accuracy, it was
clear that modern western materialist and capitalist values—the very
values that had seemed to the nineteenth century to ensure endless
progress into a material paradise—had been called into question, if
not bankrupted. The poet Ezra Pound put it best:

> Walked eye-deep in hell,
> Believing in old men's lies, then unbelieving
> Came home, home to a lie,
> Home to many deceits, home to old lies and new infamy; . . .
>
> There died a myriad,
> And of the best, among them,
> For an old bitch gone in the teeth,
> For a botched civilization, . . .
>
> For two gross of broken statues,
> For a few thousand battered books.
>
> Ezra Pound, "Hugh Selwyn Mauberly"

As we might expect, Rudolf Steiner was among the most prescient. Already in 1917, in anticipation of the inevitable, long-expected peace, he met with a well-placed German diplomat in Berlin, Otto von Lerchenfeld. Together they prepared two Memoranda, outlining a radically new approach to the nation's socio-political, economic, and cultural life—one that would never allow a similar conflict to arise. Steiner called the approach "threefold." Just as the human being was a threefold organism composed of three systems—a bodily or metabolic system, a soul or respiratory/circulatory system, and a nerve-sense (spirit) system—with three functions (willing, feeling, and thinking), so also human society was a threefold organism, composed of three similarly interlocking systems. He called them the economic, the legal-rights, and the spiritual-cultural spheres. Giving the motto of the French Revolution—*Liberté, Egalité, Fraternité*—a new meaning, Steiner proposed that, for optimum health, each of these systems should operate according to different principles: "fraternity" (or association) in the economic sphere, "equality" in the legal-rights sphere, and "freedom" in the spiritual-cultural sphere.

Although the Memoranda were read in the highest circles, the press of events and the dead weight of convention meant nothing came of them. Once the war was over, and the ensuing chaos set in, it was clear to Rudolf Steiner that what they contained must be taken up. This meant that Anthroposophy would have to transform itself to engage its mission in a new way. It had done so before. During the first, "Theosophical," phase, the esoteric foundations had been laid. Once these were established, new art forms (drama, eurythmy, architecture, painting, and sculpture) had been created to bring the fruits of esotericism into culture in artistic form. But now, with the stakes extraordinarily high, the spiritual world called for initiation knowledge to engage and permeate society in a larger sense. A consequence of this would be a much more open face for Anthroposophy, which, as the years unfolded, would be increasingly in the glare of public scrutiny.

The years following 1918 thus witnessed a proliferation of social initiatives, whose success would depend both on Rudolf Steiner's ability to convince the public and on the ability of Anthroposophists to follow him. The epistemology and insights of spiritual science would have to be translated into accessible form, that is to say, into jargon-free, ordinary language. At the same time, everyone concerned would have to develop the presence of mind to act with dedication and responsibility. It would be a struggle on two fronts, internal and external. Both would prove difficult.

1919 saw the beginning of the work to make "The Movement for the Threefolding of the Social Organism" into a popular, political movement. While Steiner and his collaborators' heroic efforts (almost daily meetings with workers, managers, owners, as well as finance ministers and other powerful people) had some initial success, in the long run the odds were against them. There was too much confusion and too many competing philosophies and ideologies. Out of the movement, however, thanks to the initiative of Emil Molt, the owner of the Waldorf Astoria Cigarette Factory, the first Waldorf school was created in Stuttgart for the factory workers' children. Thus, the threefold seed germinated the foundation of cultural renewal through education. At the same time, other initiatives—exemplary of the threefold idea—were also planned.

1920: Seeking to create other "model institutions," further exemplifying threefold principles, Steiner formed two public corporations—Der Kommende Tag [The Coming Day] in Germany and Futurum A.G. in Switzerland—to promote economic and spiritual undertakings. Accordingly, in summer, Der Kommende Tag created a publishing house. The Waldorf school meanwhile continued to develop, as Rudolf Steiner expanded his lecturing activity to include the renewal of the natural sciences, as well as the traditional academic disciplines. Education in the largest sense was seen as a key to cultural transformation. At the same time, the practical effort to renew the sciences began in earnest. Steiner gave courses on light and warmth (giving rise to scientific research projects). At the request of doctors, he gave the first medical course (thus initiating what would become Anthroposophical Medicine). "University" courses, too, were initiated. But black clouds were forming. The businesses were taking up much more of Steiner's time than he anticipated and, though it was easy, in his name, to raise investment capital, the economic future of the companies was already looking dim. Perhaps he had overestimated the ability of others. At the same time, hardly a week went by without some public attack on Anthroposophy and Rudolf Steiner himself. Considerable time had to be taken up responding. More consequentially still, an undercurrent of misunderstanding (even lack of understanding) began to rumble through the Society, especially among older members, fixed in their ways, and less able to adapt to the changing circumstances and the new approach to spiritual science.

1921 saw Rudolf Steiner focusing his considerable energies explicitly on what was now a comprehensive program of cultural renewal. He held more "university" courses. There was a great, public scientific conference. Scientific laboratories were established. Research began into light, color, and the etheric formative forces. A pharmaceutical company was formed to create remedies. At the same time, in response to the question of the renewal of religious life, Steiner held the first two courses for priests, which would lead to the formation of The Christian Community.

In the Society, meanwhile, the clouds continued to darken. A split began to appear between the old "Theosophical" members and the new, brilliant, well-educated, young scientists, doctors, and academics who were now being drawn deeper and deeper into Anthroposophy. They demanded a more practical, existential approach. Many of the older branches and members could not keep up. They could not recognize this "new" Anthroposophy. As if this was not trouble enough, the businesses continued to sputter; and scientific research was slower than anticipated. Yet the expansion continued: new clinics were opened. Therefore, more money had to be raised. At the same time, opposition expanded to include well-known writers and scientists.

By 1922, the year the lectures collected here were given, everything came to a head. The first half of the year saw the climax of the ongoing effort at cultural renewal. Two major lecture tours in January and May, organized by a concert agency, reached about 40,000 people. There were welcome visits abroad to Holland and England, where there was greater openness. While in England, Steiner attended the Shakespeare Festival in Stratford-on-Avon and made arrangements to return in August for a "New Ideals in Education" conference to be held in Oxford.

The London Times noted:

> The famous person in this year's conference was Dr. Rudolf
> Steiner, who is distinguished at present, not only in the field of
> education, but also in other fields. In the light of spiritual science
> he gives new forces of life to a number of dogmas hitherto held
> in check, and he promises to teachers relief from unnecessary dif-
> ficulty through learning to know the soul of the child with the
> help of supersensible knowledge...Dr. Steiner was able to hold
> his audience in an extraordinary manner...as he presented state-
> ments regarding the spiritual-scientific school in Dornach and
> his own researches regarding the nature of man.

June saw the so-called "West-East Congress"—The Second
International Congress of the Anthroposophical Movement for the
understanding of the "West-East Polarity." The background was still a
Europe in shambles. Inflation was out of control. A meal cost one thou-
sand kronen; a hotel room, twenty thousand kronen. Profiteers ruled.
Abject poverty and profligate riches existed side by side. Rudolf Steiner
spoke every evening for twelve days to more than two thousand people.
His themes were knowledge and right action: "Anthroposophy and the
Sciences" and "Anthroposophy and Sociology."

The Congress was a great success. Yet it marked an unexpected
turning point. For with the second half of 1922, Rudolf Steiner
turned his attention increasingly inward to the Movement and the
Society. Public lectures gradually became a thing of the past. The esoteric work needed strengthening. It had become evident that the exoteric, culture-transforming task of Anthroposophy depended on the
seriousness and effectiveness with which inner, esoteric work was carried out at the center. And the center was weakening, losing direction
and confidence. As Günther Wachsmuth put it: "As with all living
things, expansion must be followed by concentration, openness of
heart toward the outside must be supported by constant strengthening of the center of life." The turn did not of course occur overnight.
But the reversal is clear: seventy public lectures in 1922; eleven in
1923; and only two in 1924 (excluding pedagogical lectures).

Until his death, over the next year and a half, it would take enormous strength and effort to hold together a movement whose older members had entered out of occult and theosophical streams and whose younger, philosophically and scientifically astute members now came drawn by the promise of a "free" spiritual science. Rudolf Steiner would repeatedly and increasingly inveigh against division and dogmatic—fundamentalist—sectarianism, which could only sap Anthroposophy's ability to do its work.

By this point in our narrative, Rudolf Steiner had given the lectures in our volume. The rest of the year, culminating in the burning of the Goetheanum, began to witness the turn inward—away from the public, toward inner, esoteric work—that would mark the last two years of his life and which the lectures collected here so profoundly foreshadow.

Summer and early fall, then, saw the national economy course (CW 340/341), the Oxford lectures on education (CW 305), the third priests' course (CW 344), and the so-called youth course (CW 217), in which Rudolf Steiner addressed about eighty young people. These were the brightest and best of those now turning to Anthroposophy. In November, he went to Holland, where he gave an important lecture course on the supersensible human being (CW 231), before going on to London again.

Back home in Dornach, he spoke over the Holy Nights on the emergence of natural science and the spiritual communion of humanity (*The Human Being and the World of Stars*, CW 219), which is the heart of Anthroposophy. Then—

About ten o'clock, shortly after the last members had left the Goetheanum lecture hall on the evening of December 31, someone detected the smell of smoke. The fire brigade was activated. "Smoke in the White Hall!" At first, no fire could be found. A wall was broken open. Inside it, flames raged. Hoses were set in place. Water began to flood into the fire. But more and ever denser smoke continued to rise from the south wing. The rushing drone of flames could be heard pounding between the walls. Soon the smoke was too thick to breathe. Steiner ordered everyone out of the building.

The fire raged all night. The Goetheanum—fruit of countless hours of labor and love, untold spiritual and financial generosity, and most importantly spiritual knowledge and grace as had not been witnessed for millennia—was destroyed.

Rudolf Steiner watched the destruction in silence. Only once was he heard to speak. He seemed to say, "Much work, many years." At dawn, he told those gathered around him, "We shall continue to do our inner duty at the place that is left to us," and gave instructions for the workshop to be converted to a lecture hall.

Everything would go on as before.

It is against this background that the lectures in this collection, given in the first half of 1922, must be read. Echoes of the issues at play emerge constantly between the lines.

The lectures were given to Society members and therefore give the inner teaching and indicate, indeed, what Rudolf Steiner was above all striving for: the "enchristing" of the world.

It is a remarkable collection, which truly shows us what lay behind the almost frenzied activity of the previous years and motivated Rudolf Steiner in his heart of hearts.

The first two lectures constitute a kind of introduction in the form of a veiled call to arms or return to basics. The content, as always, is naturally of great interest, but most interesting perhaps is the directness of the language. Rudolf Steiner speaks from heart to heart. (This, however, disconcerted older members, who missed the familiar esoteric lore.)

The three states of consciousness—waking, dreaming, and dreamless sleep—with which he begins, hark back to early theosophical teaching. No explicit reference, however, is made to it. Nor is any reference made to its origin in the *Mandukya Upanisad*, which describes the mystic syllable *aum* in terms of its three elements—*a, u,* and *m*—explicitly identified with the waking, dream, and dreamless sleep states.

Rather than presenting the upanisadic teaching as a theory or theosophical doctrine, Steiner proceeds virtually without jargon. He speaks existentially and phenomenologically. He builds upon recognizable descriptions of actual experiences of these states—experiences that are universal, since everyone has some experience of them. We all sleep; hence, we all have something to build on. Esoteric knowledge, "clairvoyance," is thus not something alien or added to our ordinary nature, but only an enhancement of who we already are.

The ordinary functions of waking and sleep thereby take on a new and deeper meaning. The processes of human consciousness available to all—what Steiner calls "the totality of human experience"—have initiatory possibilities. In other words, the contemporary student of esoteric science can start where he or she is. No special gift is required—only attention and spiritual practice. Steiner therefore connects these fundamental human states to the states of higher knowledge—Imagination, Inspiration, and Intuition. Having done so, he connects these in turn to cognition of the cosmic ether (Imagination), spiritual beings (Inspiration), and the beings of the higher hierarchies and our own karma (Intuition). It is only a question of waking up, or becoming conscious and being able to enter intentionally, those states we are already given by virtue of being human. In this way, the ancient teaching of the *aum* is made concrete and relevant.

This is of course only the beginning. Remarkable spiritual researcher that he is, starting from the simple fact of these three states, Rudolf Steiner shows how, as a person's consciousness expands, the lineaments of the mystery of the human soul in relation to earthly and cosmic evolution are progressively revealed. It is as if from so simple a reality that we all pass from waking consciousness into dream consciousness into dreamless sleep (and back again), the entire edifice of Anthroposophy could be constructed.

The first two lectures both conclude with observations on the Mystery of Golgotha and the meaning of Christ's incarnation for earthly-human and cosmic evolution. This proves to be the central theme—indeed, in some ways, the key—woven through the entire collection, as it is through Steiner's whole work.

The next four lectures deal in different ways with the evolution of consciousness—the evolution of "worldviews"—in relation to the universal and salvific significance of the Christ event. For ancient humanity, the whole world—human consciousness—was alive and spirit-filled. For them, our world today would be a corpse. At the same time, while we today have some sense of the "I," in ancient times this sense was much more diffuse. The "science" of that time sought to enhance "I" consciousness. Breathing exercises—as in yoga—were used for this.

Into our dying—"dead"—world, the Christ descended: "a god who truly lived in a human body." Through Christ's resurrection, Christ's being entered earthly evolution. As a result, we see the world differently. In the cross, we can see "an image of the dead natural world and the human being crucified upon it." In the Risen One, we can see "the divine spirit that people of earlier times had seen when they perceived nature as pervaded by soul and spirit." We can participate in it. Where ancient humanity experienced, "Not I but the divine spirit around me," we can experience, "Not I, but the Christ in me."

With the risen Christ we reach the heart of this volume: esoteric Christianity. The earliest human beings really did not know death. For them, death was simply a transition. They saw life as extending into worlds of soul and spirit, and experienced birth and death as transformations, not beginnings and ends. As humanity evolved, death took on ever-greater meaning. Life became bounded by a beginning and an end. Consequently, intellectuality or the forces of death developed. Behind these outer facts, lay cosmic realities. To ensure humanity's intellectual evolution, the gods or spiritual hierarchies had to work with Ahriman, "wise with regard to death...the Lord of the intellect." Were he to proceed without their participation, however, he would kill the Earth. Death would rule. Therefore, to neutralize this possibility, the gods would have to know death. A god would have to know death and overcome it. For "if no god ever experienced death, the Earth would become completely intellectualized and incapable of evolving...." The most important task for human beings is to learn to overcome death by uniting with the Christ, who overcame death. The Mystery of Golgotha teaches us that Ahriman is both part of cosmic evolution and that he is overcome. Thus, Christ's resurrection esoterically is a cosmic event: death is subsumed into life. The risen Christ is present, universally, for all humanity. It is the purpose of Anthroposophy to bring this reality into world evolution, to enable all religions and all human beings to experience the new reality. In this sense, it stands for the "resurrection" of religious life, "the esoteric resurrection of humanity's inner religious sense." Humanity's survival depends upon the "enchristing" of the world. To do so is the task of Anthroposophy.

Listen to Rudolf Steiner in the last lecture:

Today we are surrounded by dead nature, and we congratulate
ourselves heartily when we understand it. We attempt to understand not only minerals but also plants and even animals in
terms of their chemistry. In other words, we see only the dead
element in everything. The ideal of our modern way of thinking
is to replace life with dead mechanics and chemistry. We like to
imagine that a plant develops tiny little processes that, when put
together, merge into what we call "life." This is not what happens. There is real life inside that plant. We must realize that we
see death all around us because our perception is completely
death-oriented.

Christianity, which frees us from the constraints of death, tells
us that souls who do not understand the resurrection, the fact
that the Christ lives, are dead souls. We must also understand
that if we relate only to dead matter, we ourselves become dead
and ahrimanic, but if we have sufficient courage and sufficient
love for all the beings around us to relate to them directly (not
to our dead ideas about them), we discover the Christ in everything and victorious spirit everywhere. When this happens, we
may need to speak in ways that seem paradoxical to our contemporaries. We may need to speak about the individual spiritual
beings that live in the solid and fluid elements, and so forth. As
long as we avoid talking about these beings, we are talking about
a dead science that is not imbued with the Christ. To speak
about them is to speak in a truly Christian sense. *We must imbue
all of our scientific activity with the Christ. More than that, we must
also bring the Christ into all of our social efforts, all of our knowledge—in short, into all aspects of our life. The Mystery of Golgotha
will truly bear fruit only through human strength, human efforts,
and human love for each other. In this sense, Anthroposophy in all
its details strives to imbue the world with the Christ....*

Over the next two-and-a-half years, Rudolf Steiner will expend his
being on this teaching.

THE SUN MYSTERY

&

THE MYSTERY OF DEATH
AND RESURRECTION

Exoteric and Esoteric Christianity

Rudolf Steiner

1

THE LIFE OF THE HUMAN SOUL
IN SLEEPING, WAKING, AND DREAMING†

BERN, MARCH 21, 1922

W E can learn about the deeper riddles of the human soul only by considering the whole of human experience. Obviously, this experience encompasses not only the time we spend in a fully conscious waking state—that is, the time between waking up and falling asleep—but also the time between falling asleep and waking up, a time we spend in a state of obscured consciousness. Of the contents of this state, only dream activity rises to the level of ordinary consciousness.

It is important to consider this alternation between sleeping and waking from a variety of perspectives. From the perspective of everyday life, the dream state is a transition from sleeping to waking. As I have often pointed out in other lectures, it is important to distinguish between a dream's imagery and its dramatic progression. We must consider not only the dream's sensory contents but also the inner drama that unfolds. As dreams progress, tension often builds, either until a resolution occurs or until we wake up at the height of the tension. We must distinguish this dramatic progression from the images the dream contains.

For example, suppose we dream we are hiking along a mountain path. We come to a cave and go inside. As we go deeper into the cave, it gets darker and darker, and we feel increasingly uneasy, until finally we are downright afraid. We know we must go on, but we cannot because we encounter an obstacle of some sort. We feel more and more afraid. (You see how the tension is building here.)

But we might also dream something like this: We see a threatening object approaching us in the distance. As it comes closer, we make out more and more details, and our anxiety increases, culminating in a state of panic. In terms of their dramatic progression, these two dreams are the same. In both cases, the inner movement is one of mounting tension, although it is clothed in different images. We must see the images and the dramatic progression of the dream as separate elements.

In most cases, we find that dream imagery is derived from daily life. Although much of what we see in dreams is transformed or masked, we can still somehow understand that our earthly circumstances and experiences reappear in the images of our dreams.

What is actually going on when we dream as we are waking up? We know that as far as the soul-spiritual part of our being—we call it the astral body and the "I"—is concerned the time between falling asleep and reawakening is spent outside of our physical and etheric bodies.[†] We are then in a world that we cannot perceive with our everyday consciousness, because the astral body and "I" have not yet developed the organs needed to perceive it. Nonetheless, time spent outside of the physical body during sleep is full of activity. Although we cannot perceive it, the life of the astral body and "I" is actually richer during sleep than it is by day, when we are awake. Everything that plays into our dreams—for example, in the form of mounting and discharging tension, fear, anger, rage, and so on, which can be clothed in a variety of images—is with us from the time we fall asleep to the time we wake up.

In these out-of-body states, we inhabit a different world and participate in its action, just as we take part in events of the outer, physical world through our senses while we are awake. When we wake up, our soul-spiritual components, the astral body and the "I," reenter the physical body and immerse themselves in its organs. In this instant, we again become able to perceive the outer world of the kingdoms of nature—minerals, plants, animals, human physical bodies. We relate to this outer world through the physical body's soul-pervaded organs. But what happens if we immerse ourselves in the etheric body and remain at that level for a moment before taking hold of the physical body completely? When that happens, forces arising from the etheric body shape the images of a dream. These images take the form of reflections or recollections of our life.

When we fall asleep, although we have already left the physical body, some momentary abnormality may also prevent us from leaving the etheric body immediately. In this case, before passing over into complete unconsciousness, we are likewise surrounded by the etheric body's dream images. But the surging activity of the astral body and "I," which is typical of the time between falling asleep and waking up, is already beginning. Consequently, we must make a distinction between the images of the dream on the one hand, and its dramatic progression or dynamic flow of forces on the other.

I have just described this essential distinction to you in theoretical terms. On a more practical level, specific soul exercises enable us to strengthen the astral body and "I" to such an extent that we remain conscious instead of slipping passively in and out of our etheric and physical bodies. When we learn to avail ourselves of the universal cosmic ether outside of the body, we arrive at perceptions that we would otherwise not have been able to have.

The ether that makes up each human etheric body is simply a portion separated off from the universal cosmic ether, which is everywhere. At some point before birth, we gather up the portion of universal ether that becomes our etheric body. We carry this portion with us from birth to death. The universal cosmic ether, however, remains imperceptible to us unless we strengthen the astral body and "I" to such an extent that we can hold on to them even outside the physical body and even when we are not asleep. Having learned to do this, we can then perceive the etheric world outside of ourselves instead of perceiving only dream images arising from the personal etheric body.

What is actually going on here? The physical world remains spread out around us, but for the moment it does not concern us. If we have done the appropriate exercises, the physical world remains present in the way that memories are present. We can survey it; we do not step outside of it (as is the case when someone hallucinates), but it does not concern us. Having strengthened our astral body and "I," we perceive what is happening in the etheric world, not the physical world. And the etheric activity that we can now perceive is actually nothing other than what you find described in part in my book *An Outline of Esoteric Science.*[†]

In other words, once the astral body and "I" have learned to achieve the body-free state (which is also our normal state every night during sleep) and become strong enough to perceive within the cosmic ether, the world that first appears to us in images is the world of Imagination.[†] The physically perceptible world is only a small portion of the cosmos. The expanded perception of body-free consciousness also makes us aware of Saturn, Sun, and Moon existence (and so forth) in addition to Earth existence.[†] We can perceive all this in the Imaginal world. This is the first stage in learning to perceive supersensible realms.

When we learn to empty our consciousness of Imaginations, we leave the etheric world. The result is a state of soul that we can control deliberately. We dwell in images, then suppress them. This is the level of experiencing the cosmos through Inspiration. The world of Inspiration is never far removed from us. We dwell in it every night during dreamless sleep, but normally we are not capable of grasping its activity with our consciousness. In this world, our perception is not limited to images that ebb and flow, arise and die away. When images arise, this world is silent, but as they fade away an inner sounding of sorts becomes evident, adding a new mode of perception. In the Inspired world, we perceive the actions and deeds of real spiritual entities. Although for the most part *Esoteric Science* describes the evolution of the cosmos, the activity of the higher hierarchies—angels, archangels, and so on—as revealed in the cosmic ebb and flow of Imaginations is also reflected there. The beings of the higher hierarchies weave in the surging waves of activity that we experience in the world of Inspiration.

During a physical life on Earth, an essential part of our existence is truly free only during the time between falling asleep and waking up. When we enter the world of Inspiration, we realize that this essential aspect of our being is incorporated into a world of supersensible beings. In fact, from the time we fall asleep to the time we wake up, we belong to this world, and our souls move among supersensible beings. Imaginal consciousness provides a limited view of their activity. In effect, the first Imaginal level of supersensible consciousness consists of the images these beings compose for us. On the second Inspirational level, instead of simply being confronted with images of supersensible beings, we also become aware of the activity of these beings in the ebb and flow of their images. At the same time, we ourselves are part of this world of active spirituality. When we break through to this level of consciousness, we are as free of the body as we are ordinarily in dreamless sleep, when we belong to a world where spiritual deeds take place. This world shows us where we are coming from when we rush toward birth to begin a new earthly existence after having spent time in the world of spirit and soul.

Essentially, although we return to it each time we fall asleep, entering earthly life at birth means that this other world is extinguished from our consciousness. In the time between death and rebirth, as a new birth approaches, the inner activity of the astral body and the "I" becomes so weak that their deepest wish is for something to come to their rescue so they can avoid perishing in spiritual inactivity. After death, the human being develops through a series of spiritual events. In the early stages of life after death, consciousness remains very alive, and the earthly consciousness of the past life may even be remembered. By participating in spiritual activity, human consciousness ascends higher and higher. Later, however, it starts to fade. As rebirth approaches, the human being's situation can be compared to that of a person near the end of an earthly life, when memory starts to fail. The person grasps at memories, but cannot find them. Similarly, a human being approaching a new earthly life snatches in vain at reality and longs to be filled with reality. At this point, feeling and will activity are strong, but ideas have become dull. Developing any inner content becomes impossible. The human being grasps at ideas, which are more and more obscured, while the will becomes increasingly powerful. Longing drives the human being into a new incarnation, into an earthly body provided by heredity. Using this body as a tool, the individual will once again be able to think, albeit only about a physical outer world. Nonetheless, the conceptual activity that has faded away will be rekindled. Thus it is the longing to be able to think again that drives a human being into physical incarnation. During the portion of an earthly life spent in sleep, the ability to live as a spiritual being gradually develops until passage through the portal of death begins the cycle anew.

What we experience next after learning to perceive the world of Inspiration is the mystery of human life in a supersensible world between death and a new birth. The next level reveals this supersensible world as it really is. As you know, a cycle of lectures I gave in Vienna in 1914, *The Inner Nature of the Human Being and Life between Death and a New Birth*† describes some aspects of events leading up to a new earthly incarnation. As the ascent continues, we enter a state that is totally inaccessible to our ordinary consciousness. In our waking consciousness, we experience three distinctly different soul conditions: thinking, feeling, and willing. There are also three such states in sleep, but we usually distinguish only two of them, light sleep (in which dreaming can occur) and dreamless sleep. The first can be compared to *thinking* in the waking state, the second to *feeling*. Very few people realize that there is also a third state of even deeper sleep. We remain unaware of the difference between the middle state (dreamless sleep) and deep sleep, which is comparable to *willing* in the waking state. Nonetheless, this third state exists.

I am certain that some people notice the difference between these two levels of deep sleep, at least when they wake up. On some nights, we experience only the two states of dreaming and dreamless sleep and we never enter the second level of deep sleep, which is clearly different from mere dreamless sleep. Some people, however, will sometimes notice that they feel totally renewed on awakening. This is an indication that they are emerging from unusually deep sleep, from deeper levels of being. I will describe this difference in detail because, as I said, we do not take it into account in our ordinary consciousness. When dreaming, we exist outside of our physical and etheric bodies in a world comparable to the sphere around the Earth where normally invisible interactions occur between blooming plants and sunlight. These interactions elude our ordinary consciousness, but this supersensible realm is all around us. It is the realm closest to the world we experience through our ordinary waking consciousness, and we are submerged in it whenever we dream.

In deeper, dreamless sleep, we are submerged in a realm that also exists all around us, but *inside* plants. In dreamless sleep we become like spirits that can creep inside plants.

In the third stage of deepest sleep, however, we are completely submerged in the mineral kingdom. During this stage, mineral processes—the alchemists of earlier times called them salt processes—are at their most intense in the human body, and we abandon the body not simply to a plantlike level of existence but also to the mineral state.

When we become capable of consciously entering the realm we ordinarily experience only in deepest sleep, we truly understand what happens inside minerals. We usually see minerals only from the outside, but living in this world is like seeing them from the inside. I am sure you will see the relationship between this statement and one of the descriptions of the spirit land in my book *Theosophy*, where this reversal of perspective is also described.† Finding our way into this reversal means finding our way into a world where we share not only in the deeds of the higher hierarchies but also in their essential nature. We get to know the beings of higher hierarchies in ways similar to the ways in which we perceive the soul qualities of human beings in the physical world. At this stage, we leave the world of Inspiration and enter the world of Intuition. We give ourselves over not only to the activities of spiritual beings but also to the beings themselves.

This is also the realm where we experience the reality of karma. If we were to suddenly become conscious each time we entered this third stage of sleep, we would perceive our own karma. We would perceive how past earthly lives flow into our present life. In deepest sleep, we experience our karma, and carry the consequences of this experience into the physical body. The human physical body itself, however, is not suited to perceiving anything of this sort. Initially, it lacks the appropriate organs of perception. We must first develop organs for internal perception, just as we once developed eyes for outer seeing and ears for outer hearing.

Developing *physical* organs of internal perception would kill us, because the human body cannot survive when the forces that produce sense organs are turned inward. If we could turn these forces inward, we would be able to view our own karma with physical organs. In reality, we can do this only with spiritual organs, through Intuitive cognition.

Human beings cannot perceive their destinies without first performing the appropriate exercises to develop this faculty. For the sake of the argument, let us assume that this is possible. Perceiving one's own destiny without preparation would immediately trigger the desire to develop organs of internal perception, such as eyes that could see and ears that could hear inside the body. The subsequent awakening would be no ordinary waking; forces brought back from sleep would transform the body internally. In other words, the body would be killed.

Owing to the unique organization of the human constitution, its soul-spiritual portion (the astral body and the "I") can spend only a moment in the etheric body alone before it must also enter the physical body. The astral body and the "I" descend into the physical body as soon as dream imagery arises through their association with the etheric body. At that point, however, the etheric body must immediately relinquish the contents of these dream images. Anything experienced outside of the physical body cannot be taken into it. The physical body must be left as it was when the unborn human being decided to use it and its organs and descended into it from the world of spirit and soul. In this sense, our experiences on the far side of the threshold, which become imperceptible when we awaken, are a reflection of what we undergo between death and a new birth.

Observations of this sort complete our picture of the human being. They also show us that without access to physical bodies for perception, human beings in the waking state of physical, earthly existence would simply drift through life as weak, lethargic spiritual beings incapable of perceiving anything. We must recognize that human souls between birth and death exist in a state of dulled consciousness and become lucid only because they avail themselves of physical bodies. Thus, a materialistic philosophy is relatively justifiable with regard to activity on Earth, because without the physical body the soul-spiritual portion of our constitution would be oblivious to earthly life.

At this point we might ask, is it possible to get a clearer look at the time between falling asleep and reawakening, the time we spend as beings of spirit and soul? During this time, we live and participate in a world where ebbing and flowing images and sounds that rise and fade away mingle with other perceptions comparable to physical sensations of taste and so on, as described in *Esoteric Science*. If our consciousness is suitably strengthened, this world also shows us our karma, our destiny, as it unfolds from one earthly lifetime to the next.

With regard to getting a closer look at this world, it is helpful to consider a being that manifests in earthly life with an astral body but no "I" to speak of. Animals are such beings. Like us, animals sleep and wake up. When an animal falls asleep, its astral body moves out of the physical body and immediately enters the world of ebbing and flowing Imaginations and sounds. When the animal awakens, the astral body moves back into the physical body. If we look more closely, however, we can perceive Imaginations and sounds ebbing and flowing in the earthly air as the animal sleeps. When it wakes up, its respiration carries the soul back into the body on waves of air. Once in the body, the soul stimulates the senses to participate in earthly life. The soul flows in and out of the body through respiratory processes. Depending on the animal species, cutaneous respiration may also be involved.

In considering the human being, however, we must take another element into account. Even as infants, human beings possess the potential for speech. Our respiratory organs, unlike those of animals, make speech possible. Their form allows air to enter in such a way that an "I," as well as an astral body, can take possession of the physical body. We can now begin to understand how an animal's astral body first unites with its physical body. During embryonic development, the astral body moves inward, and its activity then builds up the physical body, sculpting it from the inside. (In effect, this is the opposite of the process that carries the astral body out of the physical body on the rhythms of the breath.) In other words, an animal's respiratory organs determine its physical form. The bodily shapes of different animal species are the consequences of their respiratory organs, if we take "respiratory organs" in the broadest possible sense. The shape of an animal body directly reflects how the animal's soul settles into it. For example, consider an animal with a proboscis as compared to one that has a head in which the mouth is the dominant feature. The shape of the rest of the body is based entirely on how the animal breathes, because the soul lives in the ebb and flow of air in respiration.

Having understood this, we recognize a significant truth: An animal's physical body is shaped by its respiratory organs (in the broadest sense), but the human physical body is shaped by speech, by respiration transformed into words. In humans, the Word quite literally becomes flesh; that is, we owe our human form to our ability to speak. As I described earlier, during life between death and rebirth or falling asleep and waking up, human souls belong to supersensible worlds and circulate among the beings there. If we observe human souls in this state, we find that their movements can be transmitted to the ebb and flow of air. We shape the movement of air when we speak, and air movements of the same type shape *us* when we inhale. In supersensible realms, we can actually see human souls "floating" on the ebb and flow of air. This is due to the fact that the "I" takes hold of something else in addition to air. In animals, the astral body takes hold of air, including airborne warmth. Similarly, the human astral body takes hold of air and moves on its ebb and flow, but it also takes hold of warmth, or the warmth ether. Human respiration, however, is tinged by the "I," which also moves through the cosmos on the ebb and flow of the warmth ether. Working from the inside out, the "I" becomes speech; working from the outside in, it becomes the human form. If we understand the concrete aspect of the activity of speaking, the cosmic shaping of words, we recognize what it is that shapes the human body from within, first in the embryo and then in the child. We shape our own bodies through forces that work sculpturally from within. This connection between the Word and the human form is a reality that can be perceived in the way I have just described.

Another phenomenon evident to spiritual perception is the following. If you observe a person falling asleep, the astral body remains in air-filled space when it moves out on the rhythms of the breath, but the "I" "disappears" into the warmth of the outer world. The soul lives in air and in the warmth ether during the time between falling asleep and waking up. Thus, the human constitution includes the physical human body, which actually belongs entirely to the Earth; the etheric body, which has a special connection to the Earth's watery or fluid element; the astral body, which belongs to the element of air; and the "I", which belongs to the element of warmth, or fire. When the cosmic Word moves into the human body, we can see it draw together the forces of air and warmth and combine them with the forces of water and earth. This whole interplay of forces is then developed by the internalized soul when the human being descends from the world of spirit and soul to begin an earthly existence.

Although these things are apparent only to inner vision, they exist nonetheless. It is difficult to express them in the words of any of our modern languages, which are totally adapted to materialism and a materialistic worldview. But attempts to express them are important and must become increasingly successful. What the science of initiation allows us to say about higher worlds can be clothed in words that anyone can understand—in straightforward thoughts that can make themselves at home in any human soul. While it is true that these things can be discovered only through supersensible research, understanding them does not require the ability to conduct such research oneself.

I have often tried to make this distinction clear by saying that we can both appreciate and critique paintings without having to be painters ourselves. Similarly, we can assess the spiritual science of Anthroposophy without becoming spiritual researchers ourselves, although that possibility is also open to anyone, at least to a certain extent, through the indications in *How to Know Higher Worlds,* and so forth.† But the actual practical value of the contents of spiritual truths derives not from doing the research but simply from understanding them, from taking them in.

We can all taste sugar without first learning its chemical formula. Similarly, ordinary, healthy common sense is enough to allow anyone to take in ideas derived from true spiritual research. Sugar fulfills its purpose regardless of whether we know its chemical composition, and the same is true of supersensible truths. Whether or not they serve their intended purpose depends on how they are formulated in words or clothed in ideas. For many people, it is not especially helpful to know what has to happen if we are to arrive at these truths independently. It is like telling a child, "I won't give you sugar, but let me explain its chemical composition." No doubt the child would not be satisfied with the explanation. The results of spiritual research are equally unsatisfying unless they can be formulated in ideas that allow us to experience them. If our souls can take these ideas in and enliven them, the results of Anthroposophy begin to have practical significance for our lives.

By taking in what Anthroposophy has to offer—for example, the contents of the Imaginal world—we do our healthy common sense a real favor. Our personalities become freer, inwardly more independent. This is something we desperately need at present and in the near future, because people today are extremely dependent on ideas that they take in but cannot confirm.

A simple reminder should make this clear to you. Our contemporaries who attend political meetings or gatherings of other sorts are really like sheep in a herd. Taken in by buzzwords speakers throw at them, they pursue ideas without being able to confirm them. In this respect, modern human beings are terribly dependent, automatically accepting anything preexisting as a reality. Consequently, people are becoming less and less able to think. They seem to be thinking, but their thoughts are no longer illumined by spiritual light, if I may put it like that, and the results can be very strange indeed.

For example, after a recent eurythmy performance in Berlin, a very clever critic distinguished himself by saying that because the serious pieces and humorous pieces were performed using the same movements, eurythmy is clearly not a viable artistic medium.[†] Before the performance, the organizers made a point of explaining that eurythmy is speech made visible and that its contents (the movements) are to be understood as speech. What are the logical consequences of the critic's comment? Would he not also have to say that, if an orator uses ordinary speech sounds for serious poems, the same sounds should not be used for comic poems? This is no less contradictory than objecting to using the same movements for performing humorous and serious poems in visible speech. In short, it is absolute nonsense. People read statements like this without even noticing the lack of thought. There is no thinking involved here, just mental processes running their course and masquerading as thoughts. It is absolute idiocy. An example like this shows how much inner activity people have lost. Real thought life, real thinking activity, must come from familiarizing ourselves with Imaginal activity and tracking its outcomes with healthy common sense. This effort makes us more active; we revert to being personalities in the fullest sense of the word.

It is especially important, however, to tackle the revelations of Inspired consciousness. When we use healthy common sense to retrace Inspirations that have been described to us, we gradually cease to judge things as true or false and begin to assess them as healthy or pathological. I have described this phenomenon in different ways in other contexts. When something is untrue, we have a feeling that it is pathological; when something is true, we sense that it is healthy. The logic of "true" and "false" actually applies only to the physical world. As soon as we find our way into the spiritual world, we experience truth as healthy and falsehood or error as unhealthy.

Acquiring judgment of this sort by studying Inspired truths prepares us to understand the Christ event, which occurred because humankind's evolution threatened to become unhealthy. The power that emanates from the Christ event, the Mystery of Golgotha, leads the human race in the direction of truth and healing.† Inspired truths make it possible for us to acquire a feeling for religious truths, especially those of Christianity. We again learn to understand why the being of the Christ is hailed as a "savior" in the literal sense of the word—as one who truly healed and continues to heal humankind (Latin *salvus* = "safe, healthy"). When the Mystery of Golgotha occurred, ancient clairvoyant faculties still existed, so the people of that time were able to appreciate its significance. During the four centuries after the Mystery of Golgotha, these faculties faded away until only a theoretical understanding of the event remained.

Today, through our own efforts, we must again learn to appreciate the significance of this event. Until the Mystery of Golgotha, the Christ inhabited the world we observe in dream-filled sleep and was therefore perceptible to everyone in their dreams. At that time, however, it was inconceivable—as the Mystery schools taught—to reach the indwelling being of the Christ through earthly thoughts; that is, this being could not be discovered by anyone in the waking state. This became possible only through the Mystery of Golgotha, through Christ's passage through death. Since that time, we can indeed think of him as a being belonging to earthly life. The god who left the land of dreams for physical existence has become a reality for earthly life and is therefore accessible to earthly thinking. The Christ truly is the god who learned how to die, who embraced the phenomenon of death, which is otherwise foreign to the gods. The Christ is the god who descended into human nature and into the world where birth and death exist. A divinity became human. For the sake of the Earth, the Christ became the archetypal human being, that which gives meaning to human existence.

But let us suppose that the opposite also took place. At the same time that a god became human, a human being also became a god, immortal and no longer subject to the laws of earthly life. Needless to say, while the god who descended to Earth became the most perfect human being, the human being who became divine was the most abject of immortals. And, in fact, this polarity actually does exist! Alongside the Christ, who mounted the cross on Golgotha, we find Ahasuerus, the "wandering Jew."† Ahasuerus became immortal, a bumbling god who cannot die but is condemned to wander the physical plane, where he develops singular faculties that should actually be acquired only in dreamland.

Here we confront a mystery and a tremendous spiritual reality: In addition to the god who became human, there is also a human who became a god, although, of course, his divinity made him miserable. In the Earth's evolution, this human-turned-god sustains the principle that denies the descent of the divine to the physical plane. That principle is Judaism, or the Old Testament worldview. Those who understand such matters know that Ahasuerus is an actual being and that legends about him are based on actual perceptions of him as he appeared in one place or another. Ahasuerus, the man who became a god, in fact exists. He is the guardian of Judaism in the time after the Mystery of Golgotha. Initiates know that Ahasuerus walks the Earth to this day. Because he has become a god, we cannot see him in human form, of course. Nonetheless, he continues to wander through earthly existence.

To grasp the full reality of the situation, any true historical account must include a consideration of spiritual factors. Of course, these spiritual factors often manifest only in images. The point is to realize that the images correspond to realities. It is fatuous to suggest that people should not express themselves in such images, because we make use of images whenever we speak. Consider the Sanskrit word *manas*, for example. To anyone who understands this word, the sounds convey the image of the crescent Moon holding the Sun. Those who spoke the word *manas* in ancient Sanskrit experienced the human will-being as a bowl that holds the thinking-being. All words can be traced back to images; they are merely simple, more fundamental pictures. What we express through words is not inherent in the words themselves. When we attempt to characterize more complex beings that elude description with existing words, we must resort to verbal images, such as the legend of Ahasuerus, which are simply more complex forms of expression that point to the spiritual aspect of the subject.

Anyone who rails against the use of imagery in mythology should also be incensed that human beings have developed languages for expressing content. If it is somehow wrong to use images in myths, the logical next step is to forbid people to speak, because the process of clothing a content in images is exactly the same in ordinary speech as it is in accounts of events that take place on a higher level—for example, the legend of Ahasuerus. As a spiritual being active in cosmic evolution, Ahasuerus attempts to prevent the normal next step for human beings, namely, the possibility of returning, through the Christ, to the spiritual world we left when we lost the faculty of atavistic clairvoyance.

I had two reasons for telling you this today. First, I wanted to provide accurate descriptions of the sleeping and waking states in order to illustrate how we human beings are incorporated into the spiritual world. Second, I wanted to point out that spiritual beings are active in human history and must be taken into account if we wish to understand it completely.

2

The Three States
of Night Consciousness

DORNACH, MARCH 24, 1922

W E begin by knowing only with the waking state of consciousness, which serves our daily life and conventional science. This familiar territory, however, does not unveil the riddles of existence. If life's riddles could be solved in the waking state, they would cease to be riddles because the answers would be divulged continuously and it would not occur to us to ask questions.

Even if we do not formulate them precisely, the very fact that we ponder existential questions such as "What is the deeper meaning of life?" suggests that, in the depths of our souls, we have longings that are not fulfilled by ordinary consciousness. We sense that part of our human existence arises from the more or less unconscious recesses of the soul and does not become fully conscious without effort on our part. As a result, people who do not observe life very carefully are led to develop all sorts of speculative philosophies, which ultimately remain unsatisfying. Anyone who approaches these phenomena with a certain lack of bias, however, will realize that the answers to such questions—and an understanding of life's meaning—may lie concealed in sleep, which is the opposite of the waking state. I have often discussed this subject, but it is important to return to it repeatedly, because Anthroposophy can be understood only by approaching it from a variety of different aspects.

We know that dream activity arises out of sleep and that dreams unfold in pictures. When we begin observing our dreams, one of the first things we notice is that dream images refer to objects and events in our waking life and ordinary consciousness. Although we often say that we dream about things we have never experienced, I must nonetheless emphasize that the pieces of imagery that make up our dreams are derived from ordinary consciousness. Another, quite separate element of dream activity is its drama—the tension or feelings of anxiety, delight, or readiness for action that build as the dream progresses. The drama behind the sequence of dream images derives from a deeper aspect of human nature than our day consciousness. The following scenarios will show what I mean.

Suppose you dream that you come upon a cave while hiking in the mountains. You enter the cave. The dim light gives way to darkness as you go deeper into the cave. A nameless impulse forces you to keep walking, and you begin to feel increasingly anxious, afraid of falling into an abyss in the darkness. You wake up, and the feeling of fear persists for a while.

Or perhaps you dream that you are standing somewhere and see a person approaching in the distance. As the person comes near, you see the terrifying expression on his face, and you know that he is planning to attack you. Your anxiety increases as he draws closer, and the harmless instrument he showed you from the distance is transformed—dreams are great transformers—into a horrible murder weapon. Again, your anxiety increases to the point of panic, and the fear persists even after you wake up.

These images—a cave beneath a mountain or an approaching enemy—are very different, but the psychological experience is the same in both cases, even though it is very different from anything you may have experienced in waking life. We might even say that the images are unimportant compared with the dream's inherent psychological drama. Regardless of whether the dream involves an inner impulse or something approaching from outside, the important aspect is the sense of anxiety that increases until fear jolts you awake and returns you to waking consciousness. You do not perceive the mounting forces hidden behind the dream and clothed in its imagery. The two series of images I mentioned are just examples. The same psychological content could be veiled in any number of different images.

There is something happening in the soul.† We remain unaware of what is happening on this level, but we are aware of dream images. They are the aspect of the dream that becomes conscious. The more important aspect, however, is the escalation from mild to pronounced anxiety to intense fear. In both instances, the images—the mountain, the cave, the approaching enemy, the weapon—are taken from daily life. These images, however, are merely a disguise, and this disguise can be penetrated by the Imaginal consciousness I have often described. With Imaginal consciousness, we dwell in the underlying psychological forces—such as the escalation of anxiety to intense fear—and thus discover an element that is different and distinct from the imagery that veils it.

When you are asleep, your "I" and astral body are outside of your etheric and physical bodies. Normally, you pass very rapidly through the etheric body and into the physical body as you wake up. Under slightly abnormal circumstances, however, you may be detained briefly in the etheric body before entering the physical body. In deep sleep, your consciousness is empty of dream images derived from waking life. They develop only during the transitional states—waking up or falling asleep—when you are detained in the etheric body on the way into or out of the physical body.

Imaginal consciousness makes it possible for us to be active outside of the body, in the psychological forces that underlie dreams. When through deliberate effort we achieve Imaginal consciousness, we live in a different reality; we live in the world where we are between falling asleep and waking up, when we are ordinarily unconscious. To use a physical image of what happens to the soul when we fall asleep: it is like losing consciousness as we submerge in water and regaining it only when the water's buoyancy lifts us above the surface again. When the soul leaves the body, it submerges in the spiritual world and loses consciousness; on waking up and reentering the body, it emerges from the spiritual world and regains consciousness. As I mentioned earlier, dream images arise whenever we do not enter the physical body immediately, but have time to notice the transition through the etheric body. When we learn to leave the physical body and enter the spiritual world deliberately, the images that arise are neither arbitrary nor derived from daily life. We then perceive images such as those I used to describe the development of the cosmos in *Esoteric Science*. The images in *Esoteric Science* and all similar accounts all originate in the way that I have just characterized.

So what does *Esoteric Science* contain? Well, it contains thoughts. We can think its contents. As you know, I always emphasize that mentally tracing such contents requires nothing more than healthy common sense, even though the thoughts in *Esoteric Science* are not ordinary thoughts. They are thoughts that work creatively in the cosmos. We find ourselves surrounded by such thoughts as soon as we cross the threshold into the spiritual world. They are not dream images, which arise under the very different circumstances that I have just described. They are actual experiences in the spiritual world. Imagine yourself asleep. During sleep, intense, all-encompassing events take place in your soul, but they go unnoticed because you are unconscious when you sleep. In the morning, you reenter your physical body, submerging in it immediately. You then use your eyes to see colors and light, your ears to hear sounds, and so on. You become conscious.

A transitional state is also possible: You may enter the etheric body without entering the physical body immediately. This is the state in which you experience dreams. Now imagine "waking up" from deep sleep and becoming conscious before you even enter the etheric body. If that were to happen, you would "wake up" in the external ether that fills the entire cosmos, and you would become conscious of everything described in *Esoteric Science*. If you were to become conscious in the middle of the night without returning to your physical body, you would be outside of your body; you would be able to see it from the outside. But you would also perceive the cosmology portrayed in *Esoteric Science*. I call what I describe there the "formative forces of the cosmos," or cosmic thoughts. Just as we explain individual thoughts in daily life, everything that you would see in the spiritual world can be explained. For instance, the Earth evolved in this and such a way; it went through a Moon stage, a Sun stage, a Saturn stage—in short, everything I describe in *Esoteric Science*.

This is only one of three possible modes of perception in the spiritual world. In our day consciousness we can distinguish three modes of experience—thinking, feeling, and willing.† Similarly, our night consciousness (which is usually unconsciousness) encompasses three different states. We do not spend our entire waking time in one mode of experience, and the same is true of the time between falling asleep and waking. At any given time when we are awake, we may be thinking, or feeling, or willing. Similarly, we sleep in three different states. Those who have learned to acquire Imaginal consciousness perceive cosmic formative forces, but regardless of whether or not we perceive them, we all enter the realm of these forces or cosmic thoughts whenever we fall asleep. Like submerging in water when we dive in, we also submerge in cosmic formative forces when we fall asleep.

In addition to the state where we dwell in cosmic formative forces, sleep includes two other states, just as waking consciousness encompasses feeling and willing as well as thinking. Thinking, or having thoughts, corresponds to life in the cosmic formative forces during sleep. In other words, if you become conscious during the lightest stage of sleep, you "wake up" into cosmic formative forces. This is like swimming through the cosmos from one end to the other, moving through thoughts that are also flowing forces. Normally, we bring something back into our waking life (through dreams) only from this lightest stage of sleep. But as I described earlier, the images in these dreams are in no way definitive, because the same dream can be veiled in very different images. Nonetheless, the lightest stage of sleep can produce dreams; that is, we can bring something back out of this state into consciousness, or we can at least sense that we experienced something while asleep. This is true only of the lightest stage of sleep.

But there is also a deeper level of sleep, from which no dream images rise into daily consciousness unless the soul has undergone special training. Only those who achieve Inspired consciousness are capable of knowing anything about this next stage of sleep. People with this ability are not limited to perceiving what I described in *Esoteric Science*, although, in fact, some of that carries over from Inspired consciousness. It is important to understand the transition from light sleep to this deeper sleep from which we return without dreams. Anthroposophy is essential to this understanding.

Anyone capable of perception in the worlds of light or dream-filled sleep perceives the ebb and flow of thought images, or cosmic Imaginations, which reveal cosmic mysteries. They also reveal another world to which we belong, in addition to the one where we spend our conscious waking life. We all live in this world during light sleep, although we are not aware of it. This world, which I described in *Esoteric Science*, is not static, like a two-dimensional painting, but is in constant motion. At a certain point, images begin to appear in this world. As they increase in clarity and brilliance, these images reveal specific beings behind them. And then the images fade, and we are left with nothing in our consciousness except a certain sense that the images have been suppressed. Then the images reappear. As they ebb and flow, cosmic music also becomes audible—what we call the "Music of the Spheres."[†] This cosmic music is more than just melody and harmony. It represents the deeds and actions of the beings that inhabit the spiritual world. These beings are the angels, archangels, archai, and so on.[†]

On surging waves of images, we see moving beings that work out of the spirit to direct the cosmos. The second world, the world in which these beings manifest, is perceived through Inspiration. This world is the second element of sleep, just as feeling is the second element of wakefulness. During sleep, therefore, we enter not only the world of cosmic thoughts but also the world in which the deeds of the inhabitants of the spiritual world are revealed within the ebb and flow of these thoughts.

In addition to these two states of sleep, however, a third state also exists. We usually have no inkling at all of this third state. We are aware of the existence of light, dream-filled sleep and deeper, dreamless sleep. We become aware of a third type of sleep only occasionally, when we wake up with a sense of having undergone very profound experiences during sleep. This state leaves us with a sense of heaviness that we must overcome during the first few hours of wakefulness. I am certain that a number of you are familiar with this sensation of waking from a different type of sleep. This experience points to a third type of sleep that is extremely significant for human beings. Its contents can be grasped only through Intuitive consciousness.

In light sleep, much of what we experience still resembles life in the waking state. We are still involved (although differently) in our breathing. We are still involved (although from outside, not from within) in our circulation and other bodily processes. In the second stage of sleep, we are no longer involved in the life of the body. Instead, we might say that we participate in a world common to the body and the soul. In this state, some aspects of the body still play over into the soul, in a way that corresponds to the influence of light on plants as they develop in the light. During the third type of sleep, however, something inside us becomes mineral-like. Salt deposition in the body becomes especially pronounced, and the soul lives inside the mineral world.

Suppose you could perform the following experiment: You are lying in bed, first in the state of light, dream-filled and then in the deeper, dreamless sleep in which the soul still maintains a connection to the physical body. But then you enter the stage of very deep sleep, when salt deposition increases in the body and the soul is no longer involved in bodily processes. Suppose that you keep a piece of crystalline quartz on your nightstand. In this state, you can slip inside it with your soul and perceive it from the inside out. You cannot do this during sleep of the first or second type. The contents of the first type of sleep can pass over into dreams, and if you dreamed about the crystal, you would still experience it as such. Your experience, although shadowy, would still contain crystal-like elements. If you then sank into sleep of the second type, your experience would no longer be so strictly limited to the crystal. If you were still able to dream (normally, you would not be able to, but let's assume that you could), the crystal would become indistinct and transform itself into a sphere or ellipsoid of sorts before it disappeared. But if you could dream (that is, achieve the level of Intuition) during the third, deepest stage of sleep, you would experience being inside the quartz crystal. You could following its edges up to the point and then down again. You could live inside the crystal or any other mineral, experiencing not only its shape but also its intrinsic forces.

In short, the third type of sleep takes us completely outside of the body and inserts us into the spiritual world. During this third type of sleep, we experience a third mode of existence in the essential character of the spiritual world itself. We enter into the beingness of angels, archangels, and all the other beings that we otherwise perceive only from outside, through their manifestations. In the waking state, we apply our sense-based consciousness to the outer manifestations of the gods in nature. We enter the world of images in light sleep, the world of manifestations in the second stage of sleep, and the world of revelations in the third stage. In this third type of sleep, we experience divine spiritual beings from the inside.

The three types of soul activity—thinking, feeling, and willing—that we experience during waking consciousness have their counterparts during sleep, when we flow with cosmic thoughts, perceive in them the deeds of divine spiritual beings, or are taken into the beings themselves so that our soul rests in them. Thinking, or ideation, is the clearest type of day consciousness, whereas feeling—which is always dreaming, in a way—is duller by comparison, and willing is the least conscious, sleeplike state of day consciousness. Similarly, there are three levels of consciousness during sleep. The first is the state in which our ordinary consciousness experiences dreams and higher, clairvoyant consciousness perceives cosmic thoughts. At the second level, our ordinary consciousness is empty, but Inspired consciousness perceives the deeds of divine spiritual beings all around us. At the third level, Intuitive consciousness is active within these divine spiritual beings themselves. As I mentioned earlier, the ability to submerge into minerals signals this third level of consciousness. The third type of sleep is especially important for human beings.

Let us consider the second type of sleep in greater detail. As I mentioned before, at this level of higher consciousness, you discover cosmic beings—angels, archangels, and so on—moving in images that weave and surge, appear and disappear. But you also discover yourself, your own soul—not as you are now, but as you were before birth or conception. You get to know yourself as you were in life between death and a new birth. This aspect of yourself also belongs to this second world. Each time you enter dreamless sleep, you enter the world where you lived before descending to take on a physical body.

If you enter the third type of sleep and are capable of waking up in that world through Intuitive consciousness, you experience your own destiny, or karma. You understand not only why you have particular abilities in this life as a result of the character of your previous life but also why you have been brought together with certain other personalities in your present life. From a different perspective, you can recognize your own destiny in this way only when you are also able to penetrate into the interior of minerals, when you can see a quartz crystal, for example, from the inside instead of simply from outside. (You are not allowed to cut it into pieces, of course, because if you did that, you would still be seeing each fragment from the outside.) When you are able to do this, you also become capable of understanding why you encounter a particular stroke of destiny in this lifetime.

Consider a crystal, any crystal, such as an ordinary cubic salt crystal. With your ordinary consciousness, you see it from the outside. As far as this type of consciousness is concerned, your life is not transparent. But when you learn to penetrate the crystal and see it from the inside—the size of the crystal is not a limiting factor here!—you find yourself in a world that also allows you to understand your own destiny. You are in this world whenever you enter the third type of sleep.

After the Mystery of Golgotha, after the appearance of the Christ on Earth, such things were felt especially strongly in places like Central Europe, where Christianity mingled with a strong, ancient, pagan consciousness. People knew that certain individuals died by falling into this type of deep sleep and that they would not have had to die if the Christ had come to their aid. This was said of the deaths of Charlemagne and Frederick Barbarossa. (I am simply passing on to you what people sensed about their deaths. Although to all outer appearances Frederick Barbarossa drowned, it was nonetheless reported that he died in this way. The sense was even stronger with regard to Charlemagne.[†])

Where did medieval consciousness imagine that such souls went? Into crystals, inside mountains, where they waited for the Christ to come and awaken them from deepest sleep. Legends developed on the basis of such consciousness. The union of the Christ impulse with the Earth since the Mystery of Golgotha is what now causes the angeloi, archangeloi, and so on to bring human beings back when they fall into the third type of sleep, from which they cannot return by themselves. This is a fact related to the power of Christ itself, not to personal belief in it. What the Christ did on Earth is an objective, accomplished fact, and the awakening I have just described takes place regardless of an individual's religious affiliation or faith. We will talk about the importance of faith in the next few days, but this awakening is an objective fact that has nothing to do with faith.

There is something very special about this third level of sleep. For people who lived before the Mystery of Golgotha—that means all of us, in earlier lifetimes—the third type of sleep was a very common experience. But before they sank down into it, their guardian angels appeared to bring them back. As human beings, we can find our way back out of the first and second levels of sleep by ourselves, but this is not true of the third level. This is a unique attribute of the third level of sleep. Prior to the appearance of the Christ on Earth, human beings would have died if they were not brought back from this level by angels or other spiritual beings. But ever since the Mystery of Golgotha, as I have often emphasized, the power of Christ is united with the Earth. This power is what now helps us make our way back out of the third type of sleep. Without the power of Christ, we would be unable to awaken from that level. We can slip inside the crystal, but we cannot get out again without the power of Christ. When we look behind the scenes, we realize how important the Christ impulse is for earthly existence. Let me emphasize again: Without the power of the Christ, we would be able to get inside the crystal but unable to get back out.

How is this possible? It became possible because the world of the gods themselves was imbued with a new destiny. Let me characterize this changed destiny as follows: Here in the physical world, human beings are born and die. This is not true of the divine spiritual beings of the higher hierarchies. They are not born and do not die; they are simply transformed. The Christ, who lived with the other divine spiritual beings until the time of the Mystery of Golgotha, decided to experience death, to descend to Earth and become human in order to undergo death in a human constitution and to regain consciousness after death through resurrection.

For a god to undergo death for this purpose was a very significant event in the divine spiritual world. In the history of the Earth's evolution, the single most important event was that a god became human, allowing his power to pervade the very important event of being brought back from the third level of sleep. In earthly life, the god who became human has such power that he releases human souls from the interior of crystals. In speaking of the Christ, we are referring to a cosmic being, a god, who became human. The Christ descended into the human world and into death, taking on a human body in order to participate in human destiny. But where do we find his counterpart, the human being who became a god? This god would not necessarily have to be a very good god.

When we look for the opposite pole, we are looking for a human being who freed himself from death and the constraints of the human body to become a god under earthly circumstances. This human being would cease to be mortal but would continue to roam the Earth, although not under the same conditions as an ordinary human being who passes from birth to death to a new birth. We are looking for a human being who became a god on Earth and roams the Earth forever, having acquired divinity illegitimately, in contrast to the Christ, the god who became human through legitimate means. And as you know, the Christian tradition that points to the Christ Jesus as the legitimate god-become-human also associates him with Ahasuerus, the illegitimate human-become-god† who abandoned the mortality characteristic of human nature. Thus we find the polar opposite of Christ Jesus in Ahasuerus. This is the deeper foundation and meaning of the Ahasuerus legend, which describes an actual reality that must be conveyed to people. This illegitimate god, the being of Ahasuerus, actually roams the Earth, wandering from one ethnic group to another. One of his tasks is to prevent the Jewish faith from dying out.

If we truly wish to understand history, we have good reason to pay attention to its spiritual components, to see how the forces and beings of supersensible worlds play into the sense-perceptible world. The Christ's appearance in the physical world is one example. We must also understand how the sense-perceptible world plays into supersensible worlds, and in this connection we must see Ahasuerus as an actual cosmic power or being. People have always been conscious of him roaming the Earth. He has always been present, although, of course, he cannot be perceived with physical eyes but only with a certain degree of clairvoyant vision. The legends about him are based on solidly objective foundations. We fail to understand human life when we consider it from purely external perspectives, as it is described in history books, without considering its exceptional developments.

It is undeniably true that the Christ has dwelled in us since the Mystery of Golgotha. When clairvoyant vision is directed inward, we can find the Christ within ourselves. When it is directed outward, toward human life around us, Ahasuerus, the wandering Jew, appears to us. (Most people who acquire clairvoyance are able to direct their higher vision outward in this way, and it can also happen unexpectedly when someone passes over the threshold of consciousness.[†]) We may mistake Ahasuerus for some other being instead of recognizing him for who he is. Nonetheless, it is quite possible for the wandering Jew to appear to us, just as it is possible for the radiance of the Christ to light up within us when we turn our gaze inward.

These subjects touch on a few of the many cosmic mysteries that are meant to be revealed in our time.

3

The Transformation
of Worldviews

DORNACH, MARCH 25, 1922

W E have often turned our attention to times gone by, and in a certain sense we will do so again today, with the goal of establishing several vantage points for considering human history and development. If we look back thousands of years to what I call the ancient Indian epoch, we discover that the people of that time perceived the world around them very differently than we do today (to choose a much later time).† When we look back on these ancient times, we realize that people simply did not see the natural world as we see it. They still perceived spiritual beings on every part of the Earth's surface, in mountains and rivers as well as in the clouds, light, and so on, surrounding the Earth. It would have been unthinkable for them to speak about nature as we do today. To them, that would be like sitting down with a group of corpses and saying that we are in the company of human beings. This comparison, although somewhat grotesque, is certainly commensurate with the reality of the situation. Because they perceived beings of spirit and soul in everything around them, people who lived thousands of years before the beginning of the Christian era would have experienced the nature we encounter today as the mere corpse of the natural world.

As modern human beings, when we read in poetry, myths, or legends that people once believed that beings of spirit and soul inhabited springs, rivers, mountains, and so on, we think these people of ancient times were simply exercising their imagination or applying poetic license. We are naïve to think so, however. These people really did perceive soul-spiritual beings, as truly as we perceive colors or the movement of leaves on the trees. They had direct perceptions of the world of spirit and soul, and they would have dismissed what we now call "nature" as the mere corpse of the natural world. But in some respects, a few individuals in these ancient times aspired to a mode of perception that differed from that of their contemporaries.

As you know, modern people (if their circumstances allow it) may attempt to achieve a different view of the natural world through study-ing, by becoming "educated." We call this "science;" and it involves learning terms and acquiring concepts that describe the inner work-ings of things we otherwise see only from the outside. Although such science did not exist in the ancient times we are considering here, some individuals of those times aspired nonetheless to transcend the com-mon mode of perception available to them in everyday life. But they did not study in the same way we do today. Instead, they performed certain exercises—not the ones we talk about in Anthroposophy, but exercises more closely bound up with the human body. For example, some of these exercises altered respiration and made it something dif-ferent from what it was in its natural state. Instead of doing experi-ments in laboratories, the people of these ancient times experimented on themselves, so to speak, by regulating their breathing. After inhal-ing, for example, they held their breath and attempted to experience what happened inside the body as a consequence of this change.

The character of these exercises is preserved, although in weakened form, in yoga. We should not attempt to imitate such yogic breathing exercises today. At that time, however, people experienced them as a way of achieving insights on a higher level than their ordinary percep-tions of nature, which included not only what we now see in the nat-ural world, but also the spiritual and soul aspects of natural objects. When the people of ancient India deliberately altered their breathing, these spiritual and soul elements disappeared, and the natural world appeared to them as we see it today. To achieve this altered perception, the people of those ancient times had to do specific exercises, or their view of the beings and objects around them would be full of soul-spiritual entities. They banished these entities, so to speak, by altering their breathing.

As "educated" people—I use the expression we now apply to those who aspire to insights that transcend the ordinary—these individuals strove to experience the natural world as a corpse, without the beings of soul and spirit that normally pervaded it. We might also say that when these people looked out into nature, they experienced themselves within a cosmos full of weaving, surging soul-spiritual beings, but at the same time they also felt the way we modern people feel when we are having vivid dreams and cannot wake up. That is how they felt. But what did these individuals, the educated people of their times, achieve through the special exercises that extricated them from the spiritual ebb and flow of life and deadened it until they truly felt they were surrounded by its corpse? What did they hope to accomplish?

They were attempting to achieve a stronger sense of self, an enhanced experience of selfhood. Modern human beings say "I am" all the time. "I" is a word we use very frequently, as a matter of course, from morning till night. For these people of ancient times, however, saying "I" or "I am" was not something they took for granted in their ordinary, everyday experience. It was something they had to acquire through effort. To achieve an inner experience that allowed them to say "I am" with a certain degree of truthfulness—in other words, to become conscious of their own existence—they first had to perform exercises such as the breathing exercise I described. The "I am" experience, which we take for granted, was possible for the people of ancient India only when they made an inner effort to alter their breathing. To wake themselves up, so to speak, they first had to "kill off" their environment, at least as far as their perception of it was concerned. Doing so allowed them to achieve the conviction that they themselves existed, and they could then say "I am" to themselves. This "I am" gave them something that we now take for granted, namely, the inner development of the intellect, the possibility of developing internalized, detached thinking.

If we go back in time to civilizations in which the ancient Eastern mode of perception was the norm, we find that people experienced an ensouled natural world in their daily life but had a very weak, almost nonexistent sense of self. They were completely incapable of summing up this sense of self in the statement "I am." Individuals trained in Mystery Centers[†] learned to experience the "I am," but not as a matter of course, as we experience it today. They were able to say "I am" out of inner conviction and inner experience only in moments when they altered their breathing sufficiently. In these moments, they experienced something that we modern human beings also do not truly experience, at least not initially.

If you think back to your childhood, your memories reach back to a certain point, but no further. Once upon a time, you were a baby, and you have no recollection of your inner experience at that time. At this point, your memory fails you. There can be no doubt that you existed as a baby. You crawled around on the floor and flapped your hands in the air; you were cuddled by your mother and father. But your ordinary adult consciousness retains no inkling of your inner experiences at that time. Nonetheless, you were having soul experiences that were much livelier and more intense than later ones. This intense psychological activity sculpted your brain and pervaded and shaped the rest of your body. The people of ancient India felt themselves transported into this infantile state in the moments when they said, "I am."

Try to imagine what that was like. People saying "I am" did not feel themselves to be in the present moment; they felt sent back in time to when they were babies. They felt as they had when they were babies, and from this vantage point they said to their entire later life, "I am." They did not feel at all capable of saying "I am" in the present moment; to do so, they felt that they had to go back to the very beginning of this life. From that very early point in life, the force that says "I am" then spilled over into all the years that followed. This regression was a very natural experience. But when they experienced it, the people of ancient Indian times said to themselves, "I am going back into the little head I had when I was a baby, because the soul activity within it, which now becomes transparent to me, says 'I am.'" This is still true of modern human beings. We are not aware of it, but the people of ancient times were. They said of themselves, "The soul life I knew as a baby is not of this world. I brought it with me from the spiritual world, from a time when I had no body. In this soul activity, I sensed and felt and experienced my 'I am' most strongly. I brought it with me, and it flowed out into the body I acquired and shaped. After flowing out into the shaping of my body, my own soul life occupied this body from within. Prior to living in this body, however, it had lived in the world of spirit and soul."

By regulating their breathing, the yogis of ancient India went back in time to their infancy and became aware of the time before earthly life. The world that appeared as if in memory when the "I am" flashed through their souls was not their current outer world, which they had "killed off," but the "outer world" they had known before descending into the physical, earthly world. They experienced this in the same way that we remember something that happened to us ten years ago.

Let me use a modern expression again, inappropriate as it may sound when applied to those ancient times. By "studying" to become yogis, these individuals were lifted out of their present earthly existence and into soul-spiritual existence. They owed this possibility to their studies. The everyday consciousness of the yogis was different from the one we know today, but their special training enabled them to think. This was something their contemporaries could not do; they could dream, but they could not think. The yogis, however, thought their way into the supersensible world that they had left to descend into earthly existence.

This mode of perception was characteristic of the time that preceded Greco-Roman culture in the fourth post-Atlantean epoch. In ancient Greece and Rome, the "I am" pervaded the body to a greater extent during ordinary day consciousness. It is true that the "I" was still inherent in the verb in Greek and Latin and not as clearly separate as it is today. Nonetheless, the people of those times experienced the "I" quite distinctly, and this experience became a natural, self-evident fact of inner life. On the other hand, people were losing the ability to experience the natural world as ensouled. The Greeks still experienced these two perspectives side by side, even without special training. They still experienced (though less strongly than the people of earlier times) the spirit and soul in every spring, river, mountain, and tree. At the same time, however, they were able to disregard this ensouled aspect of nature and to perceive its "dead" aspect, and they also developed a sense of self. This is what gave ancient Greek culture its particular character.

The Greeks did not yet perceive the world as we do. It is true that the concepts and ideas they developed about the world were similar to ours, but they also still took perceptions conveyed in images very seriously. As a result, their life was totally different from ours. For example, we go to the theater for entertainment. In ancient Greece, this was true in Euripedes' time, but it was barely the case in Sophocles' time and not at all in Aeschylus' time or earlier.† In those times, people had other reasons for going to the theater. The ancient Greeks had a clear sense of the soul-spiritual beings living in every tree and bush, spring and river. In the moments when they experienced these beings, their sense of self was not strong. Yoga training had been needed for the ancient Indians to develop a sense of self. For the Greeks, a strong sense of self was a natural development, but it made everything around them appear dead, so that they saw only the corpse of the natural world. This experience was exhausting and consuming for the Greeks. They realized that life consumed people, and they experienced perceiving only the dead aspect of nature as a mental and physical illness of sorts.

In the early days of Greek culture, people experienced quite vividly that daily life made them ill and that they needed something to make them healthy again. That something was tragedy. People felt they were being consumed and making themselves sick, so they went to see tragedies performed in order to be healed, to become whole again. In Aeschylus' time, people still experienced the tragedian as a physician who made exhausted people well again. The feelings stirred up by the tragedies—fear, sympathy for the hero, and so on—worked like medicine. The spectators were filled with these feelings, which provoked a crisis in them, similar to the crisis in pneumonia, for example. Overcoming the crisis then led back to health. The people of ancient Greece approached the tragedies expecting to be healed, knowing that awareness of the "I" had driven the gods out of the world around them. In essence, Greek plays depicted the gods, the divine world, and the destiny that even the gods must suffer. In short, these plays presented the spiritual forces at work behind the "dead" world of nature. For the Greeks, therefore, art still involved healing.

And when the first Christians modeled their lives on the embodiment of the Christ in the person of Jesus and contemplated the contents of the Gospels—Christ Jesus' suffering and death on the cross, his resurrection and ascension—they experienced a similar inner tragedy and healing. This is why the Christ was and still is called the Savior, the physician, the great healer of the world. The Greeks of antiquity sensed this healing in their tragedies, and humankind must now gradually learn to feel the healing in the historically enacted Mystery—or great tragedy—of Golgotha.

In ancient Greece (especially in the time before Aeschylus, when rites previously celebrated only in the obscurity of the Mysteries had already become more public), what did people see in performances of the earliest tragedies? The god Dionysus† appeared onstage. Dionysus was the god who worked out of earthly forces, out of the spiritual Earth, and therefore participated in earthly suffering. As a god, Dionysus experienced on a soul level—although not on a physical level, as was the case in the Mystery of Golgotha—what it meant to live among human beings who undergo death. The Greeks felt that the god Dionysus suffered deeply as a result of his life among humans, because he saw all human suffering.

In the earliest tragedies, the only active character on stage was the suffering god Dionysus, who appeared with a choir that recited his words so that people could hear what was going on in his soul. This is how the god Dionysus was experienced in image form in ancient Greece. The single character of Dionysus gradually gave way to multiple characters, and the plays developed into dramas. Later, humankind would experience the suffering and dying god, the Christ, as a reality, as a historic fact of humankind's evolution. The tragedy depicted on Greek stages had to take place once as a historic fact for all of humankind to see and feel. But as the time approached for this historic event, the drama that had been held so sacred in ancient Greece and experienced as healing medicine for humankind came down from its pedestal, so to speak, and was transformed into

mere entertainment, as was already the case in the plays of Euripedes.†
After human perception began to see the natural world as unensouled, a time approached when humankind would need something
other than seeing the world of spirit and soul presented in images,
namely, the actual, historical Mystery of Golgotha.

The yoga students of ancient Indian culture held their breath,
retaining it in the body in order to experience in it the indwelling
divine "I"-impulse. As students of yoga, people experienced the divinity in themselves through respiration. This was no longer the case in
later times. By then, however, human beings had learned to think,
and they thought that the soul enters the human body on the breath.
For yoga students, this was a matter of direct experience, but the people of later times said, "And the Lord God ... breathed into his nos-
trils the breath of life; and man became a living soul."† When the people of Jewish antiquity said this, they experienced it somewhat
abstractly instead of concretely, as the people of still earlier times had
been able to do. Different aspects of a newer mode of perception
always develop in different parts of the globe, so while the Hebrews
of ancient times were expressing this experience in words, the Greeks
were experiencing the existence of the divine within the human being
through their drama in the form of images. In the Mystery of
Golgotha, this drama became an actual event in cosmic history.
Meanwhile, the dramatic images became increasingly separated from
the reality, devolving into mere images, just as the direct experience
of respiration yielded to thoughts expressed in words. The whole constitution of the human soul underwent a change.

It became quite natural for human beings to perceive the outer
world as dead, devoid of divinity. Human bodies, as part of the outer
world, were also seen as devoid of divinity. In consolation, however,
the Christ descended into this dead world as the god who truly lived
in a human body. Through the resurrection, the Christ impulse
passed into all of earthly evolution. As a result, human beings became
able to develop a different type of perception. They realized subcon-
sciously that they saw the world as a corpse. By contemplating the
crucified Christ Jesus, they beheld an image of the dead natural world
and the human being crucified upon it. And when they looked up to

the Risen One, whom the disciples and Saint Paul experienced as the living Christ in the cosmos, they saw the divine spirit that people of earlier times had seen when they perceived nature as pervaded with spirit and soul. In earlier times, people saw many different spiritual beings—gnomes and nymphs, sylphs and salamanders, and all of the other beings of the earthly hierarchies.[†] With the dawning of the intellect, however, people felt the urge to integrate this natural diversity into the single figure of the dead Christ Jesus on the cross. In him, they saw all the spirituality they had lost in the outer world of nature. They gazed on all this spirituality when they contemplated the fact of the Christ's resurrection as the divine spirit who overcame death. Every human soul can now participate in Christ's essential being. People had lost the ability to see the divine spirit in the natural world around them, but they had gained the ability to rediscover this divine spirit in the Christ, by contemplating the Mystery of Golgotha.

Loss of the ability to behold the spirit in nature gave human beings a sense of self, the possibility of experiencing "I"-ness. If nature had not become "dead" to human perception, we would never have internalized the "I am" experience. Having done so, however, we needed a spiritual outer world, which the Christ supplied. Nonetheless, it remains true that the "I am," "I"-ness, is founded on the corpse of the natural world.

Let me draw you a diagram.[†] At an earlier stage in humankind's development, human beings experienced the natural world around them as pervaded with soul and spirit. This is what Saint Paul sensed. Let us attempt to reconstruct it. All around him was the corpse of what people had once beheld in ancient times as the body of the divine, of the soul-spiritual element. These people beheld mountains in the same way that we behold our own fingers today. It would not have occurred to them to think of mountains as lifeless natural objects, just as it would not occur to us to consider our fingers lifeless objects. They recognized the Earth as a being of spirit and soul and mountains as its "limbs." Later, however, when people experienced the internalized "I," they perceived nature as dead. We would all stand here like hermits[†] on an Earth that is unensouled and devoid of divinity if we could not look to the Christ. But instead of contemplating the Christ only from the outside, we must now take him into the "I." Like St. Paul, we must lift ourselves out of the everyday "I am" and say, "Not I, but the Christ in me."†

In later times, people still experienced the natural world, but they also experienced the personal "I am" in contrast to unensouled nature. For this, however, they needed the image of the god-in-man, which they experienced in the god Dionysus as presented in Greek drama. Still later, when the cross was erected on Golgotha and the drama became a historical reality, people again experienced ensouled nature in the "I am." What human beings had lost reappeared within them and radiated outward: "Not I, but the Christ in me."

What was the experience of the people of ancient times? They would not have been able to formulate it in words, but what they experienced was "Not I, but the divine spirit around me, in me, everywhere." We lost this all-embracing experience, found it again within ourselves, and can now consciously formulate the originally unconscious experience as "Not I, but the Christ in me." The original reality—experienced unconsciously when human beings were not yet conscious of the personal "I"—became a conscious fact in the experience of the Christ within, in the human heart and human soul.

I hope these inadequate pictures will help you see what we must now formulate in ideas. Can you see the whole cosmos filled with the Christ-Spirit and how that spirit then descends from the cosmos to come to life within human beings? We must not underestimate the importance of sunlight in our lives. Without sunlight all around us, we would be physically unable to live. Perhaps this will help you understand when I tell you that in the ancient times I talked about today, human beings experienced themselves as light within light. They felt that they belonged to the light. Instead of saying "I am," they perceived the rays of the Sun striking the Earth and did not make a distinction between themselves and those rays of sunlight. Wherever they perceived light, they also perceived themselves, because they experienced themselves as existing within the light. Whenever light appeared, they felt themselves carried on waves of the Sun's light.

This same light worked within the being of the Christ. Through him, it also works in us. Of course, there are many passages in the Bible that compare the Christ to light, but our anthroposophical attempts to draw attention to the reality of this connection are usually rejected by academic theologians, who choose not to know about such things. It is very significant that a professor of theology named Overbeck,† who lived in Basel and was a friend of Nietzsche's, once wrote a book about whether contemporary theology was actually still Christian. His intention as a theologian was to make the point that true Christianity still existed in the 1870s, but he also acknowledged that much of what passed for Christianity, including theology, had become unchristian. That is what he attempted to prove in his book, and he succeeded to a considerable extent. Anyone who takes the book seriously puts it down convinced that although many aspects of Christianity persist to this day, modern theology has become unchristian. When theologians talk about Christ, their words are no longer Christian.

If opinions such as Overbeck's were taken as seriously as they should be, people would realize not only the need for anthroposophical activity today but also the significance of Anthroposophy as a whole. Above all else, people would become aware of the responsibility we have with regard to anthroposophical knowledge, which actually ought to form the basis of all contemporary knowledge, especially our understanding of society. When people learn that the light of the Christ lives in them ("the Christ in me") and experience it fully, they learn to see themselves as more than just part of the corpse of the natural world. The antisocial, asocial character of modern times is due to the perception that human beings belong to nature's "corpse." We can achieve a true perception that will unite all human beings in universal brotherhood-and-sisterhood, a view that will once again imbue humankind with real moral impulses, only if we come to understand the words "Not I, but the Christ in me"—in other words, when the Christ is rediscovered as an active force in human interactions. Without this insight, we cannot move forward. We need it; we must discover it. If we achieve it and then continue to move forward, all of our activity in society will become imbued with the Christ.

4

HISTORICAL CHANGES IN THE EXPERIENCE OF BREATHING

DORNACH, MARCH 26, 1922[†]

IN recent times, there has been much discussion about the difference between faith and knowledge. In particular, the case has often been made that Anthroposophy (based on what it tells us) should be considered a matter of belief, faith, or conviction rather than a science or body of knowledge. Essentially, however, all distinctions of this sort are based on a widespread lack of insight into faith as it emerged in the course of human cultural development and on an almost equal lack of understanding of what knowledge is.

Faith, along with everything associated with the word, dates back to very ancient times in human evolution when the respiratory process played a much greater role in human life than it does now. Owing to our present psychological makeup, we do not pay attention to our breathing. We experience nothing in particular when we inhale and exhale.

Breathing was important to all the belief systems of ancient times. As I pointed out yesterday, the Old Testament describes how God blew the breath of life into the first human being. You will also recall what I said about how the people of ancient India attempted to achieve higher knowledge by regulating their breathing in specific ways. These attempts made sense at that time, when people in general paid more attention to their breathing and perceived more than just the "dead" natural world that we perceive today. They beheld soul-spiritual activity in all the objects and processes of the natural world, in every spring, cloud, river, or gust of wind. They attempted to become more and more conscious of their breathing by controlling inhalation and exhalation and by holding their breath. They developed self-awareness, that is, the experience of the "I" or "I am," by controlling their breathing. At that time, however, perceiving and experiencing the breath was part of everyday life. In our ordinary consciousness, we modern human beings have almost no idea of what that was like. Let me try to describe it for you.

As you know, the breathing process can be broken down into inhaling, holding one's breath, and exhaling. Usually, breathing is regulated naturally, but the yoga masters regulated it deliberately. Just as modern students of science cultivate ways of thinking that are different from everyday thinking, the people of those ancient times cultivated a way of breathing that was different from everyday breathing. Let us focus first on the ordinary breathing, not cultivated or yogic breathing. I can do this best by drawing you a diagram.†

In the human chest, we can distinguish between inhaling, holding one's breath, and exhaling. When the people of ancient times inhaled, they felt the spiritual aspect of the beings and objects of the outer world enter them along with the inhaled air. In this stream of inhalation, they experienced gnomes, nymphs, and all the other soul-spiritual beings of their natural environment.† When they exhaled, expelling air, these beings again became invisible and disappeared into the natural world. In inhalation, people recognized the soul-spiritual element in the natural world outside them and felt connected to it, and its effect was somewhat similar to intoxication as we know it. People became intoxicated with the soul-spiritual aspect of their surroundings. When they exhaled, they grew sober again. Their life involved a constant alternation of intoxication and sobriety as they interacted with the world around them.

There was more to this experience, however. When the yogis of ancient India inhaled and felt themselves become intoxicated with spirit and soul, they also felt soul-spiritual beings filling them and uniting with their bodily existence. This feeling rose quietly from their breathing into their heads. This sensation could be expressed somewhat like this: "I inhale the soul-spiritual aspect of the world around me. It fills my head. I sense it; I perceive it as I hold my breath. When I exhale, I relinquish this sensation of spirit and soul."

This awareness of breathing, however, was intimately related to everyday life. Consider this very simple example: Here is a piece of chalk. Today, as we look at a piece of chalk, we develop the intention to pick it up, and then we do so. That is not how it worked for the people of ancient times. They looked, inhaled the spiritual aspect of the chalk, then picked it up only as they exhaled. For them, inhalation was bound up with observation and exhalation with activity. This rhythmic interaction with the environment survived into later times but without the vital, perceptive consciousness of ancient times. For example, think back to how threshing was done by hand in the countryside not so very long ago: Look, strike with the flail; look, strike; look, strike. The rhythm of the activity corresponded to a specific breathing pattern.

| inhaling | = | observing |
| exhaling | = | doing |

At later stages in humankind's evolution, this experience of inhalation was lost to human perception, and we began to perceive only the aspect of respiration that rose into the head.[†] In ancient times, people perceived how inhalation, which was intoxicating for them, continued into their heads and united with sense impressions. Later, this was no longer the case. We have lost the awareness of what happens in the chest when we breathe. We no longer perceive our breathing streaming up into our head because our sense impressions have grown stronger, extinguishing what rises into the head on the breath. The respiratory process, which was very active in the hearing and seeing of people of ancient times, is now subsumed by seeing and hearing. In modern humans, the activity of hearing and seeing is so strong that it deadens our breathing. We no longer experience the intoxicating effect of nymphs, gnomes, and undines rising into our head. These flitting nymphs, hammering gnomes, and weaving undines are now overwhelmed by visual and auditory sense impressions.

In ancient India, human beings were much more aware of the breath flowing into the head and of everything carried on the breath. This awareness persisted into the next cultural epoch, when people still perceived something of the activity of gnomes, undines, and nymphs in connection with perceptions of sound, light, and color. In the later stages of this next civilization, however, everything perceived through respiration was lost. Some individuals remained slightly aware that cosmic spirit and soul had once entered human beings through their breathing. These individuals gave the name *sophia*† to the results of the joint activity of sense perception and breathing. Breathing itself, however, was no longer perceived. Its spiritual content was deadened—"paralyzed" would be a better way to put it—by sense perception.

This mingling of ancient and modern modes of perception was especially characteristic of ancient Greek culture. The Greeks had no concept of science as we know it today. If they had been told about the type of science that is taught in modern universities, they would have felt as if their brains were being stuck full of tiny needles. It would have been incomprehensible to them that anyone could derive satisfaction from such a science. They would have experienced it as damaging to the brain, because they still attempted to perceive remnants of the comforting expansion of the intoxicating breath that streamed into them mingled with sense perception. The Greeks perceived activity in the head as I have just described it, and they called it *sophia*. Those with a special fondness for developing *sophia* in themselves called themselves philosophers. Originally, the word "philosophy" pointed to an inner experience. Our horribly pedantic "cramming" of philosophy as a way of learning about this body of knowledge was unknown to the Greeks. To them, the word "philosophy" expressed the inner experience of loving *sophia*.

In the human head, the process of inhalation is absorbed into sense perceptions. Similarly, the rest of the body absorbs the process of exhalation. In the metabolism and limbs, bodily sensations and experiences flow together with exhaled air, just as sense perceptions stream into the head together with intoxicating inhaled air. The sobering element of exhaled air, which extinguishes perception, flows together with bodily feelings that arise during walking or working. Activity is linked to exhalation. When the Greeks were active, they felt spirit and soul moving out and away from them. As a result, whenever they did anything or worked on anything, they felt as if they were allowing spirit and soul to flow into what they were doing. They experienced it like this: "I take in spirit and soul, which intoxicate my head and unite with what I see and hear. When I am active, I breathe out, and this element of spirit and soul leaves me. It goes into my work, into whatever I am hammering or grasping. I release spirit and soul from myself and allow them to stream into whatever I am doing."

This is how the early Greeks felt, but then the perception of exhalation as a sobering process faded until only a trace of it remained in Greek culture. In early Greek times, people still felt that their activity transmitted spirit to the things they handled. In the end, however, this perception of exhalation was paralyzed by internal bodily sensations, such as work-related strength, warmth, and exertion or fatigue, just as the flow of inhalation toward the head had been paralyzed. People no longer experienced exhalation as tiring. Instead, when they exhaled, they felt strength or energy pervading their bodies. This strength inside the human body was *pistis*, or faith, the feeling of divine strength that allowed one to work.

sophia   =   the spiritual content of inhalation, paralyzed by sense perception

pistis   =   the spiritual exhalation process, paralyzed by bodily sensations

Thus, wisdom and faith flowed together in the human being. Wisdom streamed toward the head, and faith lived in the entire body. Wisdom was the content, or ideas; faith was the power of this content. The two belonged together. That is why the only Gnostic work that has come down to us from antiquity is entitled *Pistis Sophia*.† *Sophia* or wisdom is diluted inhalation; *pistis* or faith is condensed exhalation. In later times, wisdom continued to be diluted until it became science. Similarly, inner strength continued to condense until people felt only their bodies and lost the awareness of what faith, or *pistis*, actually is. Because they no longer sensed the connection between *sophia* and *pistis*, people began to separate understanding based on outer sense perceptions from subjective, internal belief. First there was *sophia*, then *scientia*, or ordinary science, a diluted form of *sophia*. We might also say that *sophia* was originally an actual spiritual being that humans experienced as inhabiting their heads. Today, only the ghost of this spiritual being remains, because science has become the ghost of wisdom. Actually, we should fill our souls with this statement as if with a meditation: Science is the ghost of wisdom. And, on the other hand, what we call "faith" today is not *pistis*, the inwardly experienced faith of antiquity. "Faith" has become a subjective element closely bound up with egoism. It is a condensation of the faith of ancient times. Before faith became condensed, human beings had an objective sense of the divine element in themselves. Today faith rises up only subjectively, so to speak, like smoke from the body. Just as science is the ghost of wisdom, so to speak, modern faith is a condensed, heavier version of the faith people once experienced.

If we succeed in seeing the relationship between faith and wisdom, we will not make superficial judgments such as "Anthroposophy is a system of beliefs, not a science." People who say this do not know what they are talking about. They are unaware of the connection between faith and wisdom, ignorant of the historical fact that they were once experienced inwardly as one. In our circles, we must present history as it is presented nowhere else. Where else do we hear history talked about in this way? Where else do we hear what breathing once meant to human beings when it was a totally different experience from what it has become today? A formerly very real element of spirit and soul has become very abstract; conversely, the ensouled body has become robustly material. Where else can people become aware of these historical changes?

At a certain point in the evolution of faith, it became necessary for humanity to incorporate a very specific content into ancient beliefs. In ancient times, human beings experienced the divine through faith, in their exhalation, but eventually all awareness of this aspect of the respiratory process was lost. People were no longer conscious of a divine element leaving their bodies and entering the objects they handled. This divine element in human consciousness needed to be reenlivened, and this was accomplished by taking in an idea with no outer, earthly reality. On Earth, the idea of the dead rising up out of their graves has no outer reality. The Mystery of Golgotha has no real content if we consider Jesus' biography only up to his death. There is nothing special about that. Modern theology sees nothing special in Jesus anymore, because it describes him as a human being who underwent certain experiences and then died. There is nothing special about that. The actual mystery begins only with the resurrection, with the living activity of the Christ-Being after his physical body passed through death. To paraphrase the words of Paul, those who do not accept the idea of the resurrection into their consciousness do not receive Christianity at all. Consequently, modern Christian theology is really unchristian, since it studies only Jesus, not the Christ. Of necessity, Christianity entails an idea based on a reality that is not immediately accessible to our senses. This idea lifts human beings into the supersensible world.

The people of ancient times were lifted into the supersensible world by an inner experience. Yesterday I described how yoga students were taught to experience the inner life of a baby. In the first impressions of babyhood, they experienced the soul activity that shapes the human body—something that people otherwise know nothing about. Simultaneously, however, they also became conscious of all of their life prior to birth or conception, when the human soul lives in the spiritual world before descending to take on a physical body. Today, all that remains of this experience is an idea expressed in the Gospels (Matthew 18:3): If you do not become as little children, you cannot enter the kingdoms of the heavens. This verse is based on ancient experience, but at the time of its writing it had no real life anymore. It simply recalled a time when people could go back to their infancy to experience the heavenly kingdoms, the realms they left to descend into physical existence through birth. Most people today do not imagine anything of consequence when they read about the "heavenly kingdoms" in the Bible or any other ancient source. Their line of thinking goes something like this: "All right, I know what kingdoms are. We have kingdoms on Earth. England is a kingdom. The globe is divided into nations, many of which are or used to be kingdoms. So there are kingdoms in the heavens, just like kingdoms on Earth."

But if we imagine heavenly kingdoms as divisions similar to earthly kingdoms, we get no real sense of the meaning of the modernized expression "kingdoms of the heavens." The Gospels say that we cannot see these kingdoms, also known as the kingdom of God. Most people do not think about it at all; they simply hear the sounds of the words.

A diagram may help.† If the Earth is here in the center, the "heavens" of ancient times are the surrounding sphere of the cosmos. But what was meant by "kingdom"? Clairvoyants do not simply "see" in higher worlds; they also "hear" the cosmic Word that rings and resounds through the heavens. If we cannot become as little children, we cannot hear the Word that speaks out of the heavens. When we imagine earthly kingdoms, we should secretly imagine the rulers of those kingdoms speaking or singing so loudly that their voices are heard throughout their domains. The old custom of preceding proclamations with trumpet blasts in the four directions is a symbolic expression of the "resounding" that makes the kingdom a reality. The kingdom was not the geographical area people inhabited; it was the content of the laws proclaimed by the trumpeting angels.

All this, however, had become nothing more than a memory related to the world of ideas or thoughts. Another, more will-related idea was needed, because the will is what accompanies us when we pass through the portal of death. When we die, the energy we have developed in our will accompanies us, along with its content of cosmic thoughts. And the new idea of the risen Christ—the One who lived, although his earthly body died—addresses our will. This new and powerful idea was no mere recollection of babyhood. It pointed in the other direction, toward death, and appealed to the element that accompanies human beings through the portal of death. Thus, the dawning of the Christ idea, the Christ impulse, is founded in human evolution. It was a necessity of human evolution.

This is an extremely important, even essential, truth. Consider what Hindus or Buddhists experience in perceiving, feeling, and thinking about the world of minerals, plants, and animals. They take all this with them through the portal of death to enrich the knowledge of the gods in the supersensible world. But what do Christians take through the portal of death? They take their experiences of social relationships and connections with other human beings—in other words, everything that we can experience only as human beings in the company of other human beings, through human fellowship on Earth. We might say that Buddhists take Earth's beauty with them through the portal of death, while Christians take Earth's goodness. These contributions are complementary, but Christianity represents an advance over Buddhism in that it allows the heavenly worlds to understand earthly social circumstances.

But many people on Earth today know nothing about the Christ. To be quite honest, most of those who do know about him are poorly informed. Nonetheless, they do learn something about the Christ, even if modern materialism prevents them from developing the right ideas and feelings about him. Many people on Earth, however, are still living under older, different forms of religion. Yesterday, I hinted at the very significant question that we now confront. I said that the Mystery of Golgotha is a fact: The Christ died for all human beings. The Christ impulse is a power that is present throughout the Earth. In this objective sense, regardless of their awareness of him, the Christ is present for Jews, pagans, Christians, Hindus, Buddhists, and so on. Ever since the Mystery of Golgotha, the Christ has actually been present in the forces of earthly and human evolution. Nonetheless, it does make a difference whether an individual lives in a Christian area or a non-Christian part of the globe.

We can learn to understand the difference it makes only if we see the connection between a person's earthly life and the subsequent life between death and rebirth. Hindus or Buddhists die without having absorbed any ideas or feelings about the Christ during life on Earth. What they then take with them into the supersensible world beyond death is limited to what they learned about outer nature here on Earth. The heavens would know nothing about the natural, earthly world if they were not informed by human beings who enter the heavenly kingdoms through death. This is the only way the supersensible worlds learn about earthly minerals, plants, and animals. But those who know about the Christ—and especially those who know that the Christ lives in them, that is, those who have experienced Paul's "not I, but the Christ in me"—take with them not only information about the Earth itself but also information about human beings and their life in earthly bodies. The contributions of Christians complement those of Hindus, Buddhists, and others. Of course, it is becoming increasingly necessary for human beings to carry all of the mysteries that they can experience in and through themselves into the heavens. In other words, it is becoming ever more important for human beings to be completely imbued with the Christ. Above all else, however, it is important for the heavenly worlds to receive what human beings can experience only through Christianity and in the company of other human beings on Earth.

No matter how many people non-Christian tyrants behead, they have little impact on the world of the afterlife. Their impacts are limited to their victims' outer impressions of abhorrence and so on, which are carried through the portal of death. But the lack of love that develops as a consequence of miserable social conditions in Christian areas, for example, and false socialism's misjudgments of societal relationships are of great significance for the supersensible worlds we enter after death. People carry their terrible experiences of socialism's destructive power into the afterlife, along with the loveless human relationships of the age of materialism. Through Christianity, we are meant to carry our experiences of the outcomes of human activity in earthly evolution into supersensible worlds. Our thoughts about the risen Christ, about the being who underwent death, yet still lived, make us capable of carrying what we ourselves cultivate on Earth into spiritual worlds.

People who do not want their social deeds to be carried through death have a horror of acknowledging the risen Christ. The sense-perceptible world, however, is connected to the supersensible world, and it is impossible to understand the one separate from the other. We must again learn to understand what happens on Earth by understanding cosmic spiritual events. Instead of talking in abstract terms about spirit and matter, we must learn to contemplate how human beings once felt themselves connected to the divine spirit and soul of the cosmos through breathing. We must learn to experience cosmic soul and spirit in ways appropriate to our times. There is no other way to restore health to societal circumstances on Earth. Loudly demonstrating for improved social conditions accomplishes nothing. The decline will continue unless we become increasingly and truly imbued with the Christ, which is not simply a matter of intoxicating ourselves with words that have no content. In ancient times, it was appropriate for people to become intoxicated through breathing, but it is not appropriate for modern people to become intoxicated with words. Words must pervade us with wisdom, like *sophia*.

This is how Anthroposophy relates to modern issues of social importance. The very name "Anthroposophy"—*Anthroposophia*—is meant to express the fact that Anthroposophy is a new wisdom.[†] In ancient Greece, the individual "I" became a matter of common experience, and *sophia* was human wisdom, because human beings were still full of the wisdom of light. Our modern science is the mere ghost of *sophia*. Consequently, we must now appeal directly to the human being, the *anthropos*, through Anthroposophy. We must make people aware that Anthroposophy comes from human beings, shines out of human beings, develops out of human beings' best forces. In this sense, Anthroposophy enlivens human existence on Earth. Our experience of Anthroposohy is more spiritual but no less concrete than the ancients' experience of *sophia*. Anthroposophy, like *sophia*, is also meant to evoke *pistis*, the faith that completely pervaded human beings. Thus, Anthroposophy is not a belief system but a true body of knowledge that provides individuals with strength of a sort that was formerly accessible only through faith.

5

THE HUMAN BEING AS PORTRAYED IN GREEK ART

DORNACH, MARCH 31, 1922

T ODAY we will recall the forces that hold the members of the human constitution together during earthly life; in the next few days this knowledge will open up perspectives on several cosmological subjects. We know that the earthly human being consists of a physical body; an etheric body, or body of formative forces; an astral body; and an "I." Let us see how we can characterize these four members.

The physical body is the result of earthly forces working for the human being, so to speak. In the time between death and rebirth, we have no physical body to deal with. In last week's lectures, I noted that when the human spirit and soul descend from supersensible realms into physical incarnation, they are near death (spiritually speaking), and must restore their inner forces by experiencing life in a physical body. But the body that unites with what is descending from the world of spirit and soul is born out of the forces of the Earth. Until shortly before achieving physical incarnation, the descending human being also has no etheric body, or body of formative forces. Like the physical body, the etheric body unites with the soul-spiritual members of the human constitution, but its relationship to the cosmos is different from that of the physical body.

When we study the physical human body, we discover that the forces in it are those of planet Earth itself. When we approach the human etheric body, or body of formative forces, however, we find that its forces are cosmic forces, the forces of the entire universe. In contrast, the human astral body and "I" contain forces that are not encountered in the external space of the universe. In other words, they do not belong to the world to which the Earth belongs.

In reality, the Earth is constantly attempting to absorb and incorporate the physical human body. In contrast, the tendency of the cosmos is to disperse the etheric body, or body of formative forces, throughout the universe. From the time we fall asleep to the time we wake up, the physical body attempts to unite with the Earth, to become earthlike, to become completely earthly, while the etheric body, or body of formative forces, attempts to disperse throughout the universe. In the morning, when we wake up and rediscover our physical and etheric bodies, it is as if our physical bodies were saying to us: "All night long, the Earth tried to absorb me. The Earth wanted to turn me into dust. I remained a physical human body only because the forces of your 'I' and your astral body had held me together yesterday and on previous days, and these forces persisted through the night." Similarly, the etheric body says: "I kept my human form only because resembling you has become a habit. Actually, the forces of the cosmos wanted to throw me to the four winds during the night while you were sleeping and outside of me."

Each time we wake up, we must make an effort—through the "I"—to take possession of the physical body again in the right way, because it actually attempts to escape from us during the time we spend asleep. With appropriate training, the "I" can learn to sense its own efforts to repossess the physical body each morning, and the astral body can sense how it has to reshape the etheric body in its own image, forcing it back into human form to counteract the nonhuman form it attempted to assume during the night. We might say that during sleep the physical body loses the inclination to be possessed by the "I" and the etheric body loses the inclination to assume human form and starts to disperse. In actuality, the shape of the physical body is entirely the result of the activity of the "I" in the human constitution. Owing to the makeup of the modern human soul, we are relatively unaware of having to repossess our physical bodies anew each time we wake up. We have little sense of the physical body's efforts to escape or the etheric body's attempts to disperse.

But suppose that at one time people still clearly perceived the daily struggle between the "I" and astral body on the one hand and the physical and etheric bodies on the other. As a consequence of this awareness, people would also have known that being forced to leave one's physical and etheric bodies very suddenly would produce quite different results than would either dying or falling asleep.

Under normal earthly circumstances, people leave their physical and etheric bodies because the physical body (whether as a consequence of illness, injury, or age) has become so earthlike, so determined to unite with the Earth, that the "I" can no longer take possession of it. But what if the "I" and astral body suddenly had to leave a physical body and an etheric body that were totally healthy and uninjured? What would happen if this physical body and this etheric body retained the tendency to be possessed by the "I" and to resemble the astral body, respectively?

In ancient times, people realized that in such a case, the physical body would not be able to disintegrate automatically. The physical body's tendency to disintegrate develops only through illness or old age or the like. If the astral body and the "I" were unexpectedly forced to leave a completely healthy human physical body and the body of formative forces within it, the physical body would retain its humanlike form, because the tendency to be possessed by the "I" and astral body would still be inherent in it. The human form of the physical body would persist, immobilized like a sculpted column. Because the separation was so sudden, the physical body would not be able to disintegrate, and the etheric body would not be able to lose its resemblance to the astral body.

In fact, the early Greeks were aware of this possibility. You all know the Greek legend about Niobe,† who had seven healthy sons and seven healthy daughters. Proud of her fecundity, she taunted the mother of Apollo and Artemis, who had only two children, although she was a goddess. Niobe refused to worship the goddess, and the gods took their revenge. Niobe was forced to experience the sudden death of her seven daughters and seven sons, killed by the arrows of Artemis and Apollo.

As she gazed in pain on the corpses of her fourteen children, Niobe's "I" and astral body united with what she saw around her. You are probably familiar with the pediment sculptures† that show Niobe turned into a pillar of stone, surrounded by her dead sons and daughters. Niobe had been so full of vitality that she mocked the goddess for having only two children. Because of this tremendous inherent vitality, her physical body could not lose its penchant for her "I," and her etheric body could not cease to resemble her astral body, so Niobe became like a pillar of stone.

To the mode of perception common at that time, this imagery expressed a deeply felt truth. People sensed that if Niobe had lacked the excess vitality that prompted her to mock the goddess Latona,† she would have been able to die normally, and her physical body would have disintegrated. But she lived so completely in her physical body and was so full of vitality that she rebelled against the goddess. The genius of the Greek people recognized that her body was pre-served as if in stone because the "I" and astral body had left it so rap-idly and unexpectedly. When we look back through humankind's evolution, we find that art always reflects feelings consistent with the mode of perception of the time in question.† It would be possible to give many other examples.

Let us take another look at the need to repossess the physical body upon awakening, to prevent it from becoming earthlike. If Niobe had been able to sleep, even for one night, after her painful experience, she could no longer have been turned into a sculpted pillar of stone, because during sleep her physical body would have absorbed forces that would have made it earthlike, that is, capable of disintegrating. Each morning, the human being must repossess the physical body, and the astral body must reshape the etheric body in its own image to make it assume human form.

At a certain time in the development of Greek culture, people had a vivid sense that taking hold of the physical body each morning required the development of specific forces. Because the Greeks knew this and took a certain satisfaction in possessing physical bodies, they felt a need to strengthen the forces that take hold of the physical body and the forces that shape the etheric body in the image of the astral body.

If we could be fully conscious of the process of awaking each morning, we would experience anxiety about being able to reenter the physical body in the right way. We would be afraid of not being able to get back into the physical body properly. In ancient times, the Greeks were very familiar with this fear. They also knew that the etheric body tends to dissolve into four separate figures each night—one like an angel, one like a lion, one like an eagle, and one like an ox. Each morning, the astral body has to exert itself to synthesize these four parts of the etheric body into something truly human. The Greeks loved their life in the physical and etheric body. I have often quoted a saying that comes down to us from ancient Greece: "Better a beggar on Earth than a king in the realm of shades,"† that is, in the underworld. Because they loved physical existence, they longed to be able to take possession of their physical body and shape their etheric body more effectively. Greek tragedy developed as a result of this longing. Aristotle's definition of tragedy,† though formulated at a much later time, still clearly indicates that the Greeks did not think of their tragedies in the way that we do. Your experiences may be different, but in my experience modern people think that dramas are created so that when we are finished dealing with everything the day brings, we can sit down for a few hours and watch a more or less exciting presentation of events that are not real but just dramatic images.

This is not how the Greeks thought in the early days of the development of their culture. To the early Greeks, all life was one, and all of their contributions were intended to be living parts of the wholeness of life. In their view, the purpose of tragedy was to help people take hold of their physical body and shape their etheric body properly. Tragedy evolved in a way that allowed the audience to feel fear and compassion. Experiencing fear gave them the strength to take hold of their physical body properly each morning, and feeling compassion made their astral body stronger and more able to shape their etheric body properly. Show us tragedies, said the Greeks, so we can take hold of our physical body and build up our etheric body suitably, so we can be human in the fullest sense of the word. The function of tragedy in Greek culture was to help people become as fully human as possible in earthly existence. Of course, this means that the people of these ancient times knew how the human spirit and soul, the "I" and the astral body, interacted with the human physical and etheric bodies.

Aristotle defines tragedy as the imitation of an action that arouses fear and compassion and thus allows people to experience catharsis or crisis. "Crisis" and "catharsis" are terms borrowed from ancient Greek medicine. Even as Aristotle was developing the more pedantic aspects of Greek culture, he still sensed the healing, strengthening effects of tragedy.

The term "catharsis" originated in the Mysteries, and I have often explained what it meant in that context.† Now let us attempt to understand what it means in ordinary life. When the interior of the body becomes sick or diseased, pain appears. This pain would not be present otherwise. People who are ill begin to sense their bodies in a way that does not happen in a body that is normal or healthy. When nothing hurts, we think we are healthy. When we are ill, something begins to hurt, to cause us pain. This pain simply means that the "I" and astral body are not hooked into the physical and etheric bodies in the right way. When healing sets in, the "I" and the astral body again gain the strength to hook themselves in the right way. They have more power over the physical body than they did before healing began.

Suppose someone has a respiratory disease. That person's "I" and astral body are not properly engaged in the etheric and physical parts of the lungs. When the illness is cured, they are again properly engaged. During the "crisis," the "I" and the astral body, though not properly engaged, acquire the strength they need to shift into position properly when the crisis is past. What the Greeks saw in tragedy was the inner counterpart of this outward sequence of events.

The Greeks felt that if human beings did nothing at all to help themselves, the "I" and the astral body would become increasingly estranged from the physical and etheric bodies. They were concerned that they would become less and less capable of repossessing the physical body and shaping the etheric body, and they knew that to cure this weakness, they had to disengage the "I" and astral body so that they could then reengage correctly. They did this by allowing the astral body to be filled with perceived suffering, or compassion, and the "I" with fear. The "I" became stronger by surviving this fear. (Of course, it always did survive, because the fear was only an image.) The "I" that overcame fear instead of succumbing to it experienced a crisis or catharsis, which gave the "I" more strength to repossess the physical body each morning. Similarly, through compassion—that is, by watching suffering—the astral body gained strength to shape the etheric body ever more exactly in its own image. As the figure of Niobe illustrates, the Greeks saw their art as intimately related to the human constitution and to forces that are meant to work in human development and education. The Greeks were especially concerned with the concrete aspect of human existence, and since Greek times we have become more and more estranged from this concrete aspect.

This phenomenon becomes especially apparent when we consider Goethe's early life. At an early age, Goethe learned a great deal about the world around him and about how people think and feel. He also learned a great deal about how important and intelligent people attempt to explain the world. But for Goethe, as I have explained before, it was a struggle to grow into his cultural surroundings. We know that our culture has become ever more intellectual in the past four or five centuries, and Goethe was sensitive to the intellectualism that had overwhelmed everything. In *Faust*, he expressed his feeling that philosophy, law, medicine, and even theology had become intellectual.[†] Faust studied all these subjects, but the pure thought behind all of them seemed estranged from reality, and he attempted to experience his connection to the spiritual foundations of existence. In essence, this is also what Goethe felt. Of course, Goethe had to concede that modern human beings were becoming intellectualized, which was the whole point of that stage of cultural evolution. For Goethe, however, it was a struggle, because thinking does not embrace the whole human being. Goethe felt estranged from the exclusively thought-based culture he saw developing around him.

The young Goethe knew about Lessing[†] who was one of the people who welcomed intellectualism enthusiastically and as a matter of course. Goethe could have encountered Lessing in Leipzig but deliberately avoided him as being too intellectual and uncannily reasonable. This was not the case with Herder[†], whom Goethe met later in Strassburg. In spite of his intellectualism, Herder was full of feeling and arrived at a comprehensive worldview that Goethe found accessible.

In the same vein, we can also understand why Goethe eventually had to get out of the cultural milieu of Weimar, where everyone insisted on thinking about everything. After a certain point, he was ready to jump out of his skin, although outwardly things were going extremely well for him. He was adored at the court of Weimar, but he could not stand it anymore. The whole situation was too much for him. Even Herder, of all people, was studying Spinoza, and Spinoza's work[†], although it is a marvelous piece of mental machinery, had the effect of estranging people from the real world.

And so Goethe, hungering to experience the whole human being, had to get away and go to Italy. By experiencing the Greek art of antiquity, he hoped to discover what it meant to be human in a way that had become foreign to his contemporaries. Essentially, Anthroposophy is nothing more than a response to a similar quest. It originates in the longing to discover the true and complete nature of the human being, in attempts to answer the questions "What does it mean to be human?" and "What is our role in the greater life of the world?"

Through Anthroposophy, contributions to civilization that emerged from a feeling for the human being as a whole (such as Greek tragedy or a work of art such as the Niobe group) become increasingly transparent to us. We understand that Niobe's soul—that is, her "I" and astral body—is completely outside her body, in the sphere that is the source of her pain. Her soul has been torn out of her body by pain, but the body remains imbued with the forces of her "I" and astral body. Its form persists, held together by these forces, and Niobe is turned into a pillar of stone.

Now let us consider the opposite case: Suppose there is no intrinsic reason for the "I" and astral body to leave the physical and etheric bodies, but they are forced out because the physical and etheric bodies are destroyed from outside. In this instance, the physical and etheric bodies assume a form that reflects the forces of destruction on the one hand and the expulsion of the "I" and astral body on the other. This is not what happened to Niobe when her soul suddenly abandoned her physical and etheric bodies in the shock of witnessing the death of her children. It is what would have happened if these bodies had been so damaged that her "I" and astral body were forced out. In that case, we would not see the physical and etheric bodies hardened into a pillar of sculpted stone. Instead, we would see the fruitless attempts of the "I" and astral body to shape the etheric body. We find this situation depicted in another Greek sculpture, the death struggle of Laocoön.† We can understand this sculpture if we fill ourselves with the understanding that it depicts a situation that is the opposite of what happened to Niobe. The physical and etheric bodies are being destroyed from outside and are struggling with the "I" and astral body, which are being forced out. We can see this phenomenon in the very shape of Laocoön's mouth and face and the position of his arms and fingers.

It is important to find our way to such insights again, for if we do not, the intellectualism of modern times, although profoundly justified, will estrange us from reality, from a true perception and understanding of the natural world.

In the age of intellectualism, this ability has been completely lost. Essentially, our intellectual age has no clue about how to approach the human being as a whole and has therefore lost its standard for assessing everything else. This is what Goethe felt so strongly and why he could not stand to see intellectualism invading art. He could not stand the whole genre of Corneille and Racine because of the impact of the intellect on drama.†

Let us recall Lessing's attempts to explain the Laocoön group. With all due respect for the great Lessing, these explanations are very superficial. Essentially, he says that when a poet talks about Laocoön, it is all right for Laocoön to scream, because we cannot see him with his mouth open, but when a sculptor portrays him, we see how he opens his mouth, and this is not acceptable. It is very superficial to say that poets can do thus and so but sculptors must do something different. With all due respect for Lessing's exceptional accomplishments, we must be clear that his treatment of the Laocoön group does nothing to explain the figure of Laocoön on the basis of the underlying situation, which would require a certain ability to investigate the forces that hold the four members of the human constitution together.

Goethe instead turned to Shakespeare, whose work is full of natural contradictions. For this reason, Goethe felt that in some respects, Shakespeare spoke for the cosmic spirit itself. This was something Goethe felt very deeply, because he was so aware of the dawning of intellectualism. As you may recall, I have often said that Hamlet—Shakespeare's Hamlet, of course, not the Hamlet of Saxo Grammaticus†—can be seen as a student of Faust. Goethe had a vivid image of the ten years in Wittenberg when Faust was leading his doting students around by the nose and pulling his students' legs. Of course, Goethe did not say all this in detail, but just listen to Faust say, "Thank God, I have now studied philosophy, jurisprudence, medicine, and—to my salvation—theology."† No doubt Faust would have felt very uncomfortable when Hamlet, who has just spoken to the ghost of old Hamlet himself, mentions the land from which no traveler returns! Hamlet's memory must have been exceedingly poor if he could not remember just having talked to his father, who had indeed returned from that unknown land.

Of course, intellectuals would never write anything of the sort. I have known such people to say that *Hamlet* was not written by a single author, that someone other than Shakespeare wrote Hamlet's monologue ("To be or not to be") and then the pieces were combined. They say similar things about Homer, of course. It is very easy to "prove" that *Hamlet* could have been written by a whole series of different people, because it is full of contradictions, just like reality. Goethe felt reality to be very rich compared with the poverty of intellectualism, and it is in this sense that we must understand him.

By the way, if you want to enjoy all the terrible contradictions in *Hamlet*, I recommend reading Rümelin on the subject of Shakespeare. Rümelin† was a famous professor in Heidelberg, and his essay goes into Shakespeare's shortcomings in great detail. There is a difference, however, between Shakespeare's art, which Goethe experienced so deeply that he called the artist an interpreter of cosmic spirit, and what is passed down to us as science (even in places like Heidelberg).

If you compare what Lessing said about Laocoön to Goethe's beautiful comments on the same subject, of course you will find that

Goethe came to no real understanding of the issue, because Anthroposophy was not available to him. Nonetheless, Goethe made significant progress compared with Lessing's arguments. Goethe's work is full of traces of what I presented here today. For example, his comments on the Laocoön group can be seen as a starting point for what.I said about it. We are quite justified in saying that if Goethe's approach is carried forward in the right way, it leads straight to Anthroposophy.

6

INVESTIGATING AND FORMULATING THE COSMIC WORD IN INHALATION AND EXHALATION

DORNACH, APRIL 1, 1922

SOME spiritual realities are best approached through images. In such instances, it is necessary to refrain from using habitual abstract and intellectual ways of speaking. This is certainly the case with regard to what I will attempt to present today.

To make the matter as simple as possible, suppose we have an enclosed space with a window. Let us assume that light enters through this window and fills the space. Let us also assume that the space is filled with all sorts of transparent, domelike surfaces that reflect and transmit the light in a great variety ways. Now suppose I allow steam to flow up through this enclosed space. There is also an outlet that allows it to flow out again. This steam, however, is a living, feeling being. It flows into and through the sparkling light that is changed, reflected, and transmitted by the domes. Before leaving the enclosed space, the steam perceives whatever it can, "touching" and feeling the light to internalize an image of it.

Now let us assume that after a while, when the steam flows out, it is able to reproduce and express what it experienced inside the enclosed space in the sparkling, flickering light. Imagine an instrument of some sort that allows the steam to express its experience by sounding musical notes or the like.

Now consider a different version of this picture. Instead of the enclosure, we have the interior of the human head; and instead of the window, the eye, which admits impressions of light. The transparent domes of the first illustration are the nerves and convolutions of the brain. Instead of steam, imagine inhaled air streaming up and sensing everything that sparkles and flickers in the brain as a result of in-streaming light and is then shaped into thoughts. The air then streams downward, following the spinal cord. Instead of an instrument, it encounters the human larynx, which allows it to express its experiences. Here you have an image of what actually happens in the human head.

Now let us go back to the first drawing. Suppose we shutter the window, so it is very dark inside the enclosure when the steam flows up into it. In this case, the steam does not perceive the light that enters through the window and is dimmed and reflected in various ways. Instead, the steam perceives forms inside the enclosure itself—perhaps shapes once constructed by a carpenter, for example. What the steam senses will be the the results of the carpenter's actions, and when it flows out again, it will again be able to express what it perceived.

But now let us assume that the carpenter constructed the space in a very particular way. Let us suppose that he was the master carpenter of the universe and that he constructed the space in the image of the entire cosmos. What the steam then touches and senses when the window is shuttered is the mysteries of the entire cosmos. When the window is open, the steam perceives the light that sparkles in from outside, but when the window is shut, it perceives the room's contents, the image of the entire cosmos.

Imagine that we have here an image of the cosmos. And, in fact, the marvelous convolutions of the brain really are an image of the entire cosmos. If we shut off our senses and then allow inhaled air to flow along the spine into the head, we can touch and sense the mysteries of the brain's inner space. But we must not simply allow the air to touch things willy-nilly, in a disorganized, chaotic fashion. This must be done systematically.

You know that if we want to confirm that a certain piece of fabric is made of silk, we have to touch it in a particular way. Our touch must be appropriate to what we are attempting to perceive. If we meet what we are touching halfway, we can recognize it for what it is.

Last week, I mentioned that when the original ancient Eastern yoga was in full flower, its devotees were able to attain higher knowledge by manipulating their breathing.[†] They knew that the configuration of nerves inside the head reflected cosmic mysteries and that they could grasp these mysteries if they managed their breathing appropriately. (I am talking about the original yoga, not the decadent secondary developments we know as yoga today.) As the devotees of the original yoga inhaled, they sent their breath up inside the dome of the head, which is an image of the entire cosmos. They shaped this stream of air into a sound somewhere between *a* and *o*, or *a* and *u*. Like hands whose shape we adapt to the outer objects we touch, the sound *a-u* was adapted to touching and sensing cosmic mysteries. The resulting perception then became conscious as the air was allowed to flow out again in a mood of absolute devotion. What was accomplished by inhaling, by touching with air imprinted with the sound *a-u*, was then offered to the world in a mood of devotion, allowing exhaled air to flow out in the sound *m*. The breath, shaped inside the body into the sound *aum*, received cosmic mysteries as reflected or reproduced in the nerves inside the head.[†] Cosmic mysteries were brought to life (or to consciousness) as the air was exhaled in the sound *m*. This was the basis of the original yoga training.

A yoga student of ancient times experienced something like this: "The mysteries of the entire universe are in my head. I sense them when I inhale. When I inhale, I perceive cosmic mysteries. But I can hold on to them only as long as I maintain an attitude of absolute devotion to the cosmos. Otherwise, they remain in the unconscious."

In other words, inhalation was shaped into the Cosmic Word, which weaves and surges as the force that creates the universe. When they grasped the Cosmic Word and then breathed out in absolute devotion to the cosmos, yoga students recognized inhalation as the revelation of the Cosmic Word and exhalation as its condensation and affirmation. *Aum* unites revelation and affirmation, bringing cosmic mysteries to life within the human being.

For us today, sound has moved up a step. It is expressed in real, concrete thought, not in intellectual thoughts. Inhalation becomes thought, and exhalation becomes the deliberate, living manifestation of thought. In other words, we separate the unified experience of inhalation as revelation and exhalation as affirmation into thought exercises and will exercises. Through thinking trained in meditation, we receive revelation; through will exercises, we affirm the revelation.

For modern humanity, what was once experienced in respiration and shaped into vowel sounds (in inhalation) and consonants (in exhalation) now manifests on the level of the soul, in thought that is contemplated inwardly but pervaded with will in devoted submission to the cosmos. The process is the same, but it has been ensouled and internalized. Nonetheless, it still consists of perception and affirmation—perception of our internalized experience of cosmic mysteries and affirmation of the cosmos and its spiritual foundation.

Let us look at this from a different perspective. It can be said that human beings are born out of light and that the interior of the human head—the entire nervous system—is a product of light. In addition to the eye, all the other sense organs also convey light. The eye is simply the organ that conveys light in the most obvious sense. We cannot say that blind people are totally cut off from light. It works within them; they simply do not perceive it consciously.

Sound also works within us, in the entire body and not just in the ear, which is simply an organ for perceiving sound. When we experience a symphony, for example, we experience it with our whole body. In the inner process of listening to a piece of music, our respiration shifts into very specific rhythms. These rhythms are specific musical processes evoked by the composition. They are shapes in the element of air inside our body. As such, they bounce off the shapes of the brain, which force them back. This is what produces musical impressions. Inside us, sound is constantly touching and sensing light.

This concept is important to remember: Inside us, sound touches light. The sound in us, the sounding body, is actually an organ of touch for light. Light is the outer element, sound the inner element.

| Thought | Inhalation: | Revelation |
| Will | Exhalation: | Affirmation |

Sound (internal) touches light (external)
Human will touches cosmic thought.

The inner element touches the outer. We grasp an essential aspect of being human only when we understand that we are special beings, removed from the cosmic music of the spheres. As human beings, we feel our way around in the light; within us, sound discovers the nature of the cosmos in configurations of light. Only in our era has human will begun to touch cosmic thought. Now will replaces sound; thought replaces light. As I have said before, these things are very difficult to formulate in abstract, intellectual terms, but the image that I attempted to present will make it accessible if you contemplate it a bit. The important point about human beings' relation to the cosmos is that the human head is an image of the entire cosmos.

When a human embryo begins to develop in the womb, it is shaped in the image of the cosmos. In the earliest stages of development, the human being is essentially all brain, an image of the cosmos. You can study the cosmos by studying an early-stage embryo. Everything that is not an image of the cosmos is added later and can be described as follows: Here is the Earth, with the human being on it. A portion is taken from the embryo to add the rhythmic forces that surround the Earth and work parallel to its surface. The chest is formed out of streams of forces encircling the Earth. You can see them reflected in the ribs. The last to be added is the effect of the Earth itself, which streams upward from below and is reflected in the legs. As a result, the human body can be drawn as consisting of currents that flow upward from the Earth, currents that encircle the Earth (and are related to the chest), and the head at the top, as the image of the entire cosmos.

Throughout a human lifetime, what happens in the head remains an image of the entire cosmos. The very fact that we have a head means that each of us carries an image of the entire cosmos around with us. All we have to do is perceive it. We would not perceive it if the Earth had not organized our body in a way that makes possible the appropriate organs. In fact, the Earth perceives the cosmos through human beings, and the chest provides the connecting link. The cosmos causes inhalation; the Earth causes exhalation. The cosmos supplies pure oxygen; the Earth causes oxygen to combine with carbon, transforming it into the deadening air that we exhale. But in the process of producing dead air, we gain the ability to understand.

Understanding is always associated with death processes in the human being. Understanding kills us; the cosmos enlivens us. But we would develop very rapidly if we were subject only to the cosmos. The cosmos supplies us with the most life during the embryonic period. Later, the forces that circulate around the Earth begin to work on us and, later still, the forces streaming up from the Earth itself. These forces convey the life that the cosmos contributes to the body until our portion of cosmic life is used up. The cosmos enlivens us, but the Earth kills us, both as physical organisms and as etheric organisms. The human etheric body, however, belongs primarily to the cosmos, while the physical body belongs primarily to the Earth.

If you consider all this and recall that the people of ancient times cultivated higher knowledge by regulating respiration so they could explore cosmic mysteries within themselves, you will then realize that these people felt themselves related to the entire cosmos. You will understand how they experienced the Cosmic Word through inhalation and attempted to sacrifice to the Cosmic Word in exhalation. Through yogic breathing, they attempted to insert themselves—or rather, their consciousness—into cosmic processes, for, of course, they themselves were always involved in cosmic processes, though not consciously. No documentation exists of the original yogic breathing, and superficial modern descriptions leave us none the wiser about what it was actually meant to accomplish.

Modern anthroposophical spiritual science, however, does allow us to understand its purpose. By the time documents were produced, ancient yogic breathing no longer existed in its original form. We can never depend on historical documents to reveal the real mysteries of human origins on Earth. These mysteries are disclosed only to those who can look back on times much more ancient than those recorded in outer documents. The mystery of the Eastern *aum* prayer, if I may call it that (I could also call it the *aum* "cognition formula," for it is that, too), is revealed only when we really know how human beings relate to the cosmos through inhaling and exhaling. Air does not convey specific pitches by itself, but it certainly does so when differently tuned strings are plucked. Similarly, inhaled air sent through the brain together with the *aum* sound expresses all the mysteries of the cosmos within us.

When we know this, we understand how we as human beings are connected to the cosmos. We touch and sense how we have become the personalities we are now. Before conception, we lived in the world of spirit and soul, but in the descent to Earth, we passed through the ether of the entire cosmos as we gathered our ether body around us. In this process, we absorbed all of the mysteries of the cosmos and gradually imprinted them on our brain. Infants are still involved in this imprinting process. Later, we can rediscover these mysteries within us through deliberate effort. In ancient times, breathing exercises were used for this purpose, but now we do it through thinking.

The power of thought, which is nothing other than the diluted force of respiration, is also configured if and when when it is actually directed through the brain. Modern people do not do this. We do not guide the power of thinking through our brains. Instead, we hear words spoken in our language, words in which thoughts are inherent. What we allow to pass through us is nothing more than imitative babbling based on our nationality. This process yields no inner insight. At best, we write books about how impossible it is to understand anything through language, although it is all we have. We write critiques of language because we have no idea of what the power of thinking hits up against. We know only what is recorded in the words. Modern human beings are simply sounding boards for words. People with keen minds, like Fritz Mauthner†, then write books about the fact that words actually encompass nothing of the world's essence.

All this, however, gets us no closer to understanding either human beings or the cosmos and especially not human beings' connection to the cosmos. We must acknowledge the profound truth of the statement that human beings are "human" as a result of inhaled air, the breath of the divine. Through this inhaled air, we discover the entire cosmos in ourselves. We discover that we ourselves are a microcosm.

If you take what I have presented here today and ponder it from all aspects, you will find that you gradually arrive at very significant associations. The fact that I initially simply drew you a picture is not owing to some personal quirk. When dealing with spiritual subjects such as this, it is important to avoid the use of abstract words. Instead, we must attempt to approach the reality of the situation through images.

I believe that I have pointed to a very important chapter in anthroposophical spiritual science today. I will continue tomorrow in greater detail.

7

Exoteric and Esoteric Christianity

DORNACH, APRIL 2, 1922

Human evolution is recorded in religious documents and philosophical texts that speak to all of humanity down through the ages, and we must certainly acknowledge the exoteric impact of such documents. Nonethless, I must emphasize repeatedly that they need to be complemented by esoteric sources of information. Wherever people have talked in any deeper sense about how they view and understand the world, they have always distinguished between exoteric teachings, which convey outer knowledge, and esoteric teachings, which are accessible only to those who have undergone appropriate preparation in heart and mind. We must make the same distinction with regard to Christianity itself, and especially to its spiritual center, the Mystery of Golgotha. The Gospels present the exoteric view of Christianity for all the world to see. Alongside them, however, esoteric Christianity has always existed for those who have appropriately prepared themselves in their souls to receive it.

The most important element of esoteric Christianity is its insight into the risen Christ and his interaction with the disciples who were able to understand the resurrection. As you know, this interaction is described only briefly in the Gospels.[†] Unless we advance to the level of esoteric knowledge, these brief accounts merely hint at the fact that a new and unique element was incorporated into Earth's evolution through the resurrection.

Paul's affirmation of the Christ is an important complement to these hints, because Paul clearly states that his belief in the Christ dates from the moment the Christ appeared to him outside Damascus.† His belief is based on direct perception that the Christ has risen from the dead and is still alive and active in earthly evolution. In his experience at Damascus, Paul perceived the living Christ. It is important for us to consider the significance of Paul's affirmation of the Christ.

Why was Paul unconvinced of the legitimacy of the Christ-Being until his experience at Damascus? Paul had been initiated into Hebrew esoteric teachings in certain respects, and we must understand what it meant to a person from this tradition that the Christ Jesus had been condemned to an ignominious death on the cross. To Paul, it was initially inconceivable that ancient prophecies could refer to someone crucified by his contemporaries. In Paul's mind, before his experience at Damascus, the crucifixion was fully valid proof that Jesus of Nazareth could not have been the Messiah. Paul became convinced of the truth of the Mystery of Golgotha only when Jesus of Nazareth— or rather, the being incarnated in him—appeared outside Damascus. Hence Paul's affirmation of the Christ was extremely significant.

The accounts passed down in the first few centuries after Christ are no longer extant, except perhaps as exoteric historical notes in the hands of a few esoteric societies that do not understand them. If we want to know more about the Christ after the Mystery of Golgotha, we must turn to anthroposophical spiritual science. We must rediscover what the risen Christ said to disciples not mentioned in the Gospels. According to tradition, the disciples who encountered the Christ on the road to Emmaus, as well as those enumerated elsewhere in the Gospels, were very simple people who would not have achieved esoteric levels of knowledge. Consequently, our question is, what did the Christ say after his resurrection to the disciples who were truly initiated?

To understand this, we must begin by considering the soul makeup of the people of ancient times and how it was affected by the event of Golgotha. For modern people, it is extremely difficult to understand that the earliest human beings on Earth did not experience "knowledge" as we do today. Through their atavistic clairvoyant capabilities, these early people were able to receive the wisdom of the gods. This means that they were taught by divine beings who descended to Earth—in spiritual form, of course—from the kingdoms of the higher hierarchies. These divine beings conveyed knowledge to human souls on a spiritual level.

Being taught by divine beings was once a common occurrence in human evolution. The people of ancient times—or at least those initiated into the Mysteries—were transported into a state of rapt absorption; for the most part, their souls were outside their bodies. In this state they were not dependent on outer sense impressions or outer conversation. Instead, they were spiritually receptive to communications from the gods. They did not receive these communications through what we would now call dreams but rather through living, spiritual interaction with divine beings. This is how the people of ancient times experienced wisdom.

This wisdom included knowledge of what human souls had experienced in the divine spiritual world before their descent into earthly bodies. For people in the above-mentioned state of consciousness, becoming aware of prebirth experiences was like remembering. When the gods conveyed these experiences to them, people felt reminded of what they had experienced in the world of spirit and soul before birth or before conception. An echo of such experiences still resonates in Plato's work.†

Looking back at ancient times, we see divine spiritual wisdom that was literally conveyed by the gods. This wisdom was unique in that it did not include any knowledge of death, strange as it may sound to modern ears. Like little children, the Earth's earliest inhabitants were unaware of death. Regardless of whether they received knowledge directly from the gods or indirectly from their contemporaries who were taught by the gods, they knew that their souls had once descended from divine spiritual worlds to enter a body and would leave the body again. They saw life as extending into the world of soul and spirit, and they experienced birth and death as transformations, not beginnings or ends. In other words, the first people on Earth saw earthly life as one segment in the ongoing development of the human soul, they did not see birth and death as the beginning and the end.

Instead, they saw the uninterrupted flow of the life of the spirit and soul, though, of course, they also saw people die.

Please do not interpret what I say next to mean that I am comparing these earliest humans with animals. Although outwardly animal-like in appearance, their bodies housed human souls and spirits, as I have said here before. Nonetheless, they understood as little of death as the animals of today do when they see other dead animals. These earliest people understood only the uninterrupted flow of spirit and soul. For them, death was part of maya, the great illusion, and it made no particular impression on them. All they knew was life. Despite seeing death, they did not know death. They saw human life only from the inner perspective of the activity of the human spirit and soul, which do not die. When they looked back toward their birth, they also saw beyond it to life in the spirit before birth, and when they looked toward death, they again saw the life of spirit and soul extending beyond death. Birth and death had no meaning in their lives.

Later, humankind gradually emerged from this early state of consciousness. If we trace the development of humanity from the earliest times to the Mystery of Golgotha, we realize that people were becoming increasingly aware of death and its impact. Their souls became involved in death, and they began to wonder what happened to the souls of people who died. In the earliest times, people did not see death as an ending. At most, they wondered about what sort of transformation it entailed. They thought that perhaps the breath leaving the body carried the soul into immortality, or they developed different ideas about how life flows on into the world of spirit and soul. They thought about the ongoing flow of life, but they did not think about death as an end to life.

As the Mystery of Golgotha approached, people were beginning to sense for the first time that death had meaning and that earthly life had a beginning and an end. Of course, they did not formulate this question in philosophical or scientific terms, but the feeling weighed on their minds nonetheless. It was important for people to begin experiencing this feeling in earthly life, because the dawning of reason, or the intellect, depended on it. As I have often explained, the intellect is dependent on knowing that we die.[†]

Consequently, human beings had to become aware of death and involved in their own deaths. In ancient times when people were unaware of death, they were totally unintellectual. They did not think up ideas; they received them directly from the spiritual world. Human intellect as such did not exist; it gained a foothold in human minds only later. In soul-spiritual terms, the intellect can gain ground only when people die, when they constantly carry death forces within them. Or to put it in physical terms, we might say that death can occur only when salt—that is, solidified or dead mineral substance—is deposited not only in the rest of the body but also in the brain. The brain always has a tendency to develop salt deposits, as if bone formation were a constant unrealized potential in the brain. In other words, the brain always includes a dying-off tendency.[†] At a certain point, death had to be experienced as a reality in human life. People had to become outwardly familiar with death. If human beings had remained as unaware of death as they had been in ancient times, they would never have been able to develop their intellect, because intellect is possible only in a world ruled by death.

I have just described the human perspective on this matter. It looks rather different from the perspective of the higher hierarchies, whose intrinsic forces shaped Saturn, Sun, Moon, and finally the Earth. If these hierarchies had discussed the matter among themselves before the Mystery of Golgotha, they would have said something like this: "We can shape the Earth out of Saturn, Sun, and Moon. But if the Earth contains nothing more than what we incorporated into these earlier evolutionary stages, human beings capable of experiencing death and developing their intellect will never evolve on Earth. We higher hierarchies are capable of transforming the Moon into an Earth where people know nothing of death and cannot develop their intellect, but we cannot make the Earth supply forces that foster human intellectual development. For this, we will be forced to rely on Ahriman, a being who is very different from us and whose evolutionary path is very different from ours. We must get involved with Ahriman. If we tolerate his presence in the Earth's evolution and allow him to participate in it, he will provide the elements of death and intellect for us to incorporate into the human constitution. Ahriman knows death because he is bound up with the Earth; his path has involved him in earthly evolution. And because he is knowledgeable and wise with regard to death, he is also the lord of the intellect."

The gods were forced to come to terms with Ahriman, if I may put it like that. They had to say to themselves: "Evolution cannot continue without Ahriman. He will have to play a role in evolution, but if he does, he will become the lord of death and thus also the lord of the intellect, and the Earth will slip through our fingers. Ahriman is interested only in intellectualizing the whole Earth, and he will claim the Earth for himself."

Thus the gods were confronted with the dilemma of whether to relinquish the Earth to Ahriman in a certain respect. There was only one possible solution. The gods themselves had to become familiar with an element that was nonexistent in the divine worlds not controlled by Ahriman. Their representative, the Christ, had to experience death on Earth—death caused not by divine wisdom but by the human error that would gain ground on Earth under Ahriman's sole dominion. A god had to undergo death and overcome it. For the gods, therefore, the significance of the Mystery of Golgotha was that it enriched their wisdom with the knowledge of death. If no god ever experienced death, the Earth would have become completely intellectualized and incapable of evolving in ways determined beforehand by the gods.

In ancient times, human beings did not know death, but they gradually became familiar with it and began to sense that death (or the intellect) meant a completely new direction in human evolution. The Christ taught his initiated disciples that he came from a world where death was unknown; he learned about death on Earth and overcame it. If we understand this Christic connection between the earthly world and the divine world, we will also learn how to make our way back from intellectuality to spirituality. This is an approximate expression of the contents of the esoteric teachings the Christ imparted to his initiated disciples. He taught them to see death from the perspective of the divine world.

To understand the depth of this esoteric teaching, we must realize that the gods have defeated Ahriman by making his forces useful to the Earth and have blunted his power by learning about death through the being of the Christ. While it is true that the gods have included Ahriman in earthly evolution, they are simply using him and will not allow him to fully implement his rulership.

You know from my book *An Outline of Esoteric Science* that Ahriman has been working in the human unconscious and subconscious since Atlantean times.[†] Ever since then, he has been waiting for the moment in world history when he will also be able to work in human consciousness. To apply human expressions to divine intentions, we might say that Ahriman has been longing for the moment when he will also be able to infiltrate human consciousness with his power. Ahriman was in for a surprise, however, when he realized that the gods had decided to send the Christ, a divine being, to Earth to experience death. This decision, while it made Ahriman's intervention possible, also blunted the force of his rulership. Since that time, Ahriman takes every opportunity to make human beings rely exclusively on their intellect. He has not yet abandoned all hope of succeeding in this effort.

What would it mean if Ahriman were to realize his intentions? What if Ahriman succeeded in convincing human beings that the only possible life is life in a physical body? What would happen if we all believed that it is impossible for us to leave our bodies and exist as beings of spirit and soul? If this conviction becomes universal, the human will be completely imbued with the idea of death, and it will be easy for Ahriman to succeed in his plans.

Ahriman's heart was full of joy from the 1840s through the end of the nineteenth century, because as materialism increasingly prevailed, he again had hopes of being able to exert his dominion over all of the Earth. (Of course, it is somewhat incongruous to speak of Ahriman having a "heart." Please take this statement metaphorically. Again, I am applying human expressions to a subject that would actually require inventing new terms.)

During the late 1800s, even theology became materialistic. Last week I noted that theology has become unchristian, and I mentioned a book by the Basel theologian Overbeck, who attempted to prove that modern theology is no longer Christian at all.[†] Such things gave Ahriman grounds for hope.

By now, opposition to Ahriman exists only in teachings that flow through Anthroposophy. If Anthroposophy makes it possible for people to acknowledge the existence of the human spirit and soul independent of the body, Ahriman will be forced to abandon his hopes. The Gospels provide an inkling of the Christ's struggle against Ahriman in the story of the temptation in the wilderness. In our times, this struggle again becomes possible. But we will understand the issue completely only if we become fully aware that Lucifer played a greater role in humankind's evolution in the past, whereas Ahriman has gained influence over human consciousness only since the Mystery of Golgotha. In earlier times, his effect on human beings did not extend to consciousness.

If we look into human hearts and minds, we must conclude that the most important event in our evolution on earth is learning to overcome death within ourselves by uniting with the inherent power of the Christ impulse. From the perspective of the spiritual world outside us, this means that the hierarchies active in the evolution of Saturn, Sun, Moon, Earth, and so on, have involved Ahriman in earthly evolution but have limited his dominion by forcing it to serve their purposes. Without Ahriman, the gods would have been unable to bring intellectuality to humankind. And if they had not broken Ahriman's dominion through the Christ event, Ahriman would have made the entire Earth inwardly intellectual and outwardly material. We must see the Mystery of Golgotha as more than just an inner, mystical event. It is also an outer event, although not in the sense of superficial, materialistic historical research. The significance of this outer event is that the forces of Ahriman have been incorporated into earthly evolution but have also been overcome. A struggle between gods is played out in the Mystery of Golgotha. After the resurrection, the Christ imparted knowledge of this struggle to his initiated disciples through esoteric teachings.

In earlier stages of earthly evolution, human beings were aware of their connection to the divine worlds and learned about these worlds through divine revelations. But because death did not exist in these divine worlds, human beings were unable learn anything about death. Death was not a reality for human beings, because they recognized only the steady, constant progression of human souls through various states the gods arranged for them. Later, when death gained significance, human beings were able to overcome death by developing the inner strength to hold fast to the Christ. This is a matter of inner development, however, not of esoteric Christianity. What was the content of esoteric Christianity that the Christ conveyed to his initiated disciples? He told them that events on Golgotha reflected super-earthly events and a relationship between Ahriman and the divine worlds responsible for the evolution of Saturn, Sun, and Moon and Earth as it was before the Mystery of Golgotha. He told them that the cross on Golgotha cannot be seen simply as a manifestation of earthly factors; in fact, it has significance for the entire cosmos. This was the content of esoteric Christianity.

The esoteric teachings that the Christ conveyed to his initiated disciples were profoundly moving. To continue the conversation, the disciple might have said: "Today we are entangled in death, and we would no longer know anything about the gods if the Christ had not died and risen from the dead to share with us the gods' experiences with death. As human beings, we faced a time when we would no longer be able to know anything about the gods. But the gods sought a way to speak to us again through the Mystery of Golgotha."

Perhaps we can get a feeling for what is meant by "esoteric Christianity" by imagining the following scenario: Suppose two disciples of the Christ, who are making progress in their understanding of esoteric Christianity, are talking together as they wrestle with their doubts. One of them might say to the other: "The Christ, our teacher, came down to Earth from the spiritual worlds that people knew in ancient times. These people knew about the gods, but only the gods who could not tell them anything about death. If these gods were the only ones we ever knew, we would never have experienced the essence of death. The gods first had to send a being down to Earth so that they could learn about death through one of their own. Since his resurrection, the Christ seems to be teaching us about what the

gods had to do to guide earthly evolution toward its appropriate conclusion. He is teaching us something that earlier human beings could
not know. We are learning what the gods were doing behind the
scenes in cosmic existence in order to further the Earth's evolution in
the right way. For the benefit of humankind, they introduced
Ahriman's forces into earthly evolution but prevented these forces
from corrupting human beings."

The essential point of the esoteric Christianity imparted to the disciples was that human beings, having distanced themselves from the
gods, were now drawing closer to them again. In the early years of
Christianity, the disciples were imbued with these unsettling teachings. Some of them, whom we know only from outer historical
accounts, carried with them knowledge that they could have acquired
only from the risen Christ himself or from those he had taught. This
knowledge was passed on by word of mouth, and the early propo-
nents of Christianity placed great value on having a teacher who was
the pupil of the pupil of a disciple who had known the Lord himself
after his resurrection.

In the first few centuries of Christianity, people placed great value
on personal transmission of the tradition, but it gradually became
more and more superficial and was reduced to outer historical
accounts. In essence, however, it could be traced back to what I have
described here today. The embodiment of intellect began to be especially pronounced in the fourth and fifth centuries after the Mystery
of Golgotha and underwent a reversal in the fifteenth century, when
the fifth post-Atlantean epoch began. The development of the intellect effectively eliminated the ancient wisdom that had allowed people to recognize supersensible truths, and a new wisdom had not yet
developed. For a certain period of time, people forgot about the esoteric aspects of Christianity. As I mentioned earlier, some notes about
it were preserved by esoteric societies, but in modern times their
members no longer understand that these notes refer to teachings
conveyed by the risen Christ to certain initiated disciples.

If ancient Hebrew teachings had not undergone a regeneration
through Christianity, Paul's absolute conviction prior to the event at
Damascus would have become universal. Paul's line of thinking went

something like this: "Our traditional teachings were originally conveyed to human beings spiritually, in the form of divine spiritual revelation. Later, these teachings were preserved in Scripture. The scribes of the Jewish people knew everything that had been preserved of ancient divine wisdom. These same scribes supplied the rationale for condemning the Christ Jesus to death."

People like Saul (before he became Paul) were aware of the original divine wisdom and knew that it flowed down through the ages to the scribes of their own time, outstanding individuals who devoted themselves to the study of Scripture. To people like Saul, therefore, it seemed impossible that divine wisdom could have unjust consequences. An innocent man condemned to death? Impossible! The sequence of events that led to condemning Christ Jesus to death ruled out any possibility of his innocence. Only the Roman governor Pontius Pilate, already instinctively enmeshed in a very different worldview, was able to ask, "What is the truth?" For Paul, when he was still Saul, it was impossible to imagine that the righteous judgment of the scribes was not based on truth.

What was the new conviction that Paul struggled to achieve? He had to be convinced that it was possible for human beings to subvert divine truth into such egregious error that the most innocent of individuals was put to death on the cross. The original wisdom of the gods flows down and becomes the wisdom of the Jewish scribes who lived at the time of the Mystery of Golgotha. It was inconceivable for Saul to think that the wisdom of the scribes did not contain the truth, but it was time to think otherwise. Paul, when he was still Saul, would have said: "If the Christ who was put to death on the cross is truly the Messiah, this stream of truth must have become mingled with error. The Christ must have been nailed to the cross in error." In other words, the original divine wisdom must have been transformed into error in human beings.

Of course, Saul was able to convince himself of this only by experiencing the reality of the Resurrection. Outside Damascus, Saul experienced the Christ himself and was convinced. But what did this experience mean to Saul? It meant that ancient divine wisdom no longer existed in its original form but had absorbed an Ahrimanic element.

This is how Paul arrived at the insight that humankind's evolution had been appropriated by a foe who is the source of error on Earth. By introducing the intellect to human beings, this foe also introduces the possibility of error, and in the greatest manifestation of this error an innocent being was nailed to the cross. Paul first had to be convinced that it was possible for an innocent person to be put to death. His experience at Damascus provided an initial view of how Ahriman entered humankind's evolution and a first inkling of the Mystery of Golgotha as a supersensible, superearthly event in the development of the human "I." Esotericism is never exclusively mystical. We are gravely mistaken if we interpret mere mysticism as esotericism. Esotericism is always a recognition of realities that take place in the spiritual world as such, behind the veil of sense-perceptible reality. The balancing of the divine and Ahrimanic worlds occurred behind the veil of sense perception but was played out in Christ Jesus' death on the cross.

Through his experience at Damascus, Paul realized that the error that led to the death on the cross was possible only because the being of humanity had been appropriated by Ahrimanic forces. Only when he had understood this was he also able to grasp the truth of esoteric Christianity.

In this sense of the word, Paul was certainly an initiate. This initiation, however, gradually succumbed to the influence of intellectuality. Today we need to find our way back to an understanding of esoteric Christianity. We need to know that Christianity encompasses more than exoteric accounts. The Gospels hint at its esoteric aspect, but it is still not talked about much today. Nonetheless, humankind must return to this aspect of Christianity, despite its almost total lack of outer documentation. Anthroposohical spiritual science can teach us to understand what the Christ himself taught his initiated disciples. He was able to convey these teachings only after experiencing death on Earth as he could not experience it in the divine world, where death was nonexistent until the Mystery of Golgotha. No being from that world had ever died. In the world of the hierarchies related to the Earth's development through the Saturn, Sun, and Moon stages, the Christ is the firstborn, the first to experience death.

Through the Mystery of Golgotha, death is subsumed into life. In earlier times people knew life without death, but through the Christ we learn about death as part of life, as an experience that intensifies life. The life human beings experienced before they knew about death was a weaker form of life. We must now live more intensely if we want to pass through death and still live. In this context, death is also the intellect. Before human beings were afflicted with intellect, a relatively weak sense of life was sufficient. The people of ancient times, who received knowledge of the divine worlds through inner revelations, did not die in any inner sense. They always remained alive; they were able to laugh at death because they remained inwardly alive. The Greeks still told stories about how happy people were in ancient times, because as death approached, they became so numb inside that they did not notice they were dying. These Greek stories were the last remnant of a worldview that knew nothing of death. In more recent times, we experience the intellect, and it makes us cold and dead inside. Our intellect paralyzes us. When we develop the intellect we are not actually living. We must learn to sense that when we think we pour our life out into dead, rational images. We need to be intensely alive to sense creative life in the cultivation of dead rationality and to enter the domain where moral impulses derive from the power of pure thinking—where we learn to understand human freedom on the basis of impulses of pure thinking.

I attempted to depict this experience in my *Philosophy of Freedom*, which details a mode of moral perception that is meant to show us how to enliven, or resurrect, dead thoughts so that they become moral impulses. To this extent, inner Christianity is certainly inherent in such a philosophy of spiritual activity.

My intention today was to present certain aspects of Christianity from a specific perspective for you to ponder. In our times, when there is so much contention about the nature of Christianity on the exoteric historical level, it is essential to point to Christianity's esoteric teachings. I hope you will not take what I said today lightly but will receive it with all due seriousness. In talking about such things, it is always difficult to force them into modern, abstract words. That is why I attempted yesterday to prepare your souls by presenting images of what happens inside the human being in relationship to the cosmos. Today, we turned our attention away from the individual human being and toward the esoteric historical evolution of humankind as it absorbed the incisive event of the Mystery of Golgotha. When I come back from my trip, perhaps we will have an opportunity to consider the relationship of the human soul to the evolution of the cosmos on a different level.[†]

8

THE TEACHINGS OF THE RISEN CHRIST

THE HAGUE, APRIL 13, 1922

My subject today—the Mystery of Golgotha, the greatest mystery in human evolution on Earth—is one I have often spoken about in intimate anthroposophical gatherings. The Mystery of Golgotha is such a broad, important, and rich subject that we must repeatedly illuminate new aspects and approach it from different perspectives. To fully appreciate the appearance of the Christ, we must keep in mind all of humankind's evolution both before and after the Mystery of Golgotha, including what is still to come. We must be aware of both past and future evolutionary streams in human earthly life.

It is important to realize that the thinking of the earliest earthly human beings was dreamlike and imaginative. These people possessed faculties that allowed them to interact with the beings of a higher cosmic order, if I may put it like that. You know about these beings from accounts such as those in my book *Esoteric Science*. Today, in our ordinary consciousness, we know very little about these higher beings. Our interaction with them has been cut off. This was not the case in earlier times in humankind's evolution. Of course, an encounter with one of these beings in ancient times was completely unlike a modern meeting between two people incarnated in physical bodies. It was an interaction of a totally different sort. Speaking in the original language of the Earth, the beings of the higher hierarchies communicated the deepest mysteries of existence. These communications could be received only with spiritual organs. As these mysteries flowed into their hearts and minds, the earliest human beings became aware that in the heavens above, where we now see only clouds and stars, earthly existence is linked to divine worlds. Members of these divine worlds descended in spirit to earthly human beings and conveyed archetypal wisdom to them. These revelations contained a great deal that those earliest people would have been unable to fathom by themselves. In fact, in the earliest stages of human life on Earth, there was very little that people could understand by themselves. Perception and knowledge were kindled in them by their divine teachers.

Although these divine teachings contained a great variety of truths and insights, there was one thing they did not contain. The people of that time did not need to know it, but for modern human beings it has become one of our most important pieces of knowledge. Divine teachers told early humans nothing about the actual basis of birth and death, the events that frame human life on Earth. In the short time we have available today, I cannot possibly mention everything these divine teachers taught the human race, and, in fact, you have already heard about much of it. But I would like to state emphatically that none of these teachings contained anything about birth and death, because in those ancient times (and for a long time thereafter in humankind's evolution on Earth) people did not need to know about birth and death.

Human consciousness has changed radically in the course of earthly evolution. The first primitive humans, though they were animal-like in appearance compared with modern humans, functioned on a higher level of consciousness than we do, at least in some respects, so it would be a mistake to equate their consciousness with that of even the higher species of modern animals. Nonetheless, perhaps we can take some clues from the subhuman consciousness of modern animals. If you take an unbiased look at today's animals, you will realize that they take no interest in birth or death. They are fully involved in life and approach death (and view birth, for that matter) with disinterest and a total lack of concern. Animals accept death passively as the transition from individual existence to existence in their group soul. Death does not make as deep an incision in their lives as it does for human beings.

Despite their animal-like appearance, the first earthly humans functioned on a higher level, because their instinctive clairvoyance allowed them to interact with their divine teachers. Like modern animals, however, these early humans displayed no interest in the approach of death. It did not occur to them to pay any particular attention to death. Why should they? Their instinctive clairvoyance provided a clear view of the immortal being that descended from the spiritual world to enter the physical body at birth. Because these earliest earthly humans knew that their constitution included an immortal element, they had no interest in the transformation that took place at death. At most, they experienced it somewhat like the shedding of a snake's skin. For them, death and birth were much more a matter of course and had much less impact on life than they do for us today. With their vivid perception of the life of the soul, these early humans were completely incapable of wondering about birth and death with the intensity that we now apply to these questions.

For us today, the ability to perceive the soul has faded away, and the distinction between dreaming and sleeping has become blurred. Today, we experience dream images as belonging to sleep. We feel more asleep than awake when we dream. In contrast, the dreamlike images that the first humans received were part of their incompletely developed waking life. These people recognized the content of these dream images as reality. They experienced the soul aspect of their constitution in this way.

In the earliest stages of human earthly evolution, this state of consciousness was especially pronounced. Later, it faded away gradually. If I may put it like this, people gradually began to notice that dying had a major impact on human life, including the life of the soul. Similarly, they began to pay more attention to birth. The tenor of earthly life changed; it became increasingly important to people as their experience of soul existence faded. They felt increasingly isolated from the life of the soul and spirit during the time they spent on Earth. This change became increasingly pronounced as the Mystery of Golgotha approached. Among the Greeks, it was already so strong that they experienced life outside the physical body as a shadowy existence and viewed impending death with a certain sense of tragedy. The teachings human beings received from their divine teachers in earliest times had not prepared them to experience being born and dying. Before the Mystery of Golgotha, people were becoming increasingly aware of birth and death but did not understand these totally unfamiliar incisions in their earthly life.

Now let us suppose that around the time of the Mystery of Golgotha, those divine teachers descended to Earth again. Perhaps they would have been able to communicate their ancient divine wisdom to a few specially prepared students or mortal teachers of humankind, such as the priests of the Mysteries. Still, none of their teachings would have dealt with birth and death. Even in the Mysteries, none of the revelations of divine wisdom conveyed anything about the riddle of death. Meanwhile, in their exoteric earthly life, people were beginning to observe birth and death and to take an interest in them, but the gods had told them nothing about these important, even fundamental, aspects of their lives. Why not?

This question must be explored without preconceived ideas, so we will have to set aside some of our traditional religious ideas. It is important to realize that the higher hierarchical beings, the divine teachers of the first humans, had never experienced birth and death in their worlds. Birth and death are experienced only on Earth and only by human beings. (The deaths of plants and animals are totally different from human death.) In the divine worlds of humankind's first great teachers, birth and death do not exist. There is only transformation or metamorphosis from one form of existence into another. Hence these divine teachers had no inner understanding—there is no other way to describe it—of dying and being born. And these divine teachers include all those related to the beings we know as Yahweh, the Bodhisattva, and the founders of all ancient religions. If you read through the Old Testament, you find people confronting the mystery of death with a growing sense of tragedy. In fact, no Old Testament teachings conveyed any inwardly satisfying information about death. If nothing had changed on Earth and in the Earth-related higher worlds, human beings would have faced a terrible situation as earthly evolution continued. If the Mystery of Golgotha had not happened, people would have experienced birth and death as abrupt transitions in their lives rather than as simple metamorphoses, and they would have been unable to experience anything of the meaning of death and birth in human earthly life. Humankind had to be taught about birth and death. To this end, the being we know as the Christ, who belonged to the same Earth-related hierarchies as the great teachers of earlier times, chose a different destiny and found his way into earthly life. In compliance with the decision of the higher worlds, he incarnated into an earthly body so that a divine soul could experience earthly birth and death.

You see, the event of the Mystery of Golgotha is not simply a human or earthly affair. It also concerns the gods. Through what happened on Golgotha, the gods, who had never participated in the earthly mystery of death, became intimately familiar with it. The significance of the Mystery of Golgotha lies in the fact that a divine being decided to experience the same destiny as an earthly human being.

We modern human beings approach the Mystery of Golgotha primarily through the Gospels, the rest of the New Testament, and our religious traditions. Modern explanations of the New Testament, however, provide very few real insights into its central mystery. Exoterically acquired knowledge represents a necessary stage in the development of modern humanity, but it is also important to acknowledge its superficiality. It tells us virtually nothing about how differently people viewed the Mystery of Golgotha in the first few centuries after its occurrence. At that time, remnants of ancient, instinctive clairvoyance allowed those initiated into the Mystery of Golgotha to look back on it in a way that became impossible by the fourth century A.D. From fragments of historical traditions of the earliest church fathers and Christian teachers, we know that they placed less value on written documents than on receiving the news of the Christ Jesus' transformation from teachers who still met him face to face or, later, from students of students of the apostles and so on. This oral tradition persisted into the fourth century A.D., always invoking the living connections of teachers reaching back to the Christ himself.

For the most part, the historical documents have been destroyed, and only very careful reading turns up traces of how important it was considered to have a teacher who had a teacher and so on, always ending with an apostle who had seen the Lord himself face to face.

Much of this oral tradition has been lost, but even more has been lost of the esoteric wisdom that persisted (thanks to remnants of ancient clairvoyant insights) in the first four centuries after Christ. Our exoteric traditions have lost almost all of what was once known about the risen Christ. Like the divine teachers of old, the Christ assumed a spirit body to teach selected disciples after his resurrection. But Gospel accounts of the disciples' encounter with the Christ on the road to Emmaus, for example, give at best scant indication of the importance of the teachings the Risen One imparted to them. The experience at Damascus that changed Saul into Paul is another example of an apostle's being instructed by the risen Christ. In those ancient times, people were still aware that the risen Christ Jesus communicated very specific mysteries to human beings. In later centuries it became impossible to receive these teachings. Human beings had to develop soul forces that then led to individual freedom and the use of the intellect. This trend has been especially pronounced since the fifteenth century, but humankind has been preparing for it since the fourth century A.D.

We must now ask, what was the content of the teachings that the risen Christ was able to convey to his chosen disciples? He appeared to them as the divine teachers of old had done, but he spoke—in the language of the gods, if I may put it like that—about something that he had experienced but his divine companions had not. He was able to tell his disciples about the mystery of birth and death from the perspective of the gods. He told them that in the future, people's daily waking consciousness, which is extinguished during sleep, would not allow them to perceive the eternal human soul by day, nor would the soul appear to the mind's eye during sleep. He also explained something else, which I will attempt to clothe in the feeble, stammering words that are all our modern language makes available to us. He told them that the human body has become increasingly dense and its death forces increasingly strong. As a consequence of this change, human beings can now cultivate their intellect and freedom, but death has become an obvious incision in their life and their view of the eternal soul is extinguished during waking consciousness.

The Christ said to his disciples: "If you can simply rise to the insight that the divine descended from superearthly spheres to live among human beings on Earth, you will be able to fill your souls with the knowledge of what happened within my being. Do you realize that something exists on Earth that cannot be perceived by earthly means? Can you behold the Mystery of Golgotha as a divine intervention into earthly life, as the experience of a god? If so, you will receive this wisdom. The wisdom you derive from all other earthly events is useless for understanding human death unless you are as disinterested in death as the people of ancient times. But because you *must* be interested in death, your insight must be fortified with a strength greater than any earthly power of insight, with the strength to accept that events on Golgotha violated all earthly, natural laws. If your capacity for belief can encompass only earthly natural laws, you will indeed be able to see death, but you will never grasp its significance for human life. But if you can rise to the insight that the Earth's evolution is given meaning at its midpoint by an event that cannot be understood with earthly insight—that is, by the divine event of the Mystery of Golgotha—then you begin to develop the strength of a specific wisdom that is also faith, the power of *pistis-sophia*.† Being able to say 'Through faith, I know and believe something that I could never know or believe by earthly means' is a very potent force in your soul. This belief is much more empowering than trusting yourself to know only that which can be fathomed by earthly means. With all the science in the world, anyone whose wisdom is limited to what is comprehensible by earthly means remains a weak person. Acknowledging that a superearthly element is active in earthly life requires much greater inner strength and activity."

Contemplating the Mystery of Golgotha goads us to develop such inner activity. In ever-new variations, the original disciples of the risen Christ proclaimed that a god had experienced the human destiny of birth and death—something that the gods formerly did not experience in their own realms—and had thus become united with the Earth's destiny. This teaching is extremely powerful, as you can discover simply by thinking about it in terms of contemporary situations. We expect much less of individuals whose thinking is derived entirely from earthly circumstances and traditional religious ideas than we do of those we believe capable of rising to the understanding that entire divine hierarchies had no knowledge of death and birth until the Mystery of Golgotha, when they achieved it for the sake of humankind's salvation. It takes a certain strength to meddle in divine wisdom, so to speak, but it takes no particular strength to memorize some catechism or other: God is all-knowing, all-powerful, all-pervasive, and so on. Simply sticking "all" in front of any adjective gives us a ready-made, but nebulous definition of the divine. Our contemporaries lack the courage to meddle in divine wisdom, but it must be done. In particular, we must meddle in the divine wisdom that the gods acquired when one of their own experienced human birth and human death. It is extremely important that this mystery was entrusted to the first disciples. It is equally important that the Christ explained to them that human beings once had the inner strength to behold the eternal in their own souls.

We can never acquire such insights through "brain knowledge," the intellectual, thought-based knowledge that uses the brain as its instrument, nor can we acquire them as the people of ancient times did, with the help of nature and by cultivating the human rhythmic system. These methods were very effective for the last instinctively clairvoyant yogis, but despite all the amazing things Westerners attribute to modern Indian yoga practitioners, they no longer come close to true perception of the immortal human soul. For the most part, their experiences are illusory. They may have transitory experiences, perhaps even of something fundamental to earthly existence , but the rest is a matter of interpretation, of reading into their experience from their study of holy books. There are only two ways to acquire real, thorough, fundamental knowledge of the divine in the human soul. One is the way the first human beings did it; the other (a much more spiritual way) is through intuitive knowledge that develops on the basis of Imagination and Inspiration.

The risen Christ spoke of mysteries that still included awareness of a higher form of "substance knowledge," or metabolic knowledge, which was neither the form experienced by the first earthly humans nor the degenerate form applied by hashish users and others in their attempts to acquire otherwise unattainable knowledge through drugs. In a different way, early Christians attempted to resuscitate ancient "substance knowledge" for a specific purpose. They enveloped the Mystery of Golgotha in the cultic or mantric formulas of the Gospel, Offering, Transubstantiation, and Communion, and they gave communicants bread and wine. Not drugs, but communion wafers and wine. After the fourth section of the Mass (Communion), the true communion of the faithful was supposed to take place. The intent of the Mass was to suggest to communicants that it was time to rediscover the knowledge once achieved through ancient, instinctive metabolic perception.

For us today, it is very difficult to gain any idea of what this ancient metabolic knowledge was like. Today we no longer have a clue that birds (not to mention camels, who live entirely in their metabolism) know more than human beings, although in a dull and dreamlike way, not intellectually, abstractly, or rationally. Today, the metabolic perception of the first human beings survives only in degenerate forms such as drug use. According to early Christian teachings, however, the sacrament of Communion is intended to reawaken the urge to acquire knowledge of the eternal aspect of the human soul.

During earthly life, the thinking portion of the soul disappears after sculpting the structures of the nervous system and is no longer present as such. In the rhythmic system, it is only half present. Consequently, if we were to rely on these two systems to explore our own souls, we would discover at most some clues leading to further conclusions. The actual immortal part of the human soul is concealed only in the metabolic system, which we consider the most materialistic aspect of our earthly life. Outwardly it is indeed the most material, but just because it is so material, the spirit remains separated from it. Our other material systems, the brain and the rhythmic system, soak up or absorb spirit, so it is no longer present as such. In the most crudely material system, however, spirit is still present. If we are capable of perceiving, seeing, observing with this crudely material aspect, we can perceive the eternal soul. The first earthly human beings had this ability, and it still occurs occasionally today, although only in undesirable pathological conditions.

For example, very few people know the secret behind the style of Nietzsche's *Zarathustra.*[†] Nietzsche ingested certain toxic substances that are responsible for the unique rhythm and style of his *Zarathustra*. In other words, a certain attribute of matter was thinking in Nietzsche. This is a pathological situation, of course, even if the results are magnificent in some respects. If we want to understand Nietzsche's spirituality, we cannot have illusions about it, just as we cannot have any illusions about the opposite path (Intuition and so on). We must be aware of the effects of Nietzsche's drug use, although we must not emulate him in that respect. In the human organism, these drugs assume an independent etheric existence. They spread systematically through a person's way of thinking where they produce results such as those we find in Nietzsche's *Zarathustra*. In contrast, Intuitions make it possible to perceive soul and spirit as such, separate from matter. In the descriptions of Intuition in *How to Know Higher Worlds* and *Esoteric Science*, matter is no longer involved at all. Substance-based and substance-free perception are polar opposites.

The risen Christ conveyed this knowledge to his initiated disciples at a time when people were unable to discover it for themselves. It survived in some form for four centuries but then ossified in the Roman Catholic Church, which retained the Sacrifice of the Mass but no longer knew how to interpret it. The meaning of the Sacrifice of the Mass, which is intended as an extension of the Lord's Supper as depicted in the Bible, lies entirely in its interpretation. The Mass is a wonderful emulation of the four stages of Mystery initiation, and its adoption can be traced back to the teachings imparted by the Risen One to the disciples who were capable of grasping their higher, esoteric meaning. Traditions that survived into the early Middle Ages preserved only a rather juvenile type of instruction in the Mystery of Golgotha. The faculty that developed at that time temporarily shrouded or concealed true knowledge of the Mystery of Golgotha. Before rediscovering this knowledge, human beings first needed to solidify their relationship to death and everything related to it.

Writings preserved in some modern esoteric societies contain formulas reminiscent of the Christ's teachings to his initiated disciples,
but the members of these societies—Freemasons and so on—have no
idea of the living content and meaning of these dead letters. But now
that humankind's evolution has passed through a period of darkness
with respect to the Mystery of Golgotha, a time is coming when
human beings will again long to understand the Mystery of Golgotha
on a deeper level. This understanding will be achieved only through
Anthroposophy, through the appearance of a new knowledge that
works in purely spiritual ways. Through it, we will again achieve a fully
human understanding of the Mystery of Golgotha. We will again learn
to understand that the teachings most important for humankind were
proclaimed by the risen Christ, not by the Christ who lived in a physical body before the Mystery of Golgotha. We will gain new understanding of these words of the initiate Paul: "If the Christ did not rise
from the dead, your faith is in vain." (1 Corinthians 15:14) After his
experience at Damascus, Paul recognized the crucial importance of
understanding the risen Christ and uniting his power with human
beings so that we can truly say: "Not I, but the Christ in me."

In contrast, the emergence of a theology that no longer aspires to
know much of anything about the risen Christ was all too typical of
the nineteenth century. It is a significant symptom of the times that
Nietzsche's friend Overbeck (a professor of theology in Basel,
Switzerland) wrote a book in which he presents proof that modern
theology is no longer Christian. In his opinion, although Christianity
might still exist in some form, the theology promulgated by Christian
theologists was no longer Christian.† This is approximately the view-
point of the Christian theologist Overbeck, a view he proves quite
brilliantly in his book. At this point in humankind's understanding of
the Mystery of Golgotha, the people who have the least to say about
it are those officially employed by their churches to present it to their
contemporaries. As a result, people are experiencing an inner longing
or need to know about the Christ.

As I expressed in a recent series of lectures, Anthroposophy today
is meant to serve humankind in a variety of ways, and one of its
important functions is religious.† This does not mean that we are to

establish a new religion. In an event never to be outdone, an event that gave meaning and purpose to the Earth, a god has endured the human fate of birth and death. Since the coming of the Christ, it is obvious to anyone who understands Christianity's source that founding new religions is no longer possible. If we believe that new religions can still be established, we misunderstand Christianity. But as humankind progresses in the quest for supersensible knowledge, our understanding of the Mystery of Golgotha and of the being of the Christ will deepen. Anthroposophy's contribution to this understanding may be unique at this point in time. Where else is anyone talking about humankind's relationship to the divine teachers of ancient times, who spoke of everything except the birth and death that they had never experienced? Where else is anyone talking about the teacher who appeared to his initiated disciples in the same way as the divine teachers of old, yet was able to convey a god's experience of the human fate of birth and death?

As human beings increasingly faced the need to take an interest in death, this new divine communication was intended to give them the strength to realize that death cannot touch the soul. The purpose of the Mystery of Golgatha was to make this realization possible. Paul knew that if the Christ had not risen from the dead, human souls would have become imprisoned in the fate of the body and its earthly components. If the Christ had not risen from the dead, he would not have aligned himself with earthly forces, and the human soul would have united so completely with the body during life between birth and death that it would also have remained connected with all the body's molecules that are returned to the Earth through cremation or decomposition after death. By the end of the Earth's evolution, human souls would have gone the way of matter. But because the Christ went through the Mystery of Golgotha, he wrests human souls from this fate. The Earth will go its own way in the cosmos. But just as an individual human soul is able to leave the body and yet survive, so, too, the sum total of human souls will be able to leave the Earth and move on to a new existence in the cosmos. This is how the Christ is intimately connected to earthly existence. We can understand this mysterious connection only by approaching it as we have done today.

Perhaps it will occur to some of you to wonder, what about those who cannot believe in the Christ? Let me conclude with a few reassuring words: The Christ died for all, including those who cannot yet unite with him. The Mystery of Golgotha is an objective, accomplished fact that is not affected by what people know or do not know about it. Nonetheless, knowing about it strengthens the inner forces of the human soul. We must apply all means available to us—our human cognition, feeling, and willing—to ensure that as the Earth's evolution continues, human beings will also know subjectively, through direct experience, of the Christ's presence within them.

9

SPIRITUAL INSIGHT AND INITIATION

LONDON, APRIL 14, 1922†

ANTHROPOSOPHY, as I represent it, has the same foundations as the science of initiation of any bygone era, but Anthroposophy adapts initiation science to modern times. In the course of evolution, the constitution of the human soul has undergone various metamorphoses. Each new age in the development of civilization offers a new, primary soul constitution, and initiation science, which aspires to investigate the eternal aspect of the human being and the cosmos, must adapt accordingly. In our time, initiation science cannot be the same as it was in the Middle Ages or in ancient Greece, not to mention even older civilizations. As an initiation science corresponding to the needs and aspirations of modern human souls, Anthroposophy must start from two assumptions: first, that our modern scientific worldview does not permit us to recognize the eternal, either in ourselves or in the cosmos, and, second, that turning inward and away from exoteric science in mystic contemplation does not achieve satisfactory results. The reach of exoteric science does not extend to the eternal, and while inner contemplation can produce mystical faith, it cannot produce knowledge of the sort that modern human beings need.

I will not take the time to prove these few introductory statements in detail, because I assume that all of you here today have personally experienced the inability of exoteric natural science to lead to any satisfying conclusions about the eternal in your own soul and in the cosmos. (I will also assume that you are seeking real knowledge, not merely an inner, mystical illusion.) I will choose instead to speak in detail about the relationship of Anthroposophy, as we understand it here, to natural science on the one hand and to mysticism, as it is often practiced, on the other. Let me simply say that Anthroposophy takes the spirit and the soul constitution of modern, civilized human beings as a starting point for acquiring what I will call "exact clairvoyance." This goal is why Anthroposophy has so many opponents today. Anthroposophy is also very difficult to grasp, in spite of the fact that virtually all of our modern soul forces are longing for it. Why is this so? It is because we cannot move beyond our conscious judgments, feelings, and so on to the unconscious longing that really is already present in every thinking human soul.

This unspecific longing, this unconscious goal, demands that we aspire to more profound and higher knowledge of the eternal and that we acquire this knowledge through very specific exercises that cultivate the human soul and its capacity for knowledge. Furthermore, we must be able to formulate the perceptions that result from these exercises with the precision we have come to expect today. Anthroposophy must present itself to our contemporaries with all the precision and conscientiousness of the natural sciences. At the same time, its knowledge of the eternal, imperishable element in human beings is intended to be accessible to even the simplest, most naïve hearts and minds.

Having said this by way of preparation, let me move on to a brief description of how Anthroposophy, the modern science of initiation, arrives at its path to knowledge. Anthroposophy is based on recognizing the relationship among the three fundamental forces of the human psyche—thinking, feeling, and willing. When we talk about thinking, or ideation, we know that we are reflecting on something that makes us awake and alert. During sleep our conceptual activity is silenced from the time we fall asleep until we wake up; all of our consciousness is dimmed. We see the world brightly lit to the extent that we can take in this bright light with our ordinary consciousness, which is filled with wakeful ideas.

As for our feelings, in human terms they are perhaps the most important contents of our inner life, but they are not as clear as ideas. They well up from unknown depths and are illumined to a certain extent by our ideas and thoughts, but they are not permeated with the same clarity as ideas themselves. And everything related to human impulses of will is still less clear, in fact, very dark indeed. We will have more to say about this later. The will impulses that pervade us rise from unknown depths and induce us to act. It is very uncommon to be clearly aware of what is happening in us when a will impulse is present.

We can distinguish among these three basic forces in human soul activity on the basis of their different degrees of clarity and many other factors. Nonetheless, they form a unity within our soul activity as a whole. We might say that ideation is one pole. But we also know that will activity is involved when we string ideas together or develop one idea into another. Although will impulses represent the opposite pole, they do play into our ideas. (Feeling stands between thinking and willing.) If we did not consciously shape our life's most important actions or if ideas could not incite us to act, we would not be human. Clearly, our will is also imbued with ideas. It behooves anyone who wants to develop exact clairvoyance in the anthroposophical sense to cultivate both the life of ideas on the one hand and the life of the will on the other.

Thought exercises on the one hand and will exercises on the other—these are the practices that open the portal to the supersensible world, where we can recognize the eternal in ourselves and in the cosmos. Thought exercises entail becoming aware of the will's influence on thinking; will exercises involve observing the influence of thinking on our will. In our ordinary life, we pay no attention to the element of will, but to achieve modern initiation, we must pay particular attention to the hint of will that is present in ideation. We gradually learn to do this through the exercises I described in *How to Know Higher Worlds*. The contents of our thoughts, which we usually consider their most important aspect, must be allowed to take a backseat while we learn to consciously apply our will to our thinking.

Let me describe briefly how this works. I can indicate only the main points here today; you will find the rest in *An Outline of Esoteric Science*, *How to Know Higher Worlds*, and other books of mine.

Think of an idea that is completely clear and easy to survey, such as a mathematical triangle. Make this idea the center of a complex of ideas. The content of the idea is not important at all. What is important is the effort you apply to this thinking meditation, focusing all of your soul activity on a single complex of ideas. We must learn to disregard everything else in the world so that nothing exists in our consciousness except one idea, a single complex of ideas. It takes a great deal of mental exertion to do this, but the repeated effort strengthens a force in our souls, just as an individual muscle grows stronger through repeated use. For one person, it may take months to see results; for another, years. But if we repeatedly concentrate all our mental energy on a single central idea, this soul force will be strengthened. After a while, this effort results in an initially unsettling inner experience. We find ourselves strengthened and energized for a kind of thinking that we did not have before. What we have then accomplished is easiest to describe as follows.

When we face the ordinary, everyday world, the sense impressions we receive are very vivid. We are energetically involved with these sense impressions, with the world of colors, sounds, temperatures, and other stimuli. In our everyday consciousness, thoughts are weak in comparison to sense perceptions, as you can confirm by thinking about your own thoughts and sense perceptions. Through the exercise described earlier, however, our thought activity ultimately becomes as vivid and energetic as our everyday sensory activity. This is an important milestone in human perception, because at this point our thinking is no longer linear, as it is in our ordinary consciousness. It becomes as vivid, intense, and saturated as any outer sensory perception. We have advanced from ordinary, abstract, representational thinking to something we can call "Imaginal" thinking. In this sense, "Imaginal" does not mean that we lose ourselves in imaginations or fantasies. It means that we can behold worlds that live in our souls as if in dream images, but they are not dream images. They are filled with inner reality.

When we have practiced living in Imaginal thinking for a while, being involved in it as whole human beings, we discover that we sink down into a previously unknown world. Through Imaginal thinking, we gain access to the first level of the supersensible world. We gradually discover a second human being living within us, a second body that is just as real as the outer, spatial, physical body. The outer body is an organized structure whose individual members are mutually interdependent. The head depends on the hand and the hand on the head, and the right hand depends on the left. The limbs and organs of the spatial human body are all interdependent. Similarly, we discover a second, time body. There is nothing spatial about it. This body presents itself to the mind's eye in the form of a monumental tableau. Once we achieve an adequate level of Imaginal perception, we no longer remember by looking back on individual events. When we look back over our entire earthly life to date, back to the earliest years of childhood, we see it all at once, as if in a single image, but we know the image cannot be a spatial image. If we were to attempt to draw it, we would draw something like a flash of lightning, which can be held fast only for an instant. This is the time body, which I have also called the body of formative forces, or the etheric body. It cannot be drawn in a single image; any attempt to do so produces only a cross-section of a time organism.

In this time body, we see how we were equipped in childhood with inborn supersensible forces that sculpted our brain and then found the transition to the respiratory and circulatory systems, working their way into the entire spatial structure of the body until they mastered it completely. During childhood, the time body (which we learn to experience through Imaginal perception) increasingly takes possession of the entire spatial body. As the etheric body's forces unfold, it fills the spatial body. We are unaware of either the etheric body or its effects in our ordinary consciousness. Through Imaginal perception, however, we become conscious of this time organism. As a result, we learn to perceive why we have certain character traits and abilities. For example, we learn why one person is a talented painter, another a mathematician. These abilities are the result of something supersensible that shapes our earthly existence.

When we develop exact clairvoyance by systematically exercising our capacity for thinking in this way, we learn to explore the first level of the supersensible within ourselves. Imaginal perception is the first level of supersensible perception. Through it, we perceive the super-sensible (time) body within the physical, spatial, earthly body.

Up to this point, I have been attempting to describe how we reach the first level of supersensible existence through Imaginal perception. This first supersensible element is present within the sense-perceptible world, and we can perceive it without leaving our earthly bodies. In other words, within this earthly body lies a supersensible member of the human constitution, which I have described here, at least in broad strokes. We become familiar with it through Imaginal perception. But when we move on to the second level, we leave the physical body and approach the higher, eternal aspect of human nature, which transcends birth and death.

In ordinary life, the will's influence on our capacity for thinking is involved in achieving Imaginal perception. But to continue along the path to the supersensible world, we must perform the opposite of the first exercise. Even in everyday life, it is important not only to be able to focus on a single idea or object but also to be able to let go of it. This observation leads to the next exercise. Having systematically concentrated our mental energy on a single idea (which can lead to Imaginal perception), we must then apply even greater energy to avoid becoming caught in that idea (or complex of ideas), so we can continue along the path to higher knowledge. Once we have acquired vivid, Imaginal thoughts, we must get rid of them deliberately; we must erase them from our consciousness. With practice, we become increasingly able to empty our consciousness of the heightened ideas we developed through concentration or meditation. Ultimately, we learn to be fully awake when our consciousness is empty.

Let us consider the implications of being wide awake with an empty consciousness. Ordinarily, we fall asleep—that is, we become unconscious—in the absence of sense impressions from outside or memories from within. On the path to higher knowledge, we prevent ourselves from falling asleep by first intensifying and then extinguishing mental activity. In this state, we are awake and alert, but our consciousness is completely empty and receptive to perceptions of a new sort. These are not sense impressions—which our enhanced thinking extinguished—nor are they memories or the all-encompassing tableau of past experiences we perceived in Imaginal thinking. What now enters our consciousness is totally new and bears no resemblance to our natural surroundings. In our empty consciousness we behold a supersensible milieu all around us, just as we are normally surrounded by the physical world's colors and sounds. Spiritual beings emerge from everything around us. Instead of seeing drifting clouds, for example, we perceive the supersensible beings in them. The world we now behold is not a world "beyond" the sensory world. It lies in front of us just as the sensory world does, but it is truly supersensible and accessible only through initiation. As our consciousness submerges in this supersensible world, we learn a new way of thinking that depends neither on ordinary thinking nor on the nervous system. Although the nervous system formerly served as the instrument of our thinking, in this state we no longer need to rely on the brain. Purely mental energy now brings thoughts to life in our consciousness.

Once we are able to do this, we make many discoveries that clarify how this new thinking derives from our old thinking. Because brain-free thinking does not include memories in the usual sense, it cannot be compared to brain-bound thinking, which is healthy only if it includes memories. This may sound paradoxical, but it is true nonetheless that experiences on this supersensible level initially do not generate memories. This sometimes comes as a surprise to students of initiation science. Having achieved a certain degree of clairvoyance, they expect to be able to preserve their clairvoyant experiences in memory and recall them just as they would recollect other thoughts, and they are unhappy because they cannot do this. They are aware of having been surrounded by a supersensible world and are frustrated at being unable to remember it in their physical bodies. But this phenomenon is totally characteristic of the experience of any reality that is not merely a thought.

If I have a sensory experience, I can remember the thoughts associated with it. I can recall my thoughts about a rose, but to have the rose itself before me again in all its redness, I must go back to the real thing. Similarly, having achieved a new and higher type of perception through initiation, I must retrace my steps to a spiritual experience in order to repeat it. People who speak from even the most basic personal spiritual experience (instead of merely talking about what they have learned about the spiritual world from other sources) know that exact clairvoyance must create the experience anew in their souls each and every time. Natural scientists can depend on memory, but spiritual researchers must always retrace the steps that led to their initial experience. In this sense, each spiritual experience is always new. Thus, spiritual experiences and the experiences of ordinary consciousness also have different prerequisites.

The ability to orient ourselves in spiritual worlds and truly perceive them also requires a specific trait of character. In ordinary life we call this "presence of mind." It allows us to make decisions in any situation without hesitation. Observing the supersensible world takes a great deal of practice in developing presence of mind. Without it, we would not have time to grasp what we experience in the spiritual world; the event would be over before we got there, so to speak. As soon as we advance to brain-free thinking, we also need the faculty of extremely rapid deliberation.

With more practice in cultivating the strength to empty our consciousness while remaining awake and aware of the supersensible beings in our surroundings, we learn to extinguish not only individual ideas but also the entire etheric body. Extinguishing the etheric body empties our consciousness in a higher sense, allowing us to perceive our life in soul and spirit before we descended from supersensible worlds to take on earthly bodies. Through Inspiration, or Inspired perception, we learn to perceive life before birth. Inhalation pulls physical air into our lungs, and Inspiration pulls the spiritual world into our empty consciousness. On a spiritual level, we "inhale" the spiritual worlds we knew before descending from spiritual heights to physical, earthly existence. Through Inspired perception, we learn about one aspect of our eternal being, namely, "unbornness." No one talks about "unbornness," but it is one aspect of the eternal human soul. Its other aspect is immortality, which negates death; we will talk about it in the third section of this lecture. As human beings, we are "unborn" in the same sense that we are immortal.

As a modern science of initiation, Anthroposophy does not proceed philosophically, by drawing conclusions and building on what we already know. Instead, it prepares human souls to achieve higher perception through practice. A soul that develops to a level higher than that of ordinary life learns to perceive its own eternal nature. This is the aspect of Inspired perception that relates to our own human nature. Let me also describe its other aspect, although I can present it only sketchily today: Through Inspired perception, we also learn to perceive the outer world. For example, in the outer, sense-perceptible world, ordinary exoteric science conceives of the Sun as a self-contained body in space. This physical body, however, is only one aspect of the Sun's total being, just as the human physical body is only one member of the human constitution as a whole. In the case of human beings, we say that a being of spirit and soul lives *inside* the body. In the case of the Sun, however, the supersensible element, or spiritual aspect, is *outside*, filling the entire universe. The spiritual aspect of the Sun is everywhere, in minerals, plants, animals, and human beings. We simply perceive its physically concentrated form when we look up at the Sun. Through Inspired perception, we learn to recognize the spiritual aspect of the Sun in plants, animals, and humans and even in every detail of the human body—in lungs, liver, heart, brain, and so on.

Today I have shown you not only how we can achieve true human self-knowledge through Inspired perception but also how this Inspired perception can be applied to practical activity. I showed you this with regard to one particular field, but it is also true of others. On the one hand, initiation science provides a foundation for the human soul's most profound aspirations; on the other, it provides what we need to intervene in the cosmos on a practical level and in a deeper sense than exoteric, sense-based science permits.

In addition to the spiritual aspect of the Sun, however, we also recognize the spiritual aspects of all other outer bodies. The Moon as a whole, like the Sun, does not have sharply defined contours. The external, physical Moon is only the physical concentration of the Moon's essence, which pervades all of space. Today, such statements are considered mere superstitions, but to those able to perceive such phenomena, they are as exact as any scientific statements. Inasmuch as plants, animals, and people have physical bodies, we see them as objects in the outer, physical cosmos, but through Inspired perception, we learn about their inner nature. The same is true of individual organs—hands, lungs, liver, and so on. The spiritual aspects of the Sun and the Moon are at work in them, too—the Sun in their sprouting, germinating, and thriving and the Moon in their degeneration and decline. We could not survive without these aspects of Sun and Moon. When we recognize the Sun's effect as ascending and the Moon's as descending, we are learning to recognize their spiritual aspects in the outer world.

We can also learn to recognize pathological cosmic effects, such as whether Sun influences or Moon influences prevail in a diseased organ. The effects of Sun and Moon are present as opposing forces in plants, animals, and humans. Based on this knowledge, we can also learn to identify individual outer, natural forces that point to remedies for specific internal illnesses. This is one example of how Anthroposophy begins to influence practical activities—in this case, medicine. Medical knowledge of this sort can be cultivated by investigating how cosmic spirit influences human illness and health. I can say only a few words today about anthroposophical medical science as it already exists, but unless we move toward spiritual perception of the cosmos, all medicine, all psychology, and all therapy remain nothing more than the result of blind experimentation.

Through Inspired perception as I have just described it, we perceive for the first time the real human soul, the soul being that survives even outside the body and exists even before it descends from worlds of spirit and soul into a physical, earthly body. Our perception of the eternal soul remains one-sided, however, if we advance only to the level of Inspired perception, which allows us to perceive only the "unborn" soul, the aspect that exists before birth. To perceive the aspect that survives death, we must continue with our exercises to develop supersensible forces of perception. We do this by bringing thinking to bear on our will, just as our concentration exercises brought will to bear on our thinking. I will now give a brief description of how to do this.

Let us begin with a simple example. We sit down quietly and think about what we experienced during the day, but instead of beginning with the morning and tracing the sequence of events through the day, we review the day in reverse, beginning with the evening and continuing back through earlier events in as much detail as possible, ending with the morning. Initially, it may be necessary to select a single event to review in reverse; later, with practice, the entire tableau of the day begins to unfold as if by itself. The important point in this effort is that we are accustomed to passively abandoning our thinking to the outer succession of events; in other words, we always tend to recall events in the order in which they occurred. Limiting our thinking to the natural sequence of events does nothing to strengthen our will. We strengthen our will by doing the opposite, by freeing our thinking from that natural sequence. Reviewing the events of the day in reverse order exercises our will. Similarly, we can imagine hearing a melody or seeing a drama in reverse. The point is to free ourselves from the outer succession of events by exerting our will. This effort strengthens the will and cultivates the inner strength that drives thinking into our will, just as exercises in concentration and meditation drove will into our thinking.

I have described this will exercise in greater detail in the books I mentioned earlier, but let me mention a few additional points here to make it more understandable. What happens when we go to great lengths to educate our will? What happens when, instead of passively accepting what our outer life, upbringing, and surroundings have made of us, we undertake to educate ourselves, as adults? What happens when we take ourselves in hand to such an extent that we eliminate old habits and develop new ones through years of practice? What happens when we apply the power of our thinking, or the willpower that lives in our thinking, in attempts to develop lasting character traits that we do not possess initially—a process that may take seven years? By repeating and persisting in these efforts for decades, we strengthen our will. There are also many other will exercises that allow us to approach the supersensible world from this other side.

But how does our consciousness relate to will impulses? Let me explain it like this: A will impulse is expressed when I raise my hand or my arm. This impulse then recedes into the dark recesses of my being. It eludes my ordinary day consciousness as if I were asleep. We may say that we "dream" our feelings, but we are "asleep" with regard to our will impulses. As far as our souls are concerned, our bodies are "opaque" to will impulses. We perceive certain objects as opaque to physical light because they do not allow light to pass through them. Similarly, our bodies are "opaque" because they do not allow will impulses to show through. We cannot see into our will. Physical vision is possible because the lens of the eye is transparent, except in illnesses such as cataracts, in which case we no longer see clearly. This is not to say that the physical body is "sick" in ordinary life—Anthroposophy does not promote false asceticism—but if we could make the body transparent to the soul (not to physical vision, of course), we would truly be able to perceive will impulses flowing from our thoughts into the physical body. If the physical body were transparent in this sense, we would be able to see through to our will impulses.

In perceiving ourselves as beings of will, we would also see into the spiritual world of will to which we belong. That spiritual world of will is a world outside us that becomes transparent to us through will exercises. When we achieve this level of perception, the physical body becomes transparent to the soul, revealing the will. If we persist in these efforts, we perceive an image of the moment of death, when we surrender the physical body to the Earth and pass through the portal of death as beings of spirit and soul. We perceive this image of crossing the threshold of death when we succeed in making the physical body transparent and behold the spirit through it. We understand what leaves the physical body. We not only look into the spiritual world, we begin to live in it. This stage is Intuitive perception, true Intuitive perception. It allows us to behold immortality. When we achieve this stage by way of Imagination and Inspiration, we learn to experience ourselves as eternal spiritual beings belonging to the cosmos. We behold the spirit of the cosmos with our own eternal, spiritual souls. Like the dreaming, atavistic clairvoyance of ancient times, initiation science adapted to the constitution of the modern human soul allows us to ascend from the transitory to the eternal, but now we do so in full consciousness.

In Anthroposophy, however, the knowledge that results from spiritual perception is not restricted to those who actually do all these exercises and convince themselves of the existence of the eternal world and its beings through direct, personal experience. To do research in the spiritual world, Imagination, Inspiration, and Intuition are necessary, but modern spiritual researchers bring back what they can from this world, clothe it in ordinary logic and language, and present it to their contemporaries. What they discover can be understood by anyone with a healthy feeling for it. To understand a work of art, we do not have to be painters ourselves; we simply need a healthy artistic sense. Similarly, common sense and an unbiased approach are enough to allow us to understand all the results of spiritual research. We must simply avoid creating misunderstandings on top of misunderstandings, as has so often happened.

The Imaginal, Inspired, and Intuitive modes of perception that I described here today have often been confused with hallucinations due to pathological conditions. Conceivably, the Imaginations we seek to attain might be nothing more than hallucinations or the visions of a trance medium, but, in fact, the meditation and concentration exercises that I described are the exact opposite of the mediumistic state. Someone who is hallucinating is totally caught up in that state, but our healthy common sense is preserved when we ascend through the stages of higher perception through spiritual exercises. People who preserve their healthy common sense are always able to monitor and critique what is going on. They cannot lose themselves in unfounded fantasy or hallucinations. Such pathological states are the exact opposite of Imagination, Inspiration, and Intuition. They are the opposite of what happens when modern consciousness, or an extension of it, serves as the foundation for convincing ourselves of the reality of supersensible existence. Through the anthroposophical science of initiation, we gain supersensible knowledge that is adapted to modern life.

Modern consciousness is a stage that we must pass through. We must experience all the triumphs of exoteric perception of the world, but if we are to serve modern civilization, and especially the future, we also need to perceive the supersensible world. This need is presaged by the many, many people who now aspire to supersensible perception—and realistically so—through Anthroposophy for religious purposes. Anthroposophy hopes to answer this new call. I will say more on this subject tomorrow, when I talk about the paths of anthroposophical initiation science that lead to the Mystery of Golgotha, to a true appreciation of Christianity. Today, however, I simply wanted to describe the task of anthroposophical initiation science in general terms.

When we stand in front of a person and look at her or him with our physical eyes, we get an impression of that person's outer physiognomy. This impression is incomplete. We see the whole person only when our own heart and soul can see into that person's soul and spirit. We cannot see the whole person with our physical eyes, nor can we perceive the cosmos and humankind in their totality if we apply exclusively exoteric modes of perception. To perceive soul and spirit in the cosmos, we need an initiate's perception, not the consciousness supplied by exoteric perception. We must become convinced of this fact. Only then will we strive to meet the true needs of the human soul by complementing the great advances of the exoteric natural sciences (whose contributions Anthroposophy acknowledges wholeheartedly) with modes of perception that reveal soul and spirit within the cosmos and within human beings. Anthroposophy is intended to supplement and support exoteric modes of perception with inner, spiritual perception. Just as a complete view of any human being must encompass not only the person's exoteric existence but also the soul within, so, too, Anthroposophy hopes to be the soul and spirit, the inner aspect, of modern perception as a whole.

10

PERCEIVING THE CHRIST
THROUGH ANTHROPOSOPHY

LONDON, APRIL 15, 1922

I spoke yesterday about the modern anthroposophical path of knowledge that leads from the physical, sense-perceptible world into the supersensible. By following this path, we can cultivate the exact clairvoyance appropriate to our time. Clairvoyance has always been the foundation of initiation science, but in earlier times it was simply accepted as an elemental force rising from human beings, either with or without being deliberately cultivated. In ancient times, people who achieved spiritual knowledge through instinctive clairvoyance were usually also dependent on the authority of those who traveled this path before them. Given the current level of humankind's development and the needs of the modern human soul, we can no longer take any such principle of authority as our starting point. Over the past three to five centuries, exact science has become increasingly available to us. Of course, it does not yet include the science of initiation, but it does exercise a certain control over our methods of research and modes of thinking, not to mention our entire consciousness. Anyone who aspires to exact clairvoyance in the anthroposophical sense must constantly exercise a similar control.

Clairvoyant insight into the cosmos and the human constitution does not have the same effect on us as a theoretical worldview. Modern initiation science is more than just the sum total of what we know about spiritual, supersensible worlds. It is also an active, spiritual force that can pervade and fructify all of our human capabilities. One illustration of its effects already exists in our anthroposophical artistic work, which embodies what would otherwise remain mere ideas about the spiritual world. The Goetheanum in Dornach, which will house our independent spiritual university and is being made possible by the generosity of a number of friends of Anthroposophy, is now being built and is already in use, although not yet finished.

If the members of any other spiritual movement had reason to construct a headquarters for their society, it goes without saying that they would hire some famous architect to design a building in the Greco-Roman, Renaissance, Gothic, or other conventional style. For the Goetheanum in Switzerland, this approach was not possible. It would have been contradictory to the anthroposophical worldview, which is meant to be communicated not only through ideas but also through human activity. Of course, this building is not perfect. In that regard, I am my own harshest critic. But no matter how imperfect it may be as a building, as a work of art, and as a whole, the Goetheanum is nonetheless essential as an example to our contemporaries of a new style of architecture. The lines and shapes of this building draw on the same wellspring of life as the ideas about supersensible worlds that we convey in words.

In this building in Dornach, all of the sculpture and painting are sustained by a style that will give birth to Anthroposophy as it is meant to manifest in modern life. Anyone who visits our independent spiritual university will not only hear the anthroposophical worldview communicated in words from the podium, but will also see it expressed artistically in architecture, sculpture, and painting. Our stage presentations are also intended as simply another artistic means of revealing what can be conveyed in words. Anthroposophy is not intended to be communicated through words alone. It has deep roots in the human spirit. Theoretical Anthroposophy is only one branch of a tree with many other branches, which include our artistic and educational efforts. Anthroposophical activity is a factor in many different facets of human existence.

If you visit the school in Stuttgart that we have named the Waldorf School, you will not find children being taught Anthroposophy in the way we usually teach adults, because the school is strictly nondenominational. Catholic priests provide religious instruction for the Catholic children, Protestant pastors for the Protestants. Today, however, many Germans are not interested in denominational religious instruction, and for those pupils we offer a specially designed religious "translation" of Anthroposophy. But the Waldorf School accomplishes its intended purpose when Anthroposophy flows over into real life, specifically into the practical art of education in the broadest sense. Anthroposophy is alive in the personalities of our teachers, inspiring what they do and *how* they educate and instruct. I mention this second field of practical activity to illustrate Anthroposophy's real-life impacts on various fields of human activity.

In many respects, however, Anthroposophy has already proved especially effective with regard to human religious needs. How does Anthroposophy meet religious needs in that part of the civilized world that acknowledges the Mystery of Golgotha? That will be the focus of my lecture today, with reference to the anthroposophical path to supersensible world as I described it yesterday.

Yesterday I pointed out that Imaginative perception, the first step toward spiritual perception, can be achieved by performing specific mental exercises. When it becomes active in our souls, we learn to use the mental energy of thinking (which usually provides only shadowy, abstract thoughts) to generate images as vivid, intense, and alive as any that approach us through our senses. Through Imaginative perception, we experience our thoughts in the same way that we think in colors or sounds when we give ourselves up to visual or auditory impressions. We live in Imaginative perception when we experience our thoughts inwardly, not merely in abstract contours but as images full of meaning. Yesterday I pointed out that Imaginative perception allows us to perceive the human temporal body, or body of formative forces. But when we rise to this level of perception, we must realize that the first things we see belong to the Imaginative element within ourselves. What distinguishes anthroposophical researchers from hallucinators or mediums is exact clairvoyance, that is, the ability to recognize that these earliest images exist within the human being. At first, even when we recognize the forces that shape our earthly bodies, we are learning about something subjective and personal, namely, the body of forma-tive forces.† But as I indicated yesterday, we can use the power of sug-gestion, so to speak, to extinguish these subjective images and empty our consciousness. This state of emptied consciousness has the poten-tial to receive similar images from outside.

As anthroposophical researchers, we must be conscious of the need to deliberately erase our first Imaginations. Our consciousness is then empty, but it is so intrinsically awake and energized that it receives purely spiritual images—and only such images—from the outer world. The first image we receive is an image of our life in soul and spirit before we descended from spiritual worlds to occupy physical bodies. The objective images that we begin to perceive of the spirit and soul in our surroundings belong to the level of Inspired percep-tion. Revelations, or objective images of the spiritual world, flow into our empty consciousness just as subjective images appeared as the result of strengthening our thinking through specific exercises.

In addition to prenatal spiritual experiences, what do we learn about ourselves when Inspired perception fills our empty conscious-ness with objective Imaginations? We also experience what we brought with us into physical existence from the spiritual world. As far as our consciousness is concerned, this is initially limited to the mental energy of thinking. This is an important discovery. Philosophers spend a great deal of time thinking about how thinking comes about, but anthroposophists know that thinking cannot possi-bly be derived from the physical body. It is a force that we bring with us from the spiritual world, where we lived before descending to Earth. In that world, thinking was totally different from what it becomes in our ordinary, earthly consciousness. Here on Earth, our thoughts are abstract and suited only to thinking about dead things. At this point, anyone who takes the modern science of initiation seri-ously must confront our contemporaries with something they may not want to hear. Let me clarify this with an example.

As we all know, birth and death lie at opposite ends of our limited human life span on Earth. Through death we leave the physical body behind. Whether through cremation or decomposition, the corpse returns to its native element, the Earth. After death, the body ceases to follow the laws that the human soul imposed on it, beginning at birth. Because it no longer incorporates any aspect of the human soul and spirit, it obeys the same natural laws that prevail among minerals. This is the physical fate of the human physical body after death.

We must also acknowledge that a similar death occurs when the soul descends from existence in the world of spirit and soul to incarnate into a physical body at birth. This soul enters the physical human body in the same way that the physical human body enters the earthly element at death. As far as consciousness is concerned, our thoughts are the first thing we become aware of bringing with us from the spiritual world. The mental energy of thinking is the corpse of soul and spirit. Before our earthly existence began, our thinking led a life of its own in the world of soul and spirit, but only the corpse of this spiritual force is incorporated into our earthly existence. The physical body carries our thoughts, which are the soul corpse of our former existence, just as the Earth receives the corpse of the physical body after death. This is why modern perception is so unsatisfying. As long as we carry around this soul corpse, we grasp only the lifeless aspect of nature. It is an illusion to believe that we can discover anything other than lifeless nature through our modern experiments. Of course, we will encounter organized, living bodies as well as mere lifeless matter, but with the undeveloped thinking of personal consciousness, we will not be able to understand them. Even if we were able to create life in a laboratory, we would not understand it. As a soul corpse of its former self, our thinking is spiritually dead. It understands only dead things.

We must accept this truth with open minds, because it is important to know that human beings absorbed this dead, abstract thinking only at a specific stage in evolution. Because abstract thinking has no inherent life and imposes no constraints on the inner human being, it allows us to become free. This is why human freedom developed only once we began to experience death.

Later, we will see what we can achieve in the way of Imagination, Inspiration, and Intuition through thinking. As I indicated yesterday, this process truly enlivens our thinking: it was dead, but it comes alive in us again when we achieve Imagination through the exercises I described. Whereas our power of thinking formerly provided no idea of what we were before descending from spiritual to earthly existence, now that our thinking has been reenlivened, we look back on our Imagined and Inspired thinking in our prenatal existence in the spiritual world. We perceive the life we led in a spiritual state before being somehow "absorbed" into the physical body on Earth at conception. There, our thinking was alive†, but in the consciousness unique to the physical body, it is dead. Imagination reenlivens it. We enliven the unborn soul.

Everything we achieve through Imagination and Inspiration—the spiritual world in which we then live, our enhanced capacity for real thinking, the perception of spiritual beings and events—is nothing other than an enlivening of something that is dead to our ordinary consciousness. Within the enlivened thinking that develops into Imagination and Inspiration, something happens for modern human beings that was impossible for the ancient Greeks, not to mention the Egyptians or Persians of the time before the Mystery of Golgotha. Before the Christ descended from spiritual heights to Earth, "coming alive" through initiation science was very different from what it has since become for modern humanity. Such historical changes in the human soul are disregarded by history today, which considers only outer events. We learn of these changes only through initiation science—that is, exact clairvoyance.

After achieving Imagination and Inspiration, we recognize that something unsettling has happened in us. When we become clairvoyant, we are shocked to realize that we have become too egotistical, that the activity of the personal "I" has become too strong. (No one who has received appropriate spiritual instruction will say otherwise. Anything else is an illusion.) Before the Mystery of Golgotha, initiates had the opposite experience. They were forced to realize that initiation science weakened the "I." In a certain sense, they became unconscious or less incarnated. As a consequence of initiation, they experienced themselves less strongly as human beings; but without initiation the "I" grew stronger. In a certain sense, the healthy degree of egotism that is natural and necessary in ordinary life was extinguished in initiates who lived before the Mystery of Golgotha. They felt as if they were being poured out into cosmic heights and that the power of their consciousness was suppressed.

For modern humans, however, initiation makes the "I" stronger; we become more conscious of it. In his experience at Damascus, as described in the New Testament, Paul was the first to feel that the "I" needed something to prevent it from becoming too strong through initiation. You know this; I do not need to tell you about it. Through this experience, through the Mystery of Golgotha, Paul realized that he was granted insight into the spiritual world. In order to endure this insight safely, he had to make his "I" weaker. Paul coined a universal formula for new initiates when he said, "Not I, but the Christ in me."

When we acknowledge receiving the Christ into the overly strengthened "I," we imbue ourselves with the Christ's power, which entered the Earth through the Mystery of Golgotha. As a result, the "I" once again engages in the human constitution in the right way. Paul's words "Not I, but the Christ in me" are universally meaningful.† They offer direction and orientation for those who experience the Christ's power through modern initiation.

I pointed out that modern, abstract thinking as we know it in the physical body is a mere "corpse" of its spiritual essence in prenatal existence, and I emphasized that this is true only of modern human beings. The modern constitution of the human soul has been emerging gradually since the Mystery of Golgotha, and our thinking quietly began to assume its present character three or four centuries later. Prior to that time, among all the peoples of antiquity, thinking carried some of its soul-spiritual life and inner vitality into earthly existence. This statement can be readily confirmed by anyone who truly studies the changes in the makeup of the human soul over the course of humankind's evolution.

If we look at ancient worldviews, whether derived from initiation science or not, we find that the people of ancient times always saw the spiritual aspect of minerals, plants, animals; rivers and springs; thunder and lightning. It is trivial to think of this view of enspirited nature as the result of poetic imagination. What we call animism never actually existed. In reality, ancient modes of thinking also perceived spiritual activity whenever plants were observed, for example. Where our ordinary modern consciousness sees only the green of a leaf or the red of a flower, the people of ancient times also saw spirit and soul at work. They saw the soul-spiritual element in clouds and rivers, in mountains and valleys. We now perceive the natural world without its spiritual component, but they perceived it as inwardly imbued with spirit. They were able to do so because the living power of their thinking reached out to the spiritual element in nature just as we now reach out with our hands to touch physical objects. Their living organs of thinking explored the soul-spiritual aspect of the physical world through organs of "spiritual touch."

As time passed, the great vitality that thinking possessed in ancient times was gradually suppressed. Since the fourth century A.D., thinking has become inwardly dead and capable of perceiving only the dead aspects of living things—plants, animals, and other human beings. When the people of ancient times observed themselves, they experienced their thinking as an extension of what they had been in the spiritual world before birth. They remained aware of being surrounded by the spiritual element that had surrounded them before their lives on Earth. Around the third or fourth century A.D., this experience changed as people began to perceive dead thinking when they looked inside themselves. This gradual inner death of thinking is an all-important historical event.

For a moment, let us imagine that nothing happened to counteract thinking's gradual death in the human soul. What if earthly evolution had continued beyond the third or fourth century A.D. without the intervention of the Mystery of Golgotha? If the cross had never been erected on Golgotha, what would have happened to human souls? People would have begun to feel dead in their earthly bodies. Anticipating physical death, they would have experienced earthly birth as the beginning of soul death, because human souls would have been caught up in the death of their physical bodies if the Mystery of Golgotha had not intervened. This phenomenon would have spread gradually over the entire Earth, affecting more and more individuals and becoming increasingly pronounced. How tragic it would have been to realize that we humans were so closely bound up with the Earth that we could no longer maintain the degree of life that people had until the third or fourth century and that we were forced to follow our bodies into death. Our souls would have had to die, that is, to participate in the fate of our physical bodies. This is not what happened, however. The Mystery of Golgotha intervened, changing the course of earthly evolution.

For individuals rooted in the Christian faith, the usual first approach to the Mystery of Golgotha is through the Gospels. There is nothing wrong with this approach, but initiation science elaborates on what the Gospels communicate to even the simplest hearts and minds. In the spiritual world that appears when we ascend from Imagination to Intuition, not limiting ourselves to mere belief, the Mystery of Golgotha stands out as the greatest comfort in cosmic existence. Initiates who passed through the stages of Imagination and Inspiration in the right way formerly felt that the "I" had become too strong—not as the foundation of human freedom but as a possible obstruction to developments intended to save human beings from the consequences of dead thinking. From the perspective of initiation science, the tragedy of the death of thinking becomes all the more apparent. In the background, however, stands the truth of the Mystery of Golgotha. In historical, supersensible events at the right moment in earthly evolution, the divine being of the Christ first lived in the body of Jesus of Nazareth and then passed through death on Golgotha. If we undergo initiation in the right way, we experience both the overstrengthening of the "I" and the truth of the Mystery of Golgotha.

Through spiritual perception of the events recorded by the first Gospel writers, we discern both the Mystery of Golgotha and the origin of the Gospels. We also learn to understand the truth of what Paul said: if the Christ had not risen from the dead, our faith would be in vain and our souls dead. We realize what would have happened if the Mystery of Golgotha had not occurred, if a god had not descended to experience life and death in a human body and unite with the Earth's forces. Formerly, the Christ's forces were not active in the development of earthly humanity, but now they are. Paul's words meant that the Christ had to experience death and overcome it, emerging victorious as a living spirit. Since his resurrection, he lives with and for human beings, who would possess only dead thinking were it not for his deed. As if in memory, Paul became aware that a god, the Christ, has descended to Earth to live.

Behind our ordinary reading of Gospel contents rises an Intuitive vision, the actual source of the Gospels. Through Inspiration and Intuition, initiates develop an inner strength that leads not only to an awareness of life after death but also to objective Imaginations and truths about the outer world. Thus, initiates are not dependent on what the Gospels tell them. If the Gospels had not already been written, initiates could write them themselves. In fact, initiates take the correct view of the Gospel writers, realizing that enough of thinking's ancient vitality persisted in the first three or four centuries A.D. to allow some individuals, even noninitiates, to behold the Mystery of Golgotha and interpret it correctly. If initiates of the early Christian era had not interpreted the Mystery of Golgotha through the gnosis of the time (which is similar but not identical to modern Anthroposophy), there would be no Gospels, because the Gospels were written out of the initiation science of old.

In earlier times, the living quality of thinking was preserved in earthly life or was at least easier to "resurrect." Since the early Christian era, it is resurrected through direct perception of the Mystery of Golgotha. As a result of the Christ's death and resurrection, human thinking has been reenlivened to such an extent that the soul does not have to die along with the body, as it would have if the Mystery of Golgotha had not happened. By looking up from the excessively strong "I" to images of the Mystery of Golgotha, initiates can "read" the development of the human soul. Through their insight into this particular chapter of initiation science, they know that the Christ's resurrection has reenlivened human souls. Thus, modern anthroposophical initiation science leads to an inwardly enlivened understanding of the Mystery of Golgotha. It leads *to* the Christ, not *away* from him, as some critics would have it. It is a spiritual way of finding the Christ.

Before I conclude, please allow me to briefly outline the development of human consciousness from the perspective of modern initiation science and as it has been affected by the Mystery of Golgotha.

In very ancient times, thinking was alive, and people felt surrounded by not only the physical but also the spiritual aspects of all the beings of nature. The spirit in nature was perceived through the dreamlike consciousness of instinctive clairvoyance, which provided a primal connection to the spiritual world through living thinking. Certain outstanding individuals—analogous to today's highly educated scientists—excelled in the initiation science of those primeval times, when all knowledge was initiation science because even ordinary people possessed clairvoyance of a sort. Everyone achieved certain levels of Imagination, Inspiration, and Intuition, though not the levels I described earlier. Any degree of Intuition allowed them to experience not only images of the spiritual world but also actual spiritual beings. The "I"-being of the spiritual beholder flowed out into the surrounding spirit.

Through such initiation, human beings experienced specific beings who descended from spiritual worlds as teachers. These were not physical beings; they could not be perceived with physical senses, nor did they use words that could be heard with physical ears. Human beings could communicate with them only through spiritual perception. Mighty spiritual perceptions allowed the initiates of primeval times to contact beings that descended to them in spiritual—not physical— love and taught them about a soul-spiritual existence unknown to physical thinking. This is the essence of ancient spiritual perception and knowledge. To summarize it in a single concise sentence, the first great teachers of humanity were spiritual beings who entered into spiritual intercourse with the first initiates and communicated to them the mystery of human birth, the mystery of living souls descending from prenatal existence in supersensible, spiritual worlds.

In those ancient times, the mystery of birth was a matter of direct knowledge. It was revealed directly by the spiritual world itself. Initiates with fully developed clairvoyant perception realized what others suspected on the basis of instinctive clairvoyance, namely, that we are "unborn." Initiates learned to look back in soul and spirit to earlier destinies, to see what they had been before descending into the physical world. This is how people were taught the mysteries of birth in ancient times. Although in some ways the outward rituals of their

Mysteries prefigured the Mystery of Golgotha, death was not yet viewed as it would be after that incisive event. People acknowledged being "unborn," that is, being endowed with living souls that predate physical existence, and they counted on the fact that the living human soul would survive death. They were not yet aware of the full tragedy of death, namely, the possibility that the soul might also die at the death of the physical body. As time went on, however, thinking became less and less alive. Abstract thinking, thinking's "corpse," descended from the spiritual world as people began to experience outer death as increasingly important. Mystery rituals that foreshadowed the Mystery of Golgotha offered consolation in the idea that the gods cannot die and thus divine human souls must rise from the dead. This consoling thought, however, had yet to be transformed into knowledge through the Mystery of Golgotha.

As paradoxical as it may sound to modern human ears, the spiritual teachers of old descended from life in the spiritual world only when human beings opened their souls to them. These spiritual beings served as humanity's teachers, but they did not participate in human destinies and they themselves were ignorant of the mystery of death. The fact that the people of very ancient times learned about the mystery of birth (but not the mystery of death) from souls who had experienced only birth, not death, is an important mystery in its own right. Consequently, when early Christian initiates contemplated the Mystery of Golgotha, they saw something that no ancient Mystery wisdom could have revealed. They perceived a total absence of any knowledge of death in the worlds that proclaimed the ancient wisdom, because none of the divine teachers of humankind had ever experienced death. Human destiny was foreign to the gods, and as human thinking developed, people began to live in fear that the death of the body would also mean the death of the soul. At that point, the divine kingdoms decided to send a god down to Earth to experience death and incorporate it into their wisdom. Intuitive perception of the Mystery of Golgotha reveals that it had consequences not only for human beings but also for the gods. The gods who had been able to tell earthly human beings only about the mystery of birth realized that the Earth had gradually outgrown the divine forces implanted in it and that human souls were on the verge of succumbing to death. The gods then sent the Christ to Earth to learn about human death and overcome it with his divine power.

From the perspective of the gods, the Mystery of Golgotha looks like this: For the sake of their own destiny, the gods introduced the Mystery of Golgotha into human evolution. This event was necessary not only for human beings but also for the gods. Formerly, divine events occurred only in divine spiritual worlds, but now a god descended to Earth, and a superearthly event occurred in earthly guise. In the Crucifixion and Resurrection, a spiritual event was enacted in an earthly setting. This is the single most important thing we can learn about Christianity through modern anthroposophical spiritual science. When we look at the Mystery of Golgotha as an instance of divine participation in earthly evolution—that is, in terms of what the gods accomplished on behalf of the Earth and earthly destiny—we also behold an event that concerns the gods themselves.

As long as our human activity is restricted to earthly life, we develop earth-related forces, which are not strong enough to overcome the overly strengthened "I." The Mystery of Golgotha cannot be understood through earthly reasoning, so we must move beyond our ordinary, earthly experience in our efforts to understand it. Initiation science encourages us to see the event of Golgotha as an intervention that was at once cosmic and earthly. When we do so, we imbue ourselves with the cognitive power to come to the following realization: Through ordinary, earthly, human forces, we receive everything the Earth contributes to the human "I." When we look toward the Mystery of Golgotha, however, we are lifted away from the Earth, and a life is enkindled in us that cannot be enkindled in any other way. In turning toward the Mystery of Golgotha, we absorb a supersensible element. We recognize that humanity needs a new type of supersensible, inner feeling and perception to replace the living thinking of old. We also recognize that we can achieve such perception through the Mystery of Golgotha. We experience the deadness of our thinking, and, as a result, we realize that since the Mystery of Golgotha, it is "not I, but the Christ in me" that truly makes us alive.

The purpose of modern Anthroposophy is to encourage these real-izations and to deepen, rather than deaden, our religious life by allow-ing us to break with old traditions consciously. Spiritual scientific knowledge of the Mystery of Golgotha allows us to transcend all the grave doubts we experience in modern religious life, which result pri-marily from our scientific education. Although exoteric science has made us free and achieved great outer triumphs, it has also instilled very understandable doubts in our hearts with regard to religious feel-ing and knowledge of our own supersensible nature. Anthroposophy, which works out of the spirit of science, has taken up the task of elim-inating these doubts and implanting truly religious life in the human soul. Far from contributing to the death of religion, Anthroposophy will foster a revival of religious feeling and a new understanding of Christianity, which can be correctly understood and accepted only by turning to the Mystery of Golgotha.

Because anthroposophically-derived spiritual knowledge will not only revive old religious feelings but also enkindle new ones, it is safe to say that Anthroposophy harbors no sectarian aspirations. This is as true of Anthroposophy as it is of any other science. Anthroposophy's purpose is not to found sects. Its intent is to serve preexisting religions and to revitalize Christianity in this sense. But Anthroposophy feels called upon to do more than simply preserve old religious feelings and allow traditional religious activity to continue. Its aim is to contribute not only to reviving but also to resurrecting the religious life that has suffered so severely under modern civilization. Anthroposophy hopes to be a messenger of love that will not only revitalize old religious feel-ings but also foster an esoteric resurrection of humanity's inner reli-gious sense.

11

THE THREEFOLD SUN
AND THE RISEN CHRIST

LONDON, APRIL 24, 1922

In modern times, it is absolutely necessary for a number of people to know where we stand now in humankind's spiritual evolution and what path we must take to ensure the survival of our civilization. In purely anthroposophical terms, the spiritual powers we call the ahrimanic forces, which embrace all of our materialistic thinking and actions, are attempting to bind us to the Earth through sheer intellectualism.[†] In our times, these ahrimanic forces are very strong. They are trying to gain access to human souls in any way possible and to entrap them in a materialistic, purely intellectual understanding of the world. For this reason, it is essential for many people to understand how our evolution on Earth must continue if humankind is to achieve its earthly goal. To understand this, we must look back in time over a segment of humankind's spiritual evolution. For our purposes today, we will not need to look back any further than three or four thousand years before the Mystery of Golgotha. We will then trace humankind's development into modern times.

Let me begin with the development of the Asian civilization I called ancient Persian culture in *Esoteric Science*. During this cultural epoch, humanity's foremost teacher was Zarathustra, or Zoroaster. This is not the historical Zarathustra, who lived at a later time, but a much earlier teacher of humanity. (In those ancient times, it was common for the disciples of a great teacher to retain his name for a long period of time. Thus the historical Zarathustra was the last in the generations of disciples of the great Zarathustra.) The original Zarathustra was a great, outstanding initiate. As a result of his particular initiation into the mysteries of existence, Zarathustra knew that an all-embracing cosmic spirit inhabited the space where the Sun appears to our ordinary consciousness. What Zarathustra saw first when he looked in that direction was not the physical Sun but a great cosmic spirit who influenced him on a spiritual level. As a result, Zarathustra knew that the Sun's physical rays are accompanied by rays of divine, spiritual grace. In the human soul and spirit this divine grace rouses to life the higher being to which ordinary humans aspire. In those days, initiates were known not by their exoteric names but by names indicating what they knew, so this great initiate was known as Zarathustra, or Zoroaster, the "shining star," meaning the radiant divinity that sends rays of wisdom to Earth.[†]

Zarathustra's level of initiation was higher than all subsequent initiations. What he saw in the cosmic, spiritual Sun encompassed all the forces that allow stones to harden, plants to sprout, animal species to multiply, and human beings to grow and thrive. Through the spiritual being he experienced in the Sun, the original Zarathustra, the "shining star," knew everything that happened on Earth.

During the next cultural epoch, which I called Egypto-Chaldean culture in *Esoteric Science*, it was no longer possible for human beings to delve so deeply into the mysteries of the cosmos. The initiates of that time no longer perceived the Sun's spiritual rays. For them, Ra was the shining Sun that moved around the Earth and Osiris his earthly representative. Certain mysteries were lost, because initiates could no longer see the radiant cosmic god in full inner clarity but only primal, astral forces coming from the Sun. Where Zarathustra had been able to see an actual being, the Egyptian and Chaldean initiates saw only forces of light and movement streaming down to the Earth from the Sun. They saw something less than a spiritual being—spiritual actions, but not an actual spiritual being. And "Osiris" was the name the initiates of ancient Egypt gave to the manifestations of the Sun's forces within the human being.

Moving on to ancient Greece—that is, to the eighth through fifth centuries B.C.—we find that people no longer beheld the Sun's inner mysteries but saw only its effects in the ether surrounding the Earth. Greek initiates—not ordinary people, but initiates—gave the name "Zeus" to the Sun's effects in the ether that surrounds the Earth and pervades human beings.

We have now considered three stages of human cultural development: During the first stage, initiates beheld a divine, spiritual being in the Sun; during the second, they saw the Sun's forces in action; during the third, they perceived only the etheric effects of the Sun-being. At a later date in history, these three aspects of the Sun—the aspects known to Zarathustra, Osiris, and Pythagoras and Anaxagoras, respectively—were also known to Julian the Apostate,[†] who was as familiar with the teachings of initiation as anyone in his time. Through doctrines or traditions passed down in the Mystery Schools, rather than through direct perception, Julian learned about these three aspects. He came to know something of the unutterable glory that Zarathustra had seen, and he also grasped something of the activity of fire, light, and the cosmic forces of chemistry and life that initiates had perceived in the ancient Mysteries. He was so overwhelmed by this knowledge that Christianity seemed trivial in comparison, and he was unable to become a convert. Having experienced a certain degree of initiation into ancient Mysteries, Julian attempted to disseminate their wisdom to the general public. He then met a violent death at the hands of someone who believed that exalted initiation teachings should not be communicated to humanity at large. The intent of Julian's murderer was to restrict ordinary people's knowledge of the Sun to the exoteric statements of the day.

Julian the Apostate said that the Sun had three aspects: one belonging to the earthly ether; one belonging to heavenly light and to the forces of chemistry, heat, and light that stood behind the earthly ether; and a third, purely spiritual aspect that was a divine being. For making such statements, Julian was stabbed to death. In all fairness, it must be said that Julian lived at a moment in humankind's evolution when humanity at large really was not yet mature enough to receive such significant truths.

It is also extremely important to note that exoteric Greek culture absorbed much of what was contained in the threefold teachings of Zarathustra, Osiris, and Pythagoras and Anaxagoras about the spiritual sun, the elemental sun, and the sun in the Earth's ether. Greek art and philosophy were able to achieve such great heights only because much of this ancient wisdom flowed into the likes of Plato and Aristotle. By the time of Julian the Apostate, the ancient truths of initiation were no longer adequately protected against profanation. A great deal of initiation wisdom was conveyed to prominent Romans—specifically, to the Roman emperors—but after the time of Augustus, if not earlier, they ceased to recognize its value. That is why we find reflections of ancient esoteric wisdom in Greek art but not in Roman culture. Although it took on the outer brilliance of Greek culture, Roman civilization was completely prosaic and semi-barbarian. As a result, the spirituality that still lived in Greek civilization could not be passed on in its true form, and ancient Mystery culture was not available to Christianity, which emerged in the context of Roman civilization.

This statement must not be taken as a reproach or criticism, because this stage was necessary in the evolution of humankind. We must realize, however, that because Roman civilization did not value initiation, its ancient truths could not be passed on to the West and have not entered our ordinary, modern consciousness. Roman culture separates us from the holy truths of antiquity, which the Romans did not understand. As a result, the emperor Justinian[†] closed the philosophers' schools in Athens, and the last seven Athenian philosophers fled the Roman Empire and settled in Persia.

I am telling you all this as necessary background to the actual subject of today's lecture. Before I can continue, we must briefly consider those ancient times when spiritual teachers looked up at the starry heavens and saw the threefold Sun. This knowledge has survived only in symbols such as the threefold papal miter. Outer aspects have been preserved, but its content has been lost. Today a new form of initiation, such as Anthroposophy offers, is needed if we are to look back into those ancient times when people on Earth learned the mysteries of human spiritual evolution directly from the Sun.

When disciples of the initiates of old looked beyond the Earth and into the cosmos, they perceived the spiritual being of the Sun in the physical Sun and its effects. In essence, this being was the one who would later be called the Christ. Outside of the Earth, in the cosmic Sun, these initiates beheld the Christ. Thus, knowledge of the Christ is not the single most important aspect of the Mystery of Golgotha, because the initiates of ancient times also knew about the Christ. They simply spoke of him as a being that lived not on Earth or in earthly forces but rather in the forces of the Sun. It is totally wrong to believe that the initiates of old were talking about a being other than the Christ. Prior to the Mystery of Golgotha, the Christ was always perceived as a being from outside the Earth. This is a secret that has been entirely lost to humankind. In fact, such a view is now considered unchristian, although it was certainly the view of the early church fathers, who knew that the "heathen" wise men of ancient times were Christians in a deeper sense even before the Mystery of Golgotha occurred.

What happened through the Mystery of Golgotha? This Sun-being, formerly found only outside the Earth and perceptible only to those initiated into the heavenly mysteries, incarnated in the person of Jesus of Nazareth, lived on Earth, was crucified and buried, and appeared to his initiated disciples in the spiritual body of the Resurrected One. The essence of the Mystery of Golgotha is that the exalted Sun Being actually descended to Earth from cosmic heights and that the Christ, who passed through death and whose body was laid in the grave, taught his initiated disciples after his death and resurrection. What he taught these disciples needs to be known by many people today so that we can participate in humankind's progressive development.

All of the initiates of old were literally taught by beings from outside the Earth. In the oldest Mysteries, candidates for initiation were prepared for out-of-body perception that allowed them to recognize the superearthly beings of various hierarchies, just as Zarathustra recognized the Christ as the exalted Sun Being. In these ancient times, people were taught the spiritual language of the divine teachers who descended from spiritual worlds to instruct initiates. For those he taught after his resurrection, the Christ was one such teacher, but he was able to teach them something that earlier divine teachers could not.

Earlier divine teachers told human beings a great deal about the mysteries of birth but nothing about the mysteries of death, because at that time not a single being in the divine world had experienced death. Death could be experienced only on Earth and only by human beings. Although the gods saw human beings die, they themselves had only a superficial knowledge of death. Earlier spiritual teachers incarnated only temporarily, to appear to the human beings they taught, but the Christ-God learned about earthly death by living like a human soul in a physical, earthly human body. He learned about death by experiencing it in a human body.

But that was not all he learned. If he had experienced only the events between the baptism in the Jordan and his crucifixion and death on the cross, the Christ would not have been able to tell his initiated disciples what he told them after his resurrection. Both the earlier divine teachers who descended to Earth and the initiates of old knew all of the mysteries of the cosmos, with the exception of the mysteries of the Earth's interior. They knew that the Earth's interior was ruled by spiritual beings of a different type from the gods who descended to Earth in the time before the Mystery of Golgotha. (The Greeks, for example, were aware of these beings, known as Titans in Greek mythology.) Through his burial, however, the Christ became the first of the "upper" gods to learn about the Earth's interior. It is important to know that the Christ explored this unknown territory on behalf of the upper gods. After his resurrection, he taught his initiated disciples that gods also learn and evolve. This is what Paul learned through his natural initiation outside Damascus. In this earth-shattering experience, he understood that a force previously found only in the Sun had united with the Earth's forces.

Why had Paul, in his life as Saul, persecuted the Christ's followers? As Saul, he had learned through ancient Hebrew initiation that the Christ lives out in the cosmos, not on Earth. He was convinced that those who insisted that the Christ had lived on Earth were wrong. When illumination struck him outside Damascus, he understood for the first time that *he* was wrong, because his belief was outdated. In reality, the being who once lived only in the Sun had descended to Earth to inhabit its forces. Thus, to those who first proclaimed it, the Mystery of Golgotha was not merely an earthly event. The initiates of the early Christian era taught that it was also a cosmic event.

Early Christians who achieved a profound level of initiation knew that the Christ, the being who passed through the Mystery of Golgotha, had descended from even more exalted heights to the Sun, where he was perceived by Zarathustra. His power was then vested first in the Sun's rays, where he was perceived by Egyptian initiates, and then in the Earth's surroundings, where he was perceived by Greek initiates. Now, however, we are meant to perceive him as he was when he walked among human beings in an earthly body. We are meant to perceive him in his true form, as the Risen One who is in and of the Earth. He has perceived the mystery of the Earth and is gradually allowing it to flow into humankind's further development.

With tremendous warmth and conviction, very isolated schools in the East secretly began to spread this esoteric Christian doctrine during the first few centuries A.D. Yes, esoteric Christianity does indeed exist! The early church fathers still knew of it, but they also saw the approaching storm of Roman civilization. History underestimates the monumental clash between early Christian impulses and the antispiritual culture of Rome, which spread a mantle of superficiality over the deepest mysteries of Christianity.

Our ordinary modern consciousness has virtually no inkling of how the people of ancient times related to the forces of the cosmos. Three to five millennia before the Christian era, people knew that when they ate certain substances, the forces of the cosmos worked through these substances into their bodies. For example, when Zarathustra taught his disciples, he said something like this: "You eat of the fruits of the field, which are shone upon by the Sun. The Sun, however, is inhabited by an exalted spiritual being. From out in the cosmos, the power of this spiritual being streams into the fruits of the field on the Sun's rays. You eat the fruits of the field, and their substance is released in you. May you also be filled with the spiritual forces of the Sun, which rises in you whenever you eat of the fruits of the field. Especially when you gather in ceremonial moments, take bread made from the fruits of the field and meditate on the Sun in it until it becomes radiant. Eat it, knowing that the spirit of the Sun has descended from the widths of the cosmos to live in you."

The ritual breaking and eating of bread during Communion is a mere superficial token of this ancient knowledge. The perpetuators of the superficiality imposed on Christianity by Roman culture are also those who most vigorously contest the idea that cosmic wisdom is required in order to understand Christianity. They are also the least able to understand Paul's teachings, because Paul directly perceived the Sun's power streaming down from the clouds in the form of a superphysical being. This being is the Christ, who descended to Earth through the Mystery of Golgotha. He is the cosmic divinity of the Sun who has united with the forces of the Earth.

These Mysteries were still known in the first three or four centuries of the Christian era, but then the exoteric worldview grew so strong that even traditional accounts no longer reveal the earlier, highly spiritual view of the Mystery of Golgotha. Today, however, it is essential for humankind to remember this spiritual understanding of the central event in the development of civilization. Since those early Christian centuries, human beings have taken earthly wisdom to great heights. As a result, we have become free beings. In ancient times, not even initiates were free, because their deepest impulses were guided by the gods. The freedom we experience now is due to the exceptional degree of earthly wisdom that we have achieved, and in the immediate future this freedom will increasingly allow the anti-godly and anti-Christian forces that I call ahrimanic forces to take hold of human souls.

For all our talk about nature and the dramatic achievements of our exacting natural sciences, we have not yet seen the need to Christianize science. Nonetheless, it must happen. We must thoroughly Christianize science, or we will lose everything we need to receive from the cosmos. In Zarathustra's time, people were still receptive to cosmic influences and understood them through the very food they consumed. Over time, however, human beings became increasingly estranged from cosmic life. In the Egypto-Chaldean culture, initiates were still aware of divine forces flowing into plants and stones, and this awareness led to the emergence of the science of healing. Even today, our most effective medicine dates back to those ancient times, although we no longer know it. In this field, too, it is time to return to the source, to develop a medical science that truly explores the more profound forces in natural beings. This is a task for a modern science of initiation, and, as such, Anthroposophy hopes to provide humankind with all that can be achieved in this regard today. In the year 1899, the dark age known to prophets of old as Kali Yuga† came to an end. The living, spiritual world that surrounds us can now reveal itself. We are once again becoming able to perceive it and to hear its revelations. The purpose of Anthroposophy is to draw attention to the newly accessible spiritual world. This is a matter of concern not only to human beings but also to the entire cosmos.

When the insights of initiation science are communicated in concrete detail, we must expect some of them to be met with ridicule. In my introduction today, I said that it has become essential for people to learn about humankind's evolution in detail, on the basis of initiation science. We must avoid swimming in generalities. We must enliven our insights by acting on them, which means that they need to be directly and vitally relevant to human life. Let me illustrate this with a story.

Near the end of the Crusades, an extraordinarily gifted young monk living in an Italian monastery delved into the oral (not written) traditions that had been handed down from the early years of Christianity and survived in some monasteries. After joining one of the last Crusades, this monk fell ill in Palestine, or at least somewhere in the Near East. Lying in the hospital, he met an older monk who was initiated into the mysteries of Christianity. This encounter made the younger monk long to feel and understand Christianity's deeper mysteries, but he died with this longing unsatisfied. When he was reborn in our own era, remarkable forces emerged in his personality as a result of his previous life. (As I said before, it is understandable that such statements are subject to ridicule. Nonetheless, we do need to be able to talk about the concrete and detailed conclusions of initiation science. Eventually, people will realize that the results of spiritual research are as accurate and scientific as the facts of exoteric history.) This personality was the one we know as *Cardinal Newman*.†

If you read about his life and what he said as a young man, you can see that this strong personality was filled with a Christianity that was different from the Christianity all around him. He wanted to escape from intellectual Christianity and dreamed of the different type of consciousness experienced by the first disciples of the risen Christ. If you then follow his later life, you will come upon an important statement that Cardinal Newman made on the occasion of his investiture. He said that there will be no salvation for religion without a new revelation.

If you keep this statement in mind, you will understand that Newman's quest was based on a profound longing that resulted from previous earthly lives. He felt the welling up of spiritual forces that I mentioned before, and although he never transcended traditional Christian views, he had an inkling that a new initiation science (and thus also a new spiritual revelation) could be achieved through a specific type of self-development. I need not tell you more, here in his native country, because you can read up on Cardinal Newman for yourselves. He strove to break out of the fog of traditional Christianity into a new light, but he never actually succeeded. Deeper insight into his being reveals that this failure was not his fault. In this regard, he was a victim of his time and of what I have called the ahrimanic forces, which mounted an especially strong offensive against him, keeping his thinking imprisoned and preventing his spirituality from developing freely. Today, anyone who wants to develop free spirituality must liberate thinking from dependence on the brain.

Ahriman achieves his greatest successes by shortening the second half of human existence between death and rebirth. (The two halves of this period are depicted in my mystery dramas.†) The second half, which encompasses everything that takes place after the point I call "cosmic midnight," is the period that Ahriman attempts to shorten. In great haste and with great energy, Ahriman claws his way into the human brain, so to speak, in his attempts to restrict human beings' experience of the spiritual world and to confine our thinking to the Earth. The result of Ahriman's activity is that people are incarnating one to two hundred years too soon. It takes a great deal of energy to overcome this ahrimanic intervention. For all his strength, Cardinal Newman was unable to free his own thinking sufficiently. If he had succeeded, he would have discovered the path to a new revelation himself, instead of referring to it as something that must happen in the future.

Personalities such as Cardinal Newman illustrate why we must draw attention to the spirituality that will lead human beings to a new life. As I have already pointed out, this spirituality will allow us to understand the Mystery of Golgotha again and feel its full significance, so that it lives in the inmost depths of our souls. I mentioned Cardinal Newman as an example of a tragic personality whose life reveals what needs to be done. Because ahrimanic forces intervened, Cardinal Newman failed to achieve a spiritual life and spiritual insight or perception. It is important for people here in England to grasp the esoteric necessity of making this spiritual life and perception comprehensible to humankind again. The survival of our civilization depends on it.

It is no exaggeration to say that insight into such concrete karmic connections will motivate us to do our utmost to encourage human spiritual activity. This is the only option. But we must also be aware that the ahrimanic forces are very strong. Anthroposophy's testimony has very powerful opponents inspired by ahrimanic powers, and they are growing stronger and stronger. I am telling you this today so that you will not be surprised to learn that the budding anthroposophical movement increasingly has to battle terrible adversarial forces. Insight into the intentions behind anthroposophical endeavors must alert us to terrible aspersions and other types of attacks by enemies who do not want this movement to survive. But no matter how strong these enemies may be, our own positive energy must be equally strong. It is imperative that we disseminate the anthroposophical worldview honestly and clearly, even if many people will not be able to understand or accept what the anthroposophical movement attempts to cultivate.

Despite all distortions and obfuscations of the anthroposophical movement's intentions, I hope that many people will summon the strength to apply their own positive energy to proving the validity and relevance of this spirituality to the world, which also entails recognizing this spirituality as a necessity for the continued evolution of humankind and human civilization. If we have come any closer to agreement on the inner character of Anthroposophy and its importance for our times, then this gathering for which we waited so long will have borne the best possible fruit, in my estimation.[7] In the spirit of this accomplishment and in recalling this mutual understanding, let us remain together in soul as we go our separate ways.

12

ANTHROPOSOPHY AS AN ATTEMPT TO ENCHRISTEN THE WORLD

VIENNA, JULY 11, 1922

I must precede today's lecture with a few words of introduction. As you know, many of our older members are somewhat pained by recent changes in the anthroposophical movement, and I would like to briefly present their perspective on this transformation.

Years ago, we met in circles that were smaller than today's, but otherwise very similar. The way we talked in those circles was possible because it was safe to assume that their members were familiar with the basic elements of anthroposophical thought and, more particularly, of anthroposophical feeling. I do not mean to suggest that all members of these more intimate anthroposophical circles subscribed to specific dogmatic ideas; I simply mean that they all shared a heartfelt longing to find a path into the spiritual world. When speaking about esoteric subjects, it is always essential to know that the audience consists of people who share this longing. In the early years of our movement, even public lectures preserved this esoteric character to a certain extent, although, of course, we had to use ways of thinking and speaking that belonged to the exoteric aspect of our times. Nonetheless, our older members were able to feel that even our larger gatherings represented a continuation of the esoteric striving cultivated in smaller circles.

But when these members attend our conferences now, it seems to them that we are speaking a different language than we spoke formerly, and this experience causes a certain amount of pain. Fundamental esoteric contents that were once expressed directly are now cast in the forms of modern science. I know perfectly well what many of our older members are now thinking: Formerly, we could approach the insights and impulses of the spiritual world much faster; we achieved spiritual experiences much more quickly and in an esoterically more truthful way, and now we have virtually no interest in applying rigorous trains of thought in attempts to justify the esoteric contents our hearts received in this way. Many of these older members are less interested in this new approach, and they experience a certain loss because the anthroposophical movement has not preserved its previous forms of communication.

This change, however, was not initiated by the anthroposophical movement itself. At least as far as my own involvement is concerned, our movement has never sought popularity by conveying its message in such a way that people hear what they already know anyway. The anthroposophical movement has never pursued this goal and has always spoken in ways true to its essential character. I have always been especially gratified to hear people say that Anthroposophy certainly cannot be accused of dishonest attempts to arouse enthusiasm by taking advantage of people's preconceived notions. Our manner of speaking is certainly not as accessible as it would be if we were deliberately attempting to popularize our movement.

The present state of affairs is really not something we sought out. Although I have often been approached with requests to popularize my "theory" by rewriting it so that everyone can understand it without great effort, I have always refused to corrupt Anthroposophy in this way, because I consider such effort essential to understanding what Anthroposophy represents. It has never been my intention to transform the anthroposophical movement into a popular movement that wins people's hearts and minds by saying what they already know. Nonetheless, the anthroposophical movement's recent growth has been unexpectedly rapid for a movement of this sort, and our literature has met with a totally unprecedented reception for such difficult material. As a consequence, however, people who get their hands on our literature judge it from their own perspectives.

Scientists compare ideas introduced by Anthroposophy to the rigorous science they are accustomed to. No wonder we need to give serious thought to how we relate to science! No wonder quite a few scientifically trained friends of Anthroposophy see it as their particular task to demonstrate that Anthroposophy can indeed be presented for all the world to see on scientifically justifiable grounds in any area of knowledge. This is what the reality of our situation demands. When you hear scientific overtones today in contents that we formerly communicated in quite different terms, this is not the *fault* of the anthroposophical movement, it is its *destiny*. This is what the world demands. We have had to present Anthroposophy to the broader public, and we have been able to do so only by entering into discussion with leading personalities. For us, however, the point is not to make Anthroposophy more closely resemble science. The point is to imbue science with Anthroposophy.

On the positive side, it has been very satisfying to welcome professionally trained friends to our midst, experts who can represent our budding anthroposophically oriented sciences to the scientific community. Nonetheless, it is true that their presence among us has resulted in an internal division in our movement that we have not yet been able to bridge. It cannot be said that esotericism no longer lives in our more intimate circles. Anyone who takes part in our smaller gatherings will realize that our movement's esoteric current still survives. In particular, anyone who comes to Dornach will see how much new intellectual and esoteric wealth has been added to the old. Nonetheless, a cleft has developed between Anthroposophy as it is heard in public and Anthroposophy as it is cultivated in more intimate esoteric circles. To date, we have been unable to bridge this gap, owing to shortages of time and manpower. On the one hand, we must continue to devote ourselves to esoteric training; on the other hand, our younger members, in particular, are very actively developing the anthroposophical worldview in all its social and practical applications. It is certainly both necessary and possible to bridge the gap between our esoteric efforts and the exoteric face of Anthroposophy as it appears in our public conferences. This gap must be filled, and each of us must feel that if we simply had the necessary time and energy to do this work within our movement, it would indeed be possible to build a bridge between the purity of what we hear spoken out of the spiritual world and what we teach in harmony with exoteric science.

This should give you a picture of how I myself see the situation surrounding the current work of our anthroposophical movement. I might say that to outward appearances, this movement has outgrown us in a certain respect, but I remain hopeful that more and more friends will appear among us who are able to bridge the gap.

The purpose of these introductory remarks was to point out that we must use very different forms to convey esoteric contents and to communicate with the broader public in the context of contemporary culture. Directly communicated esoteric content would not speak to the hearts of our contemporaries who come to our movement as complete newcomers. Without seeking popularity, those of us who have been part of this movement for decades must be concerned about making Anthroposophy accessible to all who choose to hear about it. This is something that we should all inscribe in our hearts, because any member can help to make it possible.

As we make the transition today from exoteric to esoteric content, I would like to address an issue that relates to our other, larger gatherings, namely, what exoteric science—physics, chemistry, biology, and even psychology—could become if imbued with Anthroposophy. This is the only way that the gap between scientific knowledge and religious activity can be bridged. When we allow ourselves to be inundated with modern science, it is true that we lose a certain connection to the spirit weaving and surging through the cosmos. Nonetheless, we must also look at life's material forms. Spirit is present in all material manifestations of our life, which cannot persist without our participation in the spirit. Today we must understand that this spirit does not merely attempt to address the cosmos out of human longing. It attempts to flow into our earthly world from a different world. We must understand that the windows between our world and this other world have been opened, not by us alone but also by the spiritual world that surrounds us. This was not the case in the nineteenth century, before a number of superhuman, extraterrestrial spiritual powers decided to allow a wave of spiritual life to flow into earthly life. When we consider the history of our times, we must realize that human beings are now newly able to receive the spiritual world if they so desire. Consequently, cultivating the spirit on Earth is now a superearthly task, an intrinsic part of the life of the spiritual world itself. Now that human beings are again beginning to sense a dim longing to access the spirit— which was often not the case as recently as the last third of the nineteenth century—this longing, whenever it is truly willed, is being met by revelations from spiritual worlds. This sense of longing is the appropriate basic mood in which to approach anthroposophical activity.

This new accessibility of the spiritual world means that humankind now faces an important decision that cuts to the heart of every individual. For centuries, human beings have been developing their intellect, which has gradually led us away from spirituality. Although intellect *is* spirit—in fact, the very purest spirit—it no longer has a spiritual content. Instead, it has chosen the world of outer nature as its contents. In other words, the intellect is spirit but fills itself with something that cannot manifest as spirit. This is the great modern tragedy of the cosmos: In moments of introspection, we human beings must acknowledge that although intellectual activity is spiritual activity, our intellect is powerless to receive spirit directly. Instead, we fill our spirit with natural, material existence. This state of affairs is fragmenting modern human souls and turning them into a wasteland. Although we may not want to admit it, the spiritual regions of the human soul are becoming fragmented and desolate. This is the fundamental evil and the underlying tragedy of our time.

In our usual anhroposophical terminology, the spiritual powers that prevail in all natural existence and enter us when it fills our spirit are called the "ahrimanic forces." Our intellect, as it has developed over the past few centuries, is exposed to a grave risk of falling prey to ahrimanic forces. As long as it still preserved the legacy of ancient spirituality, these ahrimanic forces did not wield as much power over human beings as they do today. To all appearances, the natural world lies spread out around us, but this is an illusion. In reality, Ahriman lives in this natural world. When we perceive nature, we believe that it is governed purely by neutral natural laws, but, in fact, we are unwittingly taking in ahrimanic spiritual powers that have set themselves a specific task within the existence and evolution of the cosmos as a whole.

When we talk about the task of spiritual powers such as these, it is easy to wonder why the divine governance of the cosmos permits them to intervene. In response, we must emphasize that although everything earthly can be understood with ordinary human reason, anything of a spiritual-scientific, Earth-transcending character can be understood only through direct spiritual perception. These adversary forces exist, but how they relate to the divine spiritual powers that foster human development is something that we human beings will be able to understand only much later in our evolution, if ever. In fact, these adversary forces may always elude human understanding, because understanding them requires the application of superhuman forces. All we can say is that these powers do exist, and they reveal themselves to spiritual perception.

As I described in *Esoteric Science*, the task of these ahrimanic powers is to prevent the Earth from evolving as intended by the divine spiritual powers that have been involved with human souls from the very beginning of time. In *Esoteric Science*, I described the future evolution of our Earth as the "Jupiter" and "Venus" stages. The ahrimanic powers are attempting to prevent this future development. They want the Earth to harden and freeze as it is; they want the human race to become trapped in exclusively earthly materiality and live on in the future of the cosmos as a dead image of its own past. These powers have specific cosmic goals, and binding human beings to the Earth is certainly one of them. If the ahrimanic powers were victorious, the Earth would never achieve its spiritual goal; human beings would be estranged from their origins and from the powers that set human evolution in motion. The human body would assume an outer form still fully adapted to earthly life, but all human potential to transcend the earthly would be suppressed.

As long as our intellect remained rooted in spirit through an ancient legacy, as it was in the previous three or four centuries, the ahrimanic powers could not approach human beings. Since the beginning of the twentieth century, however, the situation has changed. Ancient Indian wisdom, divining the beginning of a new age, set the end of the Dark Age (Kali Yuga) at the end of the nineteenth century. The dawning of the new age means that from the beginning of the twentieth century onward, human hearts need no longer cling to their old legacy but can truly absorb new, pure light into our earthly life.

But this spiritual light will elude human beings unless we make a deliberate effort to receive it. As long as the old legacy prevailed, human intellect was not as damaging as it can be today. In recent times, our understanding of the solid, liquid, gaseous, and etheric elements of the natural world has evolved. When we look at the Earth and its elements, they appear as if devoid of spirit. But when we consider hydrogen, nitrogen, oxygen, and so forth and the physical laws that govern them, we give the ahrimanic powers a point of attack in the context of cosmic evolution. Because we pay no attention to the spirit around us, Ahriman can creep inside us without our knowledge and usurp that spirit. This is why we must learn about the spirit around us. It is no longer acceptable to talk about solid matter only in terms of chemical elements such as sodium and calcium. We must also be aware of the spiritual element associated with everything that is solid, or earthly, in character. We must realize that the solid, earthly matter we encounter in the outer world is associated with spirit— specifically, with a spirit that has a unique tendency to manifest as a multiplicity. Wherever physical vision sees solid matter, spiritual perception also sees many different spiritual beings.

Ancient, instinctive wisdom called these beings gnomes and the like. There is no need to retain these antiquated names, however, if people are shocked by them; we can speak about these beings in more familiar terms. The point is that we must pay attention to the spirit that manifests in every clump of solid matter. When we gather in more esoteric circles, as we are doing today, we can be more direct: Today, whenever human beings equipped with spiritual perception encounter a clump of earth, they see spiritual beings springing forth from it. These beings are not physically incarnated, so we cannot see them with physical eyes, but they can be perceived with spiritual sight. They are so many and so varied that the smallest clump of solid matter yields countless numbers of them. They consist almost entirely of the active "substance" of human reason. In other words, these beings are crafty, clever, and excessively wise.

We are surrounded by their living, spiritual cleverness, by their spiritual understanding, which is much more rapid than our own intellectual rationality. In the solid, earthly element, intellect becomes substance-like. Until we know how these spiritual beings of the solid, earthly element work together, there can be no true chemistry. Anthroposophy can understand the chemistry we have today, but we will grasp the full truth only when we discover the object of supersensible perception, the spiritual element in everything earthly. We must have the will to abandon even the solidest pillars of human deliberation. Whenever we confront the earthly element in any way that involves counting—1, 2, 3, 4—we are accustomed to seeing four items when we have counted to four. But the spiritual beings that free themselves from solid matter are so eager to diversify that we may find that three or four become seven as soon as we start to count. Counting is completely useless in this situation. In our atomistic world, objects can be counted, but the real world, where everything is alive, aims for much greater diversity. We are forced to realize that a higher intelligence scoffs at our counting. Although it is important to remain levelheaded in our intellectual approach, we must openly confront what reality presents. On the other hand, many people will say that a reality that confronts us with uncountable beings will make us go crazy! Before entering this spiritual world, therefore, it is extremely important to make sure that we are completely levelheaded and capable of assessing earthly circumstances objectively.

We all know that our waking life becomes disordered when we do not sleep properly. Given that what we experience here on Earth is like sleep compared with the reality we encounter on entering the spiritual world, it makes sense that individuals who are not fully grounded on Earth—people who succumb to spiritualist fantasies, for example—will carry pathological elements with them into the spiritual world. They will move around the spiritual world with the nervousness of someone waking from a pathological sleep. This can be prevented, however, by the striving for harmony that underlies all our anthroposophical activity. The anthroposophical movement can result in greater health and healing for individuals, but it does not result in alienation from the fullness of human life between birth and death.

Moving on to the fluid element, we find spiritual beings of a different type. While the elemental beings of solid matter resemble our human reason, the elemental beings that inhabit the fluid element more closely resemble our feeling. With our emotions and perceptions, we stand outside things: That beautiful tree is over there, but I am standing here, separate from it, as I allow it to flow into me. The elemental beings of the fluid element flow through the tree in its very sap, and their sensations flow into every leaf from the inside. They experience red and blue not from outside but from within. As a result, their sensations are much more intense than ours, just as the understanding of the elemental beings of solid matter is much more intense than our human understanding.

Similarly, the airy element contains a number of elemental beings. The more these beings approach this element, however, the more they lose their longing for diversity. We get the feeling that the concept of number becomes increasingly less applicable as we move up into the airy element, where elemental beings increasingly strive for unity. Nonetheless, the elemental beings of the air manifest in great diversity, similar to that found in human will. The elemental beings of solid matter are inwardly related to human intelligence, the beings of the fluid element to human feeling, and the beings of the airy element to human will.

The Catholic Church construes the worship of saints in its own particular way, of course, but the underlying impulse is more profound. We, however, must learn not only to find the surviving spirits of revered human beings but also to seek the spirit in everything around us, just as we seek the natural world with our physical senses. When we do this, we make our way upward to the light that streams toward us and the life that pulses through the cosmos. We make our way upward toward the beings that strive for unity and seduce human beings to perceive the spirit in the cosmos as unitary. Monotheism grew out of the etheric world's revelation to earthly human beings.

But when we make our way up to these beings of light, these elemental beings of the ether, we find ourselves in a different outer world, which consists not only of physical light but also of the spirit that streams down to us in every ray of sunlight.

Here we discover beings similar to those found in the earthly elements. Instead of attempting to bind us to the Earth, as the ahrimanic powers do, these beings of the etheric element want to prevent us from fully understanding the earthly element. They want to arrest human evolution and prevent the Earth from achieving its ultimate goal. The ahrimanic beings want the Earth to evolve to a point that serves their purposes. In contrast, these other beings are intent on holding the Earth back at earlier stages of development, preventing it from realizing its full potential. The elemental powers of the ether have decided to enter into an alliance with Lucifer. This is the second such decision that confronts us when we look up into higher spheres. Ahriman and his forces gain access to human beings when we shut ourselves off from perceiving and understanding the spirit; Lucifer, along with the powers that live in the ether, moves into us when we neglect the right sort of inner absorption In short, we are now confronted with adversarial forces both from above and from below.

This whole choir of beings that surrounds us in stones, plants, animals, and physical human bodies can either reveal itself to us (if we willingly receive the spirit) or remain inaccessible to our consciousness. If we choose to know nothing of the spiritual world, this whole choir succumbs to the ahrimanic powers; Ahriman forms an alliance with the spirits of nature. The preeminent decision in the spiritual world today is to forge an alliance between the ahrimanic forces and the forces of nature. The only way to prevent this alliance is for human beings to learn to perceive the spiritual world and become as familiar with nature spirits as we are now familiar with the chemical elements of oxygen, nitrogen, hydrogen, calcium, sodium, and so forth. To our scientific understanding of the sense-perceptible, physical world, we must add a science of the spirit, and we must be absolutely serious about it. We cannot approach the spirit through mere pantheistic talk. We must avoid the lack of courage that prevents people from talking about concrete spiritual beings. What would have happened in human evolution if the people of the Old Testament and others had adhered to the pantheistic view of a vague, universal spirit and had not dared to talk about individual spiritual beings? Through its worship of saints, the Catholic Church has forged a transition on behalf of humankind. In this case, the object of devotion is the human soul-spiritual element that survives in the spiritual world.

The powers that live in warmth, ebbing and flowing in the alternation between summer and winter, also live in our blood, which pervades our bodies with warmth. These powers mediate between the luciferic and ahrimanic elements. In the outer world, these mediating forces ebb and flow regularly and rhythmically, like our blood circulation, not irregularly, as warmth does in meteorology. In the objective ebb and flow of warmth in our circulation, we are also enveloped by the ebb and flow not only of these elemental spirits but also of the entire elemental world. We can extract ourselves only by finding our way into the spiritual world in full consciousness, which is possible only if we are not afraid to look that world squarely in the face.

At this point, however, we encounter an obstacle to the continued existence of our anthroposophical movement. Let me illustrate what I mean with one of many possible concrete examples. Today, what we as anthroposophists have to say about the field of medicine, for example, must tie in with exoteric medicine. This is what the world demands of us. We must talk about the etiology of specific diseases in relationship to outer, material forces of nature—for example, how rickets relates to the air around us. We must use materialistic statistical methods to quantify how many people with rickets live in places with northern or southern exposures. When we do this, we may not be at all conscious of the element with which we are getting involved. Let us consider how the same statistical methods apply to the issue of insurance. In outer, physical reality, life insurance is possible only because individual life expectancies can be calculated, but, of course, we realize that actuarial tables cannot predict how long any individual will live. It is quite possible for reality to make a mockery of the statistics. Nonetheless, anthroposophical scientists must use statistics so that their descriptions of scientific phenomena are at least outwardly in harmony with conventional science. This is entirely appropriate, because nowadays we must speak in terms that resonate with natural science.

Having determined that rickets occurs when the forces of the lower human body develop in the absence of forces of light (when the patient lives in a dark basement, for example), we must also take into account the choices of soul-spiritual human beings who descend from a spiritual world to live in specific physical bodies. Taking on a specific body is not arbitrary. When we descend to Earth, we incarnate into a particular ethnic group and a particular family because we are attracted to the individual forces that prevail among human beings in a specific place. This attraction works right into the details of the life a child will experience—living in a room with a northern or southern exposure, for example. Under certain circumstances, a soul may actively choose to develop in darkness.

The presence or absence of light and air is not the only factor we must consider. We must also consider the being of spirit and soul and its attraction to a particular milieu. We must question whether we can attempt to cure rickets entirely on the basis of our assumptions about and understanding of the physical world. In fact, we cannot. We must realize that if medication does nothing more than make the patient physically healthy, his or her destiny—the reason for choosing to live in a world with inadequate light—is forced down into the soul's unconscious depths. We will be able to establish a holistic science of medicine only if we also target this suppressed, unconscious factor— that is, if we enable patients to become conscious of what they must do to fulfill their destiny. We must be able to consider the whole person—body, soul, and spirit.

The tragedy of the present moment in the life of the anthroposophical movement is that the multiple perspectives we must consider make it possible for critics to discover contradiction after contradiction within our movement; as a result, it is easy to accuse us of inconsistency. This inconsistency is resolved, however, when the entire truth of the matter is seen. Wherever people who work within the anthroposophical movement link to the material element, they also discover spiritual tasks. Our physicians must become different people;

they must view the world in a different spirit. Though inundated with exoteric science, they must avoid increasingly assuming its character simply out of habit. Although they must reach compromises with exoteric science, they must also rise above it.

This is something we can and must realize when we have spent a certain amount of time in the anthroposophical movement. We face many other, similar difficulties. The point is not to shed light on these difficulties from a critical perspective but to feel our way into them and learn to understand them so thoroughly that they are replaced with complete harmony. In real life, that is how we must work together in all our fields of activity. When a Waldorf School teacher talks to a physician from the Clinical-Therapeutic Institute, their conversation is different from a conversation between any two individuals outside our movement. Our Waldorf teachers speak from the perspective of psychological hygiene; they give voice to what we must do to become healers for our children. This becomes tremendously illuminating when it resonates in the mind and soul of someone who works in the Clinical-Therapeutic Institute. The reverse is also true: what we learn in the Clinical-Therapeutic Institute must influence the activity of our Waldorf School teachers. We must work toward the harmony demanded by matters themselves; we must avoid the disharmony that develops when individuals' activities are not coordinated. Anthroposophy will not be able to develop to serve humankind if individuals working within our movement cannot come together. As such, Anthroposophy demands human fraternity—fellowship—in the most profound depths of human souls. Outside our movement, fellowship may be a moral imperative; within our movement, it is essential to the growth of Anthroposophy. Anthroposophy can grow and thrive only in the fertile ground of practical fellowship, where each individual offers others whatever he or she has and can do.

This fellowship is also the foundation of other new insights. It is time to take seriously the words of a professor of theology in Basel, who wrote a book that heavily influenced his friend Nietzsche. The professor was Franz Overbeck, and the book was *On the Christianity of Theology.* Overbeck was neither an anthroposophist nor an atheist; he was employed by the university to teach theology. The premise of his book is that although individuals often still behave in a Christian manner, our theology as such is no longer Christian. In other words, theology—especially self-professed liberal theology—has lost the true concept of the Christ. The person who arrived at this conclusion was not some heretical Anthroposophist but a teacher and theologian of the Christian church.

This is one point I wanted to make. The other is something you already know well, not from tradition but from true insight, namely, the anthroposophical perspective on the Mystery of Golgotha. You can read a great deal about it in various lecture cycles of mine, but what I want to emphasize today is this: Modern liberal theologians pay little attention to the cosmic Christ-Being who passed through the Mystery of Golgotha and later communicated with initiates and disciples. How little attention they pay to the resurrected Christ, who remained visible to his initiated disciples! Those who approach Anthroposophy, however, gradually achieve a living view of the Mystery of Golgotha and learn what the Christ communicated to his initiated disciples *after* his resurrection. As we find our way into this mystery, the spiritual world around us becomes more and more tangible, because the Mystery of Golgotha can be understood only in spiritual terms. For most people, the Mystery of Golgotha is very difficult to understand, because they approach it in materialistic terms.

A great deal of what the Christ himself imparted to his initiated disciples after his resurrection survived among the early church fathers. Today I will single out only one aspect of this legacy. You see, prior to the Mystery of Golgotha humankind possessed a certain kind of primeval wisdom. When we look back on the early stages of the Earth's development, we find human beings who were primitive but not at all animal-like, or at least only in their outward appearance. These primitive humans received primeval wisdom from superhuman, divine-spiritual beings. This wisdom was no illusion; it really existed. Early humans were filled with wisdom, not ignorance, but this wisdom, which we admire so greatly when we rediscover it consciously on the basis of Anthroposophy, was then quite dreamlike. People experienced it in images that were not associated with a strong sense of self. At the beginning of the Earth stage of evolution, a

tremendously profound archetypal wisdom prevailed among outwardly animal-like human beings, who received this wisdom from
divine spiritual beings and became conscious of it only in images.

Apropos "animal-like," let me note in passing that when we finally
achieve a holistic view of the natural world in all its complexity, we
will judge animals differently than we do today. For example, when
we look at a coiled snake lying as if paralyzed while digesting its prey,
we will see an expansive inner life, like a cosmic dream, and we will
realize that even the snake's digestive abilities are provided by the
world of images, by the cosmos itself. We will also discover the spirit
within the ahrimanic principle.

But let us get back to the primeval wisdom of early humans.
Because their wisdom was dreamlike in character, these people did
not experience death to the extent that we do today, with our emphasis on exoteric perception. Although our early earthly forebears did
not see themselves and each other as animals, there was something
animal-like in their relationship to death. They did not experience
death in the depths of their souls, as their descendants would do.
Although these people lived and then ceased living, they remained
virtually untouched by life's end because they were illumined by the
spirit that worked through their primeval wisdom during life.
Because they never felt totally separated from the spirit, death was not
an especially meaningful event. They experienced it only as the cast-
ing off of the body, similar to the sloughing off of a snake's skin. They
did not experience death with our degree of clarity. To look at death
as modern humanity does would have required spiritual forces that
these early humans did not possess. In ancient times before the
Mystery of Golgotha, death emerged only gradually as the riddle that
now confronts human beings.

Let us imagine for a moment that the Mystery of Golgotha had
not happened. Without it, the ancient wisdom would have become
increasingly unconscious as humankind's evolution continued.
Human beings, left with exclusively exoteric perception, would have
been inconsolable in the face of death and its terrible consequences.
As the millennium of the Mystery of Golgotha approached, human
souls increasingly faced the possibility of their own deaths. But as the

risen Christ told his initiated disciples, humans received their primeval wisdom from divine spiritual beings at a time when the gods themselves were not familiar with death. Because the divine worlds knew only metamorphosis, not death, ancient wisdom supplied no perspective on death and overcoming it. The resurrected Christ told his disciples that those loyal to God the Father had sent him to Earth to live in a physical body and experience death—an impossibility in the world of the gods. He told them that he had come down to Earth so that the gods could experience death and so that all human beings who truly understand Christianity can learn to understand the spirit's victory over earthly death. These teachings of the resurrected Christ survived for four centuries, until exoteric views of Christianity triumphed.

The Christ called out to humankind to understand death as the freeing of spirituality from the human body when its time in the earthly world is over. Through the Mystery of Golgotha, however, the gods themselves also gained this understanding. Thus, the erection of the cross on Golgotha was also a cosmic event. One of the most important cosmic events was actually enacted on Earth. The cross not only rose up from the Earth but also descended to it. An agreement forged by the gods was implemented on Earth for human beings to behold. This is how the true Christ should be seen, but this view is lost to modern theology. If you read Harnack, for example, you could simply cross out the name "Christ" wherever it occurs and replace it with the generic "God," because Harnack does not talk about the living, risen Christ and fails to recognize the superearthly significance of the Mystery of Golgotha. When we embrace this significance, we become increasingly comfortable with the idea that spirituality *needs* death, that human beings would fail to achieve their evolutionary goals if they did not repeatedly pass through the portal of death. Through the Mystery of Golgotha, the beginnings of an understanding of human death entered all future earthly evolution. We must go still further, however. There is something else we must understand.

Today we are surrounded by dead nature, and we congratulate ourselves heartily when we understand it. We attempt to understand not only minerals but also plants and even animals in terms of their chemistry. In other words, we see only the dead element in everything. The ideal of our modern way of thinking is to replace life with dead mechanics and chemistry. We like to imagine that a plant develops tiny little processes that, when put together, merge into what we call "life." This is not what happens. There is real life inside that plant. We must realize that we see death all around us because our perception is completely death-oriented.

Christianity, which frees us from the constraints of death, tells us that souls who do not understand the resurrection, the fact that the Christ lives, are dead souls. We must also understand that if we relate only to dead matter, we ourselves become dead and ahrimanic, but if we have sufficient courage and sufficient love for all the beings around us to relate to them directly (not to our dead ideas about them), we discover the Christ in everything and victorious spirit everywhere. When this happens, we may need to speak in ways that seem paradoxical to our contemporaries. We may need to speak about the individual spiritual beings that live in the solid and fluid elements and so forth. As long as we avoid talking about these beings, we are talking about a dead science that is not imbued with the Christ. To speak about them is to speak in a truly Christian sense. We must imbue all of our scientific activity with the Christ. More than that, we must also bring the Christ into all of our social efforts, all of our knowledge—in short, into all aspects of our life. The Mystery of Golgotha will truly bear fruit only through human strength, human efforts, and human love for each other. In this sense, Anthroposophy in all its details strives to imbue the world with the Christ. We raise the sign of the Christ over all of our efforts.

If we look out over the natural world and find no god in nature, that can be due only to a pathological condition within ourselves. A contemplative approach to nature reveals God everywhere. Nature itself tells us: *Ex deo nascimur*. Inner inability to realize that we are born out of God is an illness. In the course of our earthly life, however, we must find the Christ through our own soul forces, so that we may die properly, because the Christ alone allows modern humanity to experience life in death. It is simply a matter of human destiny whether we are able to find and receive the Christ, to learn to understand the Mystery of Golgotha, and to say in our inmost being: *In Christo morimur.*

It is an illness to be unable to come to God the Father and a miserable fate to be unable to come to God the Son. The consequence is also a weakness of spirit, however, because if we imbue ourselves with understanding and love for the Father-God and the Christ, something in us awakens into living spirituality, in spite of death and the deadness of nature. Through the power of the Father-God and the power of the Christ, we realize that we are reborn in the Holy Spirit: *Per spiritum sanctum reviviscimus.*

As the result of clear insight, not of nebulous aspiration, we know:

Ex deo nascimur—We are born out of God.

In Christo morimur—We die in Christ.

Per spiritum sanctum reviviscimus—We will reawaken in the spirit-self through the Holy Spirit.†

EDITORIAL AND REFERENCE NOTES

1.

The Life of the Human Soul in Sleeping, Waking, and Dreaming

Page 1, "title"
The three states invoked in this and the following lecture echo the Manduka Upanisad:

> *Aum*, this syllable is all this...all that is the past, the present and the future, all this is only the syllable *Aum*...
> All this is verily *Brahman*. This self is *Brahman*. This same self has four quarters.
> The first quarter is *Vaisvanara*, whose sphere is the waking state, who cognizes external objects...
> The second quarter is *Taijasa*, whose sphere is the dream state, who cognizes internal objects...
> ...The third quarter is *Prajna*, whose sphere is the state of deep sleep, who has become one, who is verily, a mass of cognition, who is full of bliss and who enjoys bliss, whose face is thought
> This is the lord of all, this is the knower of all, this is the inner controller; this is the source of all; this is the beginning and end of beings.

To these three, the *Mandukya Upanisad* adds a fourth, *Turiya*, which, though Steiner does not mention it, is implicit:

> (*Turiya* is) not that which cognizes the internal, not that which cognizes the external, not what cognizes both of them, not a mass of cognition, not cognitive, not non-cognitive. Unseen, incapable of being spoken of, without distinctive marks, unthinkable, unnamable, the essence of the knowledge of the one self, that into which the world is resolved, the peaceful, the benign, the non-dual, such they think is the fourth quarter. He is the self; He is to be known.
> This is the self, which is of the nature of the syllable *Aum* in regard to its elements.

Page 2, "We know that...physical and etheric bodies."
See Rudolf Steiner, *Sleep and Dreams: A Bridge to the Spirit* (edited and introduced by Michael Lipson). For Rudolf Steiner, the human being is composed of four members: the physical body, the etheric body or body of formative forces, the astral body, and the "I." For descriptions of these, see especially his books, *Theosophy* (CW 9) and *A Way of Self- Knowledge* (CW 16).

Page 4, *"An Outline of Esoteric Science."*
See Bibliography.

Page 4, "Imagination"
For Rudolf Steiner, the three stages of "higher" consciousness are called Imagination, Inspiration, and Intuition. See *Stages of Higher Knowledge* (CW 12).

Page 4, "Earth existence."
In Rudolf Steiner's evolutionary cosmology, our present Earth stage or state of evolution (or consciousness) has evolved or metamorphosed through three previous states or stages called the Saturn, Sun, and Moon stages or states. For a concise outer description of these stages, see *An Outline of Esoteric Science* (CW 13); for an "inner" description of the stages as states, see *Truth of Evolution* (CW 132).

Page 6, *"The Inner Nature of the Human Being..."*
Eight lectures, April 1914 (CW 153).

Page 7, "Theosophy...described."
See Bibliography. The idea of a reversal of perspective between the spiritual and the physical worlds appears often in Steiner's work. The specific reference here to *Theosophy* is unclear, although several sections of Chapter Three, "The Three Worlds," imply this reversal.

Page 11, *"How to Know Higher Worlds*, and so forth."
Besides *How to Know Higher Worlds*, see the chapters on the path of knowledge in *Theosophy* and *An Outline of Esoteric Science*. Also *Start Now: A Book of Soul and Spiritual Exercises*.

Page 12, "For example...artistic medium."
Eurythmy or "visible speech" is the new art of movement created by Rudolf Steiner in 1912 in response to a request from a young woman, Lory Smits.

Page 13, "The power...of truth and healing."
"The Mystery of Golgotha" is Rudolf Steiner's way of referring to what was for him the central event of earthly evolution: Christ's incarnation, death, resurrection, and ascension. See throughout his work, but especially *The Christian Mystery*.

Page 14, "And, in fact...the wandering Jew."
Ahasuerus or the "Wandering Jew" is a figure from Christian folklore. It first appears in print in a German pamphlet in 1602, but the legend goes back into the Middle Ages. Often thought to be founded on the words given in Matthew 16:28 —"Verily, I say unto you, there be some standing here, which shall not taste of death, till they see the Son of Man coming in his kingdom"—there are many other theories. Some see the figure as that of St. John, who was also to "tarry till I come;" also Malchus, whose ear St. Peter cut off; Peter in the Garden of Gethsemane, who

is sometimes conflated with the figure (also sometimes called Cartaphilus) who, when Jesus was carrying the Cross, told him to go quicker and was told in reply, "I go; but thou shalt wait till I come." Generally, the figure has been assimilated to the Jews of the Diaspora—also waiting. From the Renaissance on, there were sightings or appearances of Ahasuerus. He became a popular figure in literature. Many poems, tragedies, and novels were written about him.

2.

The Three States of Night Consciousness

Page 19, "There is something happening in the soul."
At this point in the lecture, Rudolf Steiner illustrated what he was saying with a blackboard drawing

Page 21, "thinking, feeling, and willing."
The idea of human "threefoldness" is central to Rudolf Steiner's philosophy and practice. Just as we are tripartite beings of body, soul, and spirit, so as an organism we are constituted of three interlocking organic systems (the metabolic, the circulatory, and the nerve-sense systems), and three cognitive functions: thinking, feeling, and willing.

Page 22, "Music of the Spheres."
For the "Music (or Harmony) of the Spheres," see, for instance, *Mysteries of the East and of Christianity* (CW 144), Lecture Three "The Gifts of Isis" (also in *Isis Mary Sophia: Her Mission and Ours*): "Everything that has to be poured out from the spiritual world into the physical world, so that it may partake of a psychic, inner character, is poured in from the harmony of the Spheres resounding through space The Harmony of the Spheres gradually assumes such a form that it can be understood in its inner significance as the Cosmic Word...."

Page 22, "These beings..."
Rudolf Steiner is here referring, following Dionysius the Areopagite, to the ninefold (3 x 3) spiritual Hierarchies, as follows—*Seraphim* or Spirits of Love, *Cherubim* or Spirits of Harmony, *Thrones* or Spirits of Will; *Kyriotetes* (Dominions) or Spirits of Wisdom; *Dynamis* (Virtues) or Spirits of Movement; *Exusiai* (Powers) or Spirits of Form; *Archai* (Principalities) or Spirits of Personality; *Archangels; Angels.* For more, see, *Spiritual Hierarchies and their Reflection in the Physical World* (CW 110) and *Spiritual Beings in the Heavenly Bodies and Kingdoms of Nature* (CW 136).

Page 25, "Charlemagne..."
Charlemagne (742-814), King of the Franks (768) and Holy Roman Emperor (800) and Frederick "Barbarossa" (c. 1123-1190), Frederick I von Hohenstaufen, German King and Holy Roman Emperor. Frederick is the subject of many legends,

including that of a sleeping hero. He is said not to be dead, but asleep with his knights in a cave in Kyffhäuser Mountain in Thuringia, Germany, and that when ravens should cease to fly around the mountain he would awaken and restore Germany to its ancient greatness. According to the story his red beard has grown through the table at which he sits. His eyes are half closed in sleep, but now and then he raises his hand and sends a boy out to see if the ravens have stopped flying. Similar stories (collected by the Grimm Brothers) are attached to Charlemagne.

Page 27, "the illegitimate human-become-god…"
Ahasuerus: see note in previous lecture with the different, more positive emphasis given there.

Page 28, "…threshold of consciousness."
Threshold: threshold of the spiritual world. See Rudolf Steiner, *A Way of Self-Knowledge* and *The Threshold of the Spiritual World* (CW 16/17).

3.
The Transformation of Worldviews

Page 29, "If we look back thousands of years…"
Throughout his work, Rudolf Steiner unfolds the historical evolution of consciousness leading from Atlantis through a sequence of four cultural epochs that he names "Ancient Indian," "Ancient Persian," Egypto-Chaldean," and "Greco-Roman" to the present "fifth post-Atlantean" epoch. See, for instance, *An Outline of Esoteric Science*.

Page 32, "Mystery Centers…"
For Mystery Centers, see for instance, Rudolf Steiner, *Mystery Knowledge and Mystery Centres*, 14 lectures, Dornach, November 23 to December 23 1923, (CW 232).

Page 34, "In ancient Greece…in Aeschylus' time…"
Aeschylus (c. 525-456 B.C.E.); Sophocles (c. 496-406 B.C.E.)

Page 35, "The god Dionysus…"
"Dionysus (also known as Bacchus), the son Zeus, is a god of the Greek Mysteries, such as those of Demeter and Persephone at Eleusis and of his own rites, which were the most secret of all. His origins have been traced to Crete. For Steiner on Dionysus, see Rudolf Steiner, *Wonders of the World*, (CW 129). Also, as would have been well known to Steiner, Friedrich Nietzsche, *The Birth of Tragedy*. Also Walter F. Otto, *Dionysus: Myth and Cult*.

Page 36, "…Euripides."
Euripides (c. 484-406 B.C.E.)

Page 36, "And the Lord God…"
Genesis 2:7 (King James version)

Page 37, "In earlier times…of the earthly hierarchies."
See *Spiritual Beings in the Heavenly Bodies and in the Kingdoms of Nature.*

Page 37, "Let me draw…"
Rudolf Steiner here draws on the blackboard.

Page 37, "We would all stand here like hermits…"
One of Rudolf Steiner's chief themes is that human beings must cease to be "cosmic hermits" and become "cosmic citizens." See: *The Archangel Michael: His Mission and Ours.*

Page 38, "Not I, but Christ in me."
See Galatians 2:20.

Page 39, "Overbeck…"
Franz Overbeck, 1837–1905, *On the Christianity of Theology*, translated with an introduction and notes by John Elbert Wilson, San Jose, CA: Pickwick Publications, 2002. Professor at Basel, Overbeck was the closest friend of Friedrich Nietszche, whose *Untimely Meditations* appeared at the same time as Overbeck's book. They shared the same views and corresponded frequently.

4.

Historical Changes in the Experience of Breathing

Page 40, "lecture"
Parts of this lecture seem difficult to understand, probably due to the transcription. We have made every effort to make it consistent and understandable.

Page 41, "I can do this best…"
Rudolf Steiner at this point began to draw on the blackboard.

Page 41, "gnomes, nymphs, and all the other…environment"
So-called elemental beings. See *Harmony of the Creative Word: The Human Being and the Elemental, Animal, Plant and Mineral Kingdoms* (CW 230).

Page 42, "At later stages…into the head."
This passage was particularly confusing.

Page 43, *"sophia…"*
For *sophia* (Greek, wisdom), see lectures collected in Rudolf Steiner, *Isis Mary Sophia* (C. Bamford, ed.).

Page 44, *"Pistis Sophia"*
See, Violet MacDermot, *The Fall of Sophia, A Gnostic Text on the Redemption of Universal Consciousness.* Also: G.R.S. Mead, *Pistis Sophia: A Gnostic Miscellany.*

Page 47, "A diagram…"
Steiner draws again on the blackboard.

Page 50, "a new wisdom"
See, "The Being Anthroposophia" in Rudolf Steiner *Isis Mary Sophia.*

5.

The Human Being as Portrayed in Greek Art

Page 53, "about Niobe…"
Niobe, the Queen of Thebes, was the daughter of Tantalus and a goddess (no one seems sure which goddess). She was married to Amphion, King of Thebes. They had fourteen children. One day, in honor of the feast of Leto, who had only two children, Apollo and Artemis, Niobe bragged about how many children she had, and mocked Leto for having only two. In retaliation, Leto sent Apollo and Artemis to kill Niobe's children. At the sight of his dead children, Amphion committed suicide (or Apollo killed him, too). So Niobe was left alone, her whole family dead in a matter of minutes. She fled to Mt. Sipylon in Asia Minor, where she turned to stone and her tears formed a stream that flowed from the rock. Niobe became a symbol for eternal mourning, her tears flowing to this day.

Page 54, "You are probably familiar with…sculptures…"
The Niobe group, a Roman copy of an original Hellenistic work of the third to second centuries B.C., were found in 1583 and purchased by Cardinal Medici in that year. Until 1770 they remained in the Villa Medici in Rome. Then they were moved to Florence, where they are now in the Niobe room of the Uffizi Gallery.

Page 54, "the goddess Latona…"
Latona is the Latin form of Leto.

Page 54, "When we look…the time in question."
See, *Art and Human Consciousness* and Van James, *Spirit and Art.*

Page 55, "Better a beggar…in the realm of shades."
Homer, *Odyssey*, Book 11

Page 55, "Aristotle's definition…"
Aristotle, *Poetics:* "Tragedy, then, is an imitation of an action that is serious, complete, and of a certain magnitude; in language embellished with each kind of

artistic ornament, the several kinds being found in separate parts of the play; in the form of action, not of narrative; with incidents arousing pity and fear, wherewith to accomplish its katharsis of such emotions...."

Page 56, "The term...in that context."
See, for instance, Rudolf Steiner, "The Nature of the Virgin Sophia and the Holy Spirit," in *The Gospel of St. John* (CW 103).

Page 57, "In *Faust*..."
Faust, Part One, "Night: Faust's Study":
Philosophy have I digested
The whole of Law and Medicine,
From each its secrets I have wrested,
Theology, alas, thrown in.

Page 57, "Lessing..."
Gotthold Ephraim Lessing (1729-1781), one of the most influential figures of the Enlightenment, was a German philosopher, dramatist, religious thinker, and critic, who revolutionized all the fields he worked in. At the center of his thinking was the insistence on human of freedom. He wrote literary criticism (most importantly *Laocoön, An Essay on the Limits of Painting and Poetry* (1766), plays (among which, *Minna von Barnheim* (1772), and *Nathan the Wise* (1779), and at the end of his life, *The Education of the Human Race* (1880), which Rudolf Steiner always associated (and so Lessing himself) with a Rosicrucian impulse.

Page 57, "This was not the case with Herder..."
Johann Gottfried von Herder (1744-1803) was an extremely influential German philosopher. Hegel's philosophy, for instance, may be seen as an elaborate systematic development of Herderian ideas (especially concerning God, the mind, and history); so too does Schleiermacher's (concerning God, the mind, interpretation, translation, and art); Nietzsche, too, was deeply influenced by Herder (concerning the mind, history, and values); so too was Dilthey (in his theory of the human sciences); even J.S. Mill has important debts to Herder (in political philosophy). Indeed, Herder can claim to have virtually established whole disciplines, which we now take for granted. For example, it was mainly Herder who established fundamental ideas about an intimate dependence of thought on language. Through his broad empirical approach to languages, his recognition of deep variations in language and thought across historical periods and cultures, he inspired W. von Humboldt to found modern linguistics. Herder was also the father of modern hermeneutics, or interpretation-theory. In doing so, he established the methodological foundations of nineteenth-century German classical scholarship and hence modern classical scholarship generally. Arguably, too, it was Herder who did more than anyone else to establish the general conception and the interpretive methodology of our modern discipline of anthropology. Finally, Herder also made vital contributions to the progress of

modern biblical scholarship. Beyond philosophy, Goethe was transformed into a great artist largely through the early impact on him of Herder's ideas. (From the *Stanford Encyclopedia of Philosophy*.)

Page 58, "Spinoza's work."
Baruch Spinoza (1632-1677), extremely influential Portuguese Marrano philosopher, who lived in Holland, constantly at odds with the authorities. The heart of his philosophy, expressed in geometric, logical form, was the unitary, monistic nature of the universe and God. He held that a unique, single substance—*Deus sive natura*, "God or nature"—comprises all of reality.

Page 59, "struggle of Laocoön..."
Laocoön, a minor figure from Greek mythology, was a Trojan priest of Poseidon. When the Wooden Horse approached Troy, he presciently warned against bringing it into the city and hurled his spear into its flank. Soon after this, as he was sacrificing to Poseidon, a pair of giant sea serpents emerged from the sea and enveloped Laocoon and his sons. This tragic scene was immortalized in a dramatic, even baroque and emotional—and extraordinarily influential—Hellenistic sculpture ("Laocoön and his Sons") by Hagesandros, Athenodorus and Polydorus of Rhodes (175-150 B.C.), now in the Vatican.

Page 59, "intellect on drama."
Pierre Corneille (1606-1684) and Jean Racine (1639-1699) are considered the creators of French classical tragedy.

Page 60, "Hamlet of Saxo Grammaticus...."
"Saxo Grammaticus (c.1150-1220) was the Danish Chronicler who was Shakespeare's source for *Hamlet*.

Page 60, "medicine...theology."
See note for page 57, above.

Page 60, "Rümelin..."
Gustav Rümelin (1815-1889), writer and statesman.

6.
Investigating and Formulating the Cosmic Word
in Inhalation and Exhalation

Page 64, "Last week...breathing"
Rudolf Steiner draws on the blackboard.

Page 64, "The breath...inside the head."
Rudolf Steiner draws another diagram and then draws three sketches on the blackboard while he is speaking. See text on following two pages.

Page 68, "minds like Fritz Mauthner…"
Fritz Mauthner (1849-1923), prolific author, cultural critic, and editor of the
Berliner Tageblatt, best known for his nominalist critiques of language question-
ing the value of language in the search for knowledge.

7.

Exoteric and Esoteric Christianity

Page 70, "As you know…"
Canonical references to the disciples' experience of the resurrected Christ are
extraordinary brief. Besides the experiences at the empty tomb, we have only
Matthew 28:17-20; Mark 16:19-11 (Mary Magdalene), and 14-20; Luke
24:13-40; John 20:10-30, and 21:1-23. Conversely, there are many apocryphal
and so-called Gnostic texts of dialogs with the Risen One.

Page 71, "Paul's affirmation…Damascus."
Acts 9:3-9

Page 72, "Plato's work."
See, for example, Plato, *Phaedo.*

Page 73, "As I have often explained…that we die."
Rudolf Steiner here draws on the blackboard.

Page 74, "In other words…tendency."
See, for instance, lecture March, 4, 1921 (CW 204).

Page 76, "You know from my book…"
See *An Outline of Esoteric Science*, pp. 247 ff. and also *The Influences of Lucifer
and Ahriman.*

Page 83, "When I come back…a different level."
Rudolf Steiner left soon after this lecture for Holland and England.

8.

The Teachings of the Risen Christ

Page 90, "…power of *pistis-sophia*."
See notes for pages 43 and 44, above.

Page 93, "For example…*Zarathustra*."
Friedrich Nietzsche, *Thus Spoke Zarathustra.* See also, Rudolf Steiner, *Friedrich
Nietzsche, Fighter for Freedom.*

Page 94, "It is a significant symptom...no longer Christian."
See note for page 39, above.

Page 94, "important function is religious."
On March 10 a conference entitled "The Decline of Religion in Contemporary Theology and its New Foundation through Anthroposophy" was held at the Goetheanum. Rudolf Steiner spoke, as well as Emil Bock, Friedrich Rittelmeyer, and Johannes Geyer.

9.
Spiritual Insight and Initiation

The transcripts for this lecture and the following one are of uneven quality and may even contain lacunae. Steiner's lectures in England were given in German, in three parts, after each of which he paused to allow his translator George Adams to speak an English version.

10.
Perceiving the Christ through Anthroposophy

Page 114, "...the body of formative forces."
Or: etheric body

Page 116, "There, our thinking was alive."
Galatians 2:20: "I am crucified with Christ: nevertheless I live; yet not I, but Christ lives in me..."

Page 117, "Paul's words..."
I Corinthians 15:14-15: "But if there be no resurrection of the dead, then Christ is not risen; and if Christ be not risen, then is our preaching vain and your faith is also vain."

11.
The Threefold Sun and the Risen Christ

Page 126, "divinity that sends rays of wisdom to Earth."
Zarathustra or Zartost, usually known in English as Zoroaster, was an Iranian (perhaps born in Afghanistan) prophet, founder of the Zoroastrian religion contained in the Gathas of the holy book, the Zend Avesta. The core teaching is *Humata, Hukhta, Huvarshta* (Good Thoughts, Good Words, Good Deeds). This is the way to participate in the cosmic struggle between "The Truth" and "The Lie, the Light and the Darkness," represented by Ahura Mazda and

Ahriman. The dating of this particular historical Zoroaster has proved difficult. Dates vary widely from between 2000 and 1000 B.C. The problem is compounded by the fact that there has evidently been a sequence of incarnations, dating back to 7,000 B.C. and the origins of agriculture. Plato, for instance, speaks of Zoroaster as having lived five thousand years before the Trojan War. Another Zoroaster (Zaratas) was the reputed teacher of Pythagoras during the Babylonian captivity under Cyrus. For Rudolf Steiner, the Old Persian Epoch begins with the first Zoroaster, while the Matthew Jesus represents Zoroaster's last (?) incarnation. See Andrew Welburn, *The Book with Twelve Seals*.

Page 127, "Julian the Apostate..."

The Emperor Julian (331-363), called the Apostate, because (though trained as a Christian) he "abandoned" Christianity, was the nephew of the first Christian Emperor. He came at a time when ancient pagan Temple mysteries were in decline, and he gave his life to revive them through a combination of Mithraism and Neo-Platonism. As a young man, Julian studied philosophy deeply, traveling widely in search of teachers to (among others) Constantinople, Nicomedia, Pegamum, and Athens. He was enormously cultured and mystical. He might have accomplished much, but his reign was only twenty months. Beginning in December 361, he rebuilt the Temples and reinstituted the sacred rites. He issued his famous edict of religious freedom. He invited all those who had been exiled for religious reasons to return. He rescinded the special privileges of the Christian bishops and priests. Julian lived austerely like a true philosopher and died on his way to Persia, where, according to legend, he hoped to meet the prophet Mani. Julian is well known for his Orations on the Sun and the Mother of the Gods.

Page 128, "the emperer Justinian..."

Justinian (527-565) is best known for his jurisprudence, the "Justinian Laws"— the *Codex Justinianus,* the *Institutes,* and the *Digest.* His early years as Emperor equally marked the course of Western culture. He legislated against the Manicheans, pagans, and Samaritans. Pagans were barred from civil service; Christians who lapsed back into paganism were put to death, as was anyone caught sacrificing to the gods. Pagan teachers were denied stipends. If they did not convert, their property was taken and they were banished into exile. As part of this process, he closed down the Platonic Academy in Athens. As a result, many philosophers, alchemists, theurgists, heretical Christians, and mystics of every stripe fled east to Persia, where their wisdom lay awaiting the coming of Islam.

Page 133, "the dark age known as Kali Yuga..."

There are four Yugas: the Satya Yuga or Golden Age; the Treta Yuga or Silver Age; the Dvapara Yuga or Bronze Age; and the Kali Yuga or Iron Age. There are many different ways of calculating these. For Rudolf Steiner, the Kali Yuga ended in 1900.

Page 133, "Cardinal Newman..."

John Henry Cardinal Newman (1801-1890), churchman, philosopher, man of letters, leader of the Oxford Movement, and one of the greatest stylists in the

English language, was the most illustrious English convert to Catholicism. See his so-called "Biglietto" speech delivered in Rome, May 12, 1879, on his elevation to the rank of Cardinal: "Hitherto the civil power has been Christian. Even in countries separated from the Church, as in my own, the dictum was in force, when I was young, that 'Christianity was the law of the land.' Now everywhere the goodly framework of society, which is the creation of Christianity, is throwing off Christianity. The dictum to which I have referred...is gone or is going everywhere; and by the end of the century, *unless the Almighty interferes*, it will be forgotten..." (Emphasis added). See also, Rudolf Steiner, *The Influences of Lucifer and Ahriman*.

Page 134, "my mystery dramas."
See, Rudolf Steiner, *Four Mystery Dramas* (CW 14).

12.

Anthroposophy as an Attempt to Enchristen the World

Page 154, "through the Holy Spirit."
Ex deo Nascimur, In Christo Morimur, Per Spiritum sanctum Reviviscimus represent the so-called Rosicrucian signature going back to the original seventeenth century documents and taken up by Rudolf Steiner for whom they constituted the essential heart of Anthroposophy. See also, Rudolf Steiner, *The Secret Stream* and *Start Now* (both edited by C. Bamford).

BIBLIOGRAPHY

Rudolf Steiner:

Steiner, Rudolf, *A Way of Self-Knowledge*, Great Barrington, MA: SteinerBooks, 2006.

_____, *An Outline of Esoteric Science*, Great Barrington, MA: Anthroposophic Press, 1997.

_____, *Four Mystery Dramas*, London: Rudolf Steiner Press, 1997.

_____, *Friedrich Nietzsche, Fighter for Freedom*, Blauvelt, NY, Spiritual Science Library, a division of Garber Communications, Inc., 1985.

_____, *How to Know Higher Worlds*, Hudson, NY: Anthroposophic Press, 1994.

_____, *Truth of Evolution* (formerly *Inner Realities of Evolution*), Great Barrington, MA: SteinerBooks, 2006.

_____, *Isis Mary Sophia: Her Mission and Ours,* Great Barrington: SteinerBooks, 2003.

_____, *Sleep and Dreams: A Bridge to the Spirit*, Great Barrington: SteinerBooks, 2003.

_____, *Mysteries of the East and of Christianity*, Blauvelt, NY: Spiritual Science Library, a division of Garber Communications, Inc., 1989.

_____, *Spiritual Beings in the Heavenly Bodies and in the Kingdoms of Nature*, Hudson, NY: Anthroposophic Press, 1992.

_____, *Spiritual Hierarchies and the Physical World*, Great Barrinton, MA: SteinerBooks, 2006.

_____, *The Stages of Higher Knowledge*, Hudson, NY: Anthroposophic Press, 1967.

_____, *Start Now: A Book of Soul and Spiritual Exercises*, Great Barrington, MA: SteinerBooks, 2004.

_____, *The Archangel Michael: His Mission and Ours*, Hudson, NY: Anthroposophic Press, 1994.

_____, *The Christian Mystery*, Great Barrington, MA: Anthroposophic Press, 1998.

_____, *The Influences of Lucifer and Ahriman*, Hudson, NY: Anthroposophic Press, 1993.

_____, *Theosophy*, Hudson, NY: Anthroposophic Press, 1994.

_____, *Wonders of the World, Ordeals of the Soul, Revelations of the Spirit*, Hudson, NY: Anthroposophic Press, 1983.

Other Authors:

MacDermot, Violet, *The Fall of Sophia, A Gnostic Text on the Redemption of Universal Consciousness*, Great Barrington, MA: Lindesfarne Books, 2001.

Mead, G.R.S., *Pistis Sophia: A Gnostic Miscellany*, Blauvelt, NY: Spiritual Science Library, a division of Garbor Communications, Inc., 1984.

Nietzsche, Friedrich, *The Birth of Tragedy and Other Writings*, Cambridge and New York: Cambridge University Press, 1999.

_____, *Untimely Meditations*, Cambridge and New York: Cambridge University Press, 1997.

_____, *Thus Spoke Zarathustra: A Book for All and None*, New York: Random House, Inc., 1995.

Otto, Walter F., *Dionysus: Myth and Cult*, Bloomington, IN: Indiana University Press, 1965.

Overbeck, Franz, 1837–1905, *On the Christianity of Theology*, translated with an introduction and notes by John Elbert Wilson, San Jose, CA: Pickwick Publications, 2002.

Richter, Gottfried, *Art and Human Consciousness*, Great Barrington, MA: SteinerBooks/Anthroposophic Press, 1985.

James, Van, *Spirit and Art*, Great Barrington, MA: Anthroposophic Press, 2001.

Lessing, G.E. *Laocoon, An Essay on the Limits of Painting and Poetry*, Baltimore, MD: John Hopkins University Press, 1984.

_____, "Education of the Human Race," In *Literary and Philosophical Essays*, Vol. 32, The Harvard Classics Series, New York: P.F. Collier & Son, 1909-1914. On-line edition: www.Bartleby.com, 2001.

Welburn, Andrew, *The Book with Fourteen Seals*, London: Rudolf Steiner Press, 1991.

SIGNIFICANT EVENTS
IN THE LIFE OF RUDOLF STEINER

1829: June 23: birth of Johann Steiner (1829-1910)—Rudolf Steiner's father—in Geras, Lower Austria.

1834: May 8: birth of Franciska Blie (1834-1918)—Rudolf Steiner's mother—in Horn, Lower Austria. "My father and mother were both children of the glorious Lower Austrian forest district north of the Danube."

1860: May 16: marriage of Johann Steiner and Franciska Blie.

1861: February 25: birth of *Rudolf Joseph Lorenz Steiner* in Kraljevec, Croatia, near the border with Hungary, where Johann Steiner works as a telegrapher for the South Austria Railroad. Rudolf Steiner is baptized two days later, February 27, the date usually given as his birthday.

1862: Summer: the family moves to Mödling, Lower Austria.

1863: The family moves to Pottschach, Lower Austria, near the Styrian border, where Johann Steiner becomes stationmaster. "The view stretched to the mountains...majestic peaks in the distance and the sweet charm of nature in the immediate surroundings."

1864: November 15: birth of Rudolf Steiner's sister, Leopoldine (d. November 1, 1927). She will become a seamstress and live with her parents for the rest of her life.

1866: July 28: birth of Rudolf Steiner's deaf-mute brother, Gustav (d. May 1, 1941).

1867: Rudolf Steiner enters the village school. Following a disagreement between his father and the schoolmaster, whose wife falsely accused the boy of causing a commotion, Rudolf Steiner is taken out of school and taught at home.

1868: A critical experience. Unknown to the family, an aunt dies in a distant town. Sitting in the station waiting room, Rudolf Steiner sees her "form," which speaks to him, asking for help. "Beginning with this experience, a new soul life began in the boy, one in which not only the outer trees and mountains spoke to him, but also the worlds that lay behind them. From this moment on, the boy began to live with the spirits of nature...."

1869: The family moves to the peaceful, rural village of Neudorfl, near Wiener-Neustadt in present-day Hungary. Rudolf Steiner attends the village school. Because of the "unorthodoxy" of his writing and spelling, he has to do "extra lessons."

1870: Through a book lent to him by his tutor, he discovers geometry: "To grasp something purely in the spirit brought me inner happiness. I know that I first learned happiness through geometry." The same tutor allows him to draw, while other students still struggle with their reading and writing. "An artistic element" thus enters his education.

1871:   Though his parents are not religious, Rudolf Steiner becomes a "church child," a favorite of the priest, who was "an exceptional character." "Up to the age of ten or eleven, among those I came to know, he was far and away the most significant." Among other things, he introduces Steiner to Copernican, heliocentric cosmology. As an altar boy, Rudolf Steiner serves at Masses, funerals, and Corpus Christi processions. At year's end, after an incident in which he escapes a thrashing, his father forbids him to go to church.

1872:   Rudolf Steiner transfers to grammar school in Wiener-Neustadt, a five-mile walk from home, which must be done in all weathers.

1873-75: Through his teachers and on his own, Rudolf Steiner has many wonderful experiences with science and mathematics. Outside school, he teaches himself analytic geometry, trigonometry, differential equations, and calculus.

1876:   Rudolf Steiner begins tutoring other students. He learns bookbinding from his father. He also teaches himself stenography.

1877:   Rudolf Steiner discovers Kant's *Critique of Pure Reason*, which he reads and rereads. He also discovers and reads von Rotteck's *World History*.

1878:   He studies extensively in contemporary psychology and philosophy.

1879:   Rudolf Steiner graduates from high school with honors. His father is transferred to Inzersdorf, near Vienna. He uses his first visit to Vienna "to purchase a great number of philosophy books"— Kant, Fichte, Schelling, and Hegel, as well as numerous histories of philosophy. His aim: to find a path from the "I" to nature.

October 1879-1883: Rudolf Steiner attends the Technical College in Vienna—to study mathematics, chemistry, physics, mineralogy, botany, zoology, biology, geology, and mechanics—with a scholarship. He also attends lectures in history and literature, while avidly reading philosophy on his own. His two favorite professors are Karl Julius Schröer (German language and literature) and Edmund Reitlinger (physics). He also audits lectures by Robert Zimmerman on aesthetics and Franz Brentano on philosophy. During this year he begins his friendship with Moritz Zitter (1861-1921), who will help support him financially when he is in Berlin.

1880:   Rudolf Steiner attends lectures on Schiller and Goethe by Karl Julius Schröer, who becomes his mentor. Also "through a remarkable combination of circumstances," he meets Felix Koguzki, an "herb gatherer" and healer, who could "see deeply into the secrets of nature." Rudolf Steiner will meet and study with this "emissary of the Master" throughout his time in Vienna.

1881:   January: "… I didn't sleep a wink. I was busy with philosophical problems until about 12:30 a.m. Then, finally, I threw myself down on my couch. All my striving during the previous year had been to research whether the following statement by Schelling was true or not: *Within everyone dwells a secret, marvelous capacity to draw back from the stream of time—out of the self clothed in all that comes to us from outside—into our innermost being and there, in the immutable form of the Eternal, to look into ourselves.* I believe, and I am still quite certain of it, that I discovered this capacity in myself; I had long had an inkling of it. Now the whole of idealist philosophy stood before me in modified form. What's a sleepless night compared to that!"

Rudolf Steiner begins communicating with leading thinkers of the day, who send him books in return, which he reads eagerly.

July: "I am not one of those who dives into the day like an animal in human form. I pursue a quite specific goal, an idealistic aim—knowledge of the truth! This cannot be done offhandedly. It requires the greatest striving in the world, free of all egotism, and equally of all resignation."

August: Steiner puts down on paper for the first time thoughts for a "Philosophy of Freedom." "The striving for the absolute: this human yearning is freedom." He also seeks to outline a "peasant philosophy," describing what the worldview of a "peasant"—one who lives close to the earth and the old ways—really is.

1881-1882: Felix Koguzki, the herb gatherer, reveals himself to be the envoy of another, higher initiatory personality, who instructs Rudolf Steiner to penetrate Fichte's philosophy and to master modern scientific thinking as a preparation for right entry into the spirit. This "Master" also teaches him the double (evolutionary and involutionary) nature of time.

1882: Through the offices of Karl Julius Schröer, Rudolf Steiner is asked by Joseph Kurschner to edit Goethe's scientific works for the *Deutschen National-Literatur* edition. He writes "A Possible Critique of Atomistic Concepts" and sends it to Friedrich Theodore Vischer.

1883: Rudolf Steiner completes his college studies and begins work on the Goethe project.

1884: First volume of Goethe's *Scientific Writings* (CW 1) appears (March). He lectures on Goethe and Lessing, and Goethe's approach to science. In July, he enters the household of Ladislaus and Pauline Specht as tutor to the four Specht boys. He will live there until 1890. At this time, he meets Josef Breuer ((1842-1925), the coauthor with Sigmund Freud of *Studies in Hysteria*, who is the Specht family doctor.

1885: While continuing to edit Goethe's writings, Rudolf Steiner reads deeply in contemporary philosophy (Edouard von Hartmann, Johannes Volkelt, and Richard Wahle, among others).

1886: May: Rudolf Steiner sends Kurschner the manuscript of *Outlines of Goethe's Theory of Knowledge* (CW 2), which appears in October, and which he sends out widely. He also meets the poet Marie Eugenie Delle Grazie and writes "Nature and Our Ideals" for her. He attends her salon, where he meets many priests, theologians, and philosophers, who will become his friends. Meanwhile, the director of the Goethe Archive in Weimar requests his collaboration with the *Sophien* edition of Goethe's works, particularly the writings on color.

1887:   At the beginning of the year, Rudolf Steiner is very sick. As the year progresses and his health improves, he becomes increasingly "a man of letters," lecturing, writing essays, and taking part in Austrian cultural life. In August-September, the second volume of Goethe's *Scientific Writings* appears.

1888:   January-July: Rudolf Steiner assumes editorship of the "German Weekly" (*Deutsche Wochenschrift*). He begins lecturing more intensively, giving, for example, a lecture titled "Goethe as Father of a New Aesthetics." He meets and becomes soul friends with Friedrich Eckstein (1861-1939), a vegetarian, philosopher of symbolism, alchemist, and musician, who will introduce him to various spiritual currents (including Theosophy) and with whom he will meditate and interpret esoteric and alchemical texts.

1889:   Rudolf Steiner first reads Nietzsche (*Beyond Good and Evil*). He encounters Theosophy again and learns of Madame Blavatsky in the Theosophical circle around Marie Lang (1858-1934). Here he also meets well-known figures of Austrian life, as well as esoteric figures like the occultist Franz Hartman and Karl Leinigen-Billigen (translator of C.G. Harrison's *The Transcendental Universe*.) During this period, Steiner first reads A.P. Sinnett's *Esoteric Buddhism* and Mabel Collins's *Light on the Path*. He also begins traveling, visiting Budapest, Weimar, and Berlin (where he meets philosopher Edouard von Hartman).

1890:   Rudolf Steiner finishes volume 3 of Goethe's scientific writings. He begins his doctoral dissertation, which will become *Truth and Science* (CW 3). He also meets the poet and feminist Rosa Mayreder (1858-1938), with whom he can exchange his most intimate thoughts. In September, Rudolf Steiner moves to Weimar to work in the Goethe-Schiller Archive.

1891:   Volume 3 of the Kurschner edition of Goethe appears. Meanwhile, Rudolf Steiner edits Goethe's studies in mineralogy and scientific writings for the *Sophien* edition. He meets Ludwig Laistner of the Cotta Publishing Company, who asks for a book on the basic question of metaphysics. From this will result, ultimately, *The Philosophy of Freedom* (CW 4), which will be published not by Cotta but by Emil Felber. In October, Rudolf Steiner takes the oral exam for a doctorate in philosophy, mathematics, and mechanics at Rostock University, receiving his doctorate on the twenty-sixth. In November, he gives his first lecture on Goethe's "Fairy Tale" in Vienna.

1892:   Rudolf Steiner continues work at the Goethe-Schiller Archive and on his *Philosophy of Freedom*. *Truth and Science*, his doctoral dissertation, is published. Steiner undertakes to write introductions to books on Schopenhauer and Jean Paul for Cotta. At year's end, he finds lodging with Anna Eunike, née Schulz (1853-1911), a widow with four daughters and a son. He also develops a friendship with Otto Erich Hartleben (1864-1905) with whom he shares literary interests.

1893:   Rudolf Steiner begins his habit of producing many reviews and articles. In March, he gives a lecture titled "Hypnotism, with Reference to Spiritism." In September, volume 4 of the Kurschner edition is completed. In November, *The Philosophy of Freedom* appears. This year, too, he meets John Henry Mackay (1864-1933), the anarchist, and Max Stirner, a scholar and biographer.

1894:   Rudolf Steiner meets Elisabeth Förster Nietzsche, the philosopher's sister, and begins to read Nietzsche in earnest, beginning with the as yet unpublished *Antichrist*. He also meets Ernst Haeckel (1834-1919). In the fall, he begins to write *Nietzsche, A Fighter against His Time* (CW 5).

1895:   May, *Nietzsche, A Fighter against His Time* appears.

1896:   January 22: Rudolf Steiner sees Friedrich Nietzsche for the first and only time. Moves between the Nietzsche and the Goethe-Schiller Archives, where he completes his work before year's end. He falls out with Elisabeth Förster Nietzsche, thus ending his association with the Nietzsche Archive.

1897:   Rudolf Steiner finishes the manuscript of *Goethe's Worldview* (CW 6). He moves to Berlin with Anna Eunike and begins editorship of the *Magazin fur Literatur*. From now on, Steiner will write countless reviews, literary and philosophical articles, and so on. He begins lecturing at the "Free Literary Society." In September, he attends the Zionist Congress in Basel. He sides with Dreyfus in the Dreyfus affair.

1898:   Rudolf Steiner is very active as an editor in the political, artistic, and theatrical life of Berlin. He becomes friendly with John Henry Mackay and poet Ludwig Jacobowski (1868-1900). He joins Jacobowski's circle of writers, artists, and scientists—"The Coming Ones" (*Die Kommenden*)—and contributes lectures to the group until 1903. He also lectures at the "League for College Pedagogy." He writes an article for Goethe's sesquicentennial, "Goethe's Secret Revelation," on the "Fairy Tale of the Green Snake and the Beautiful Lily."

1888-89: "This was a trying time for my soul as I looked at Christianity. . . . I was able to progress only by contemplating, by means of spiritual perception, the evolution of Christianity . . . . Conscious knowledge of real Christianity began to dawn in me around the turn of the century. This seed continued to develop. My soul trial occurred shortly before the beginning of the twentieth century. It was decisive for my soul's development that I stood spiritually before the Mystery of Golgotha in a deep and solemn celebration of knowledge."

1899:   Rudolf Steiner begins teaching and giving lectures and lecture cycles at the Workers' College, founded by Wilhelm Liebknecht (1826-1900). He will continue to do so until 1904. Writes: *Literature and Spiritual Life in the Nineteenth Century; Individualism in Philosophy*; *Haeckel and His Opponents; Poetry in the Present;* and begins what will become (fifteen years later) *The Riddles of Philosophy* (CW 18). He also meets many artists and writers, including Käthe Kollwitz, Stefan

Zweig, and Rainer Maria Rilke. On October 31, he marries Anna Eunike.

1900: "I thought that the turn of the century must bring humanity a new light. It seemed to me that the separation of human thinking and willing from the spirit had peaked. A turn or reversal of direction in human evolution seemed to me a necessity." Rudolf Steiner finishes *World and Life Views in the Nineteenth Century* (the second part of what will become *The Riddles of Philosophy*) and dedicates it to Ernst Haeckel. It is published in March. He continues lecturing at *Die Kommenden*, whose leadership he assumes after the death of Jacobowski. Also, he gives the Gutenberg Jubilee lecture before 7,000 typesetters and printers. In September, Rudolf Steiner is invited by Count and Countess Brockdorff to lecture in the Theosophical Library. His first lecture is on Nietzsche. His second lecture is titled "Goethe's Secret Revelation." October 6, he begins a lecture cycle on the mystics that will become *Mystics after Modernism* (CW 7). November-December: "Marie von Sivers appears in the audience...." Also in November, Steiner gives his first lecture at the Giordano Bruno Bund (where he will continue to lecture until May, 1905). He speaks on Bruno and modern Rome, focusing on the importance of the philosophy of Thomas Aquinas as monism.

1901: In continual financial straits, Rudolf Steiner's early friends Moritz Zitter and Rosa Mayreder help support him. In October, he begins the lecture cycle *Christianity as Mystical Fact* (CW 8) at the Theosophical Library. In November, he gives his first "Theosophical lecture" on Goethe's "Fairy Tale" in Hamburg at the invitation of Wilhelm Hubbe-Schleiden. He also attends a tea to celebrate the founding of the Theosophical Society at Count and Countess Brockdorff's. He gives a lecture cycle, "From Buddha to Christ," for the circle of the *Kommenden*. November 17, Marie von Sivers asks Rudolf Steiner if Theosophy does not need a Western-Christian spiritual movement (to complement Theosophy's Eastern emphasis). "The question was posed. Now, following spiritual laws, I could begin to give an answer...." In December, Rudolf Steiner writes his first article for a Theosophical publication. At year's end, the Brockdorffs and possibly Wilhelm Hubbe-Schleiden ask Rudolf Steiner to join the Theosophical Society and undertake the leadership of the German section. Rudolf Steiner agrees, on the condition that Marie von Sivers (then in Italy) work with him.

1902: Beginning in January, Rudolf Steiner attends the opening of the Workers' School in Spandau with Rosa Luxemburg (1870-1919). January 17, Rudolf Steiner joins the Theosophical Society. In April, he is asked to become general secretary of the German Section of the Theosophical Society, and works on preparations for its founding. In July, he visits London for a Theosophical congress. He meets Bertram

Keightly, G.R.S. Mead, A.P. Sinnett, and Annie Besant, among others. In September, *Christianity as Mystical Fact* appears. In October, Rudolf Steiner gives his first public lecture on Theosophy ("Monism and Theosophy") to about three hundred people at the Giordano Bruno Bund. On October 19-21, the German Section of the Theosophical Society has its first meeting; Rudolf Steiner is the general secretary, and Annie Besant attends. Steiner lectures on practical karma studies. On October 23, Annie Besant inducts Rudolf Steiner into the Esoteric School of the Theosophical Society. On October 25, Steiner begins a weekly series of lectures: "The Field of Theosophy." During this year, Rudolf Steiner also first meets Ita Wegman (1876-1943), who will become his close collaborator in his final years.

1903:   Rudolf Steiner holds about 300 lectures and seminars. In May, the first issue of the periodical *Luzifer* appears. In June, Rudolf Steiner visits London for the first meeting of the Federation of the European Sections of the Theosophical Society, where he meets Colonel Olcott. He begins to write *Theosophy* (CW 9).

1904:   Rudolf Steiner continues lecturing at the Workers' College and elsewhere (about 90 lectures), while lecturing intensively all over Germany among Theosophists (about a 140 lectures). In February, he meets Carl Unger (1878-1929), who will become a member of the board of the Anthroposophical Society (1913). In March, he meets Michael Bauer (1871-1929), a Christian mystic, who will also be on the board. In May, *Theosophy* appears, with the dedication: "To the spirit of Giordano Bruno." Rudolf Steiner and Marie von Sivers visit London for meetings with Annie Besant. June: Rudolf Steiner and Marie von Sivers attend the meeting of the Federation of European Sections of the Theosophical Society in Amsterdam. In July, Steiner begins the articles in *Luzifer-Gnosis* that will become *How to Know Higher Worlds* (CW 10) and *Cosmic Memory* (CW 11). In September, Annie Besant visits Germany. In December, Steiner lectures on Freemasonry. He mentions the High Grade Masonry derived from John Yarker and represented by Theodore Reuss and Karl Kellner as a blank slate "into which a good image could be placed."

1905:   This year, Steiner ends his non-Theosophical lecturing activity. Supported by Marie von Sivers, his Theosophical lecturing—both in public and in the Theosophical Society—increases significantly: "The German Theosophical Movement is of exceptional importance." Steiner recommends reading, among others, Fichte, Jacob Boehme, and Angelus Silesius. He begins to introduce Christian themes into Theosophy. He also begins to work with doctors (Felix Peipers and Ludwig Noll). In July, he is in London for the Federation of European Sections, where he attends a lecture by Annie Besant: "I have seldom seen Mrs. Besant speak in so inward and heartfelt a manner...." "Through Mrs. Besant I have found the way to H.P. Blavatsky."

September to October, he gives a course of thirty-one lectures for a small group of esoteric students. In October, the annual meeting of the German Section of the Theosophical Society, which still remains very small, takes place. Rudolf Steiner reports membership has risen from 121 to 377 members. In November, seeking to establish esoteric "continuity," Rudolf Steiner and Marie von Sivers participate in a "Memphis-Misraim" Masonic ceremony. They pay forty-five marks for membership. "Yesterday, you saw how little remains of former esoteric institutions." "We are dealing only with a 'framework'... for the present, nothing lies behind it. The occult powers have completely withdrawn."

1906:   Expansion of Theosophical work. Rudolf Steiner gives about 245 lectures, only 44 of which take place in Berlin. Cycles are given in Paris, Leipzig, Stuttgart, and Munich. Esoteric work also intensifies. Rudolf Steiner begins writing *An Outline of Esoteric Science* (CW 13). In January, Rudolf Steiner receives permission (a patent) from the Great Orient of the Scottish A & A Thirty-Three Degree Rite of the Order of the Ancient Freemasons of the Memphis-Misraim Rite to direct a chapter under the name "Mystica Aeterna." This will become the "Cognitive Cultic Section" (also called "Misraim Service") of the Esoteric School. (See: *From the History and Contents of the Cognitive Cultic Section* (CW 264). During this time, Steiner also meets Albert Schweitzer. In May, he is in Paris, where he visits Edouard Schuré. Many Russians attend his lectures (including Konstantin Balmont, Dimitri Mereszkovski, Zinaida Hippius, and Maximilian Woloshin). He attends the General Meeting of the European Federation of the Theosophical Society, at which Col. Olcott is present for the last time. He spends the year's end in Venice and Rome, where he writes and works on his translation of H.P. Blavatsky's *Key to Theosophy*.

1907:   Further expansion of the German Theosophical Movement according to the Rosicrucian directive to "introduce spirit into the world"—in education, in social questions, in art, and in science. In February, Col. Olcott dies in Adyar. Before he dies, Olcott indicates that "the Masters" wish Annie Besant to succeed him: much politicking ensues. Rudolf Steiner supports Besant's candidacy. April-May: preparations for the Congress of the Federation of European Sections of the Theosophical Society—the great, watershed Whitsun "Munich Congress," attended by Annie Besant and others. Steiner decides to separate Eastern and Western (Christian-Rosicrucian) esoteric schools. He takes his esoteric school out of the Theosophical Society (Besant and Rudolf Steiner are "in harmony" on this). Steiner makes his first lecture tours to Austria and Hungary. That summer, he is in Italy. In September, he visits Edouard Schuré, who will write the introduction to the French edition of *Christianity as Mystical Fact* in Barr, Alsace. Rudolf Steiner writes the autobiographical statement known as the "Barr Document." In *Luzifer–Gnosis*, "The Education of the Child" appears.

1908:   The movement grows (membership: 1150). Lecturing expands. Steiner makes his first extended lecture tour to Holland and Scandinavia, as well as visits to Naples and Sicily. Themes: St. John's Gospel, the Apocalypse, Egypt, science, philosophy, and logic. *Luzifer-Gnosis* ceases publication. In Berlin, Marie von Sivers (with Johanna Mücke (1864-1949) forms the *Philosophisch-Theosophisch* (after 1915 *Philosophisch-Anthroposophisch*) *Verlag* to publish Steiner's work. Steiner gives lecture cycles titled *The Gospel of St. John* (CW 103) and *The Apocalypse* (104).

1909:   *An Outline of Esoteric Science* appears. Lecturing and travel continues. Rudolf Steiner's spiritual research expands to include the polarity of Lucifer and Ahriman; the work of great individualities in history; the Maitreya Buddha and the Bodhisattvas; spiritual economy (CW 109); the work of the spiritual hierarchies in heaven and on Earth (CW 110). He also deepens and intensifies his research into the Gospels, giving lectures on the Gospel of St. Luke (CW 114) with the first mention of two Jesus children. Meets and becomes friends with Christian Morgenstern (1871-1914). In April, he lays the foundation stone for the Malsch model—the building that will lead to the first Goetheanum. In May, the International Congress of the Federation of European Sections of the Theosophical Society takes place in Budapest. Rudolf Steiner receives the Subba Row medal for *How to Know Higher Worlds*. During this time, Charles W. Leadbeater discovers Jiddu Krishnamurti (1895-1986) and proclaims him the future "world teacher," the bearer of the Maitreya Buddha and the "reappearing Christ." In October, Steiner delivers seminal lectures on "anthroposophy," which he will try, unsuccessfully, to rework over the next years into the unfinished work, *Anthroposophy (A Fragment)* (CW 45).

1910:   New themes: *The Reappearance of Christ in the Etheric* (CW 118); *The Fifth Gospel; The Mission of Folk Souls* (CW 121); *Occult History* (CW 126); the evolving development of etheric cognitive capacities. Rudolf Steiner continues his Gospel research with *The Gospel of St. Matthew* (CW 123). In January, his father dies. In April, he takes a month-long trip to Italy, including Rome, Monte Cassino, and Sicily. He also visits Scandinavia again. July-August, he writes the first mystery drama, *The Portal of Initiation* (CW 14). In November, he gives "psychosophy" lectures. In December, he submits "On the Psychological Foundations and Epistemological Framework of Theosophy" to the International Philosophical Congress in Bologna.

1911:   The crisis in the Theosophical Society deepens. In January, "The Order of the Rising Sun," which will soon become "The Order of the Star in the East," is founded for the coming world teacher, Krishnamurti. At the same time, Marie von Sivers, Rudolf Steiner's coworker, falls ill. Fewer lectures are given, but important new ground is broken. In Prague, in March, Steiner meets Franz Kafka (1883-1924) and Hugo Bergmann (1883-1975). In April, he delivers his paper to the

Philosophical Congress. He writes the second mystery drama, *The Soul's Probation* (CW 14). Also, while Marie von Sivers is convalescing, Rudolf Steiner begins work on *Calendar 1912/1913*, which will contain the "Calendar of the Soul" meditations. On March 19, Anna (Eunike) Steiner dies. In September, Rudolf Steiner visits Einsiedeln, birthplace of Paracelsus. In December, Friedrich Rittelmeyer, future founder of the Christian Community, meets Rudolf Steiner. The *Johannes-Bauverein*, the "building committee," which would lead to the first Goetheanum (first planned for Munich), is also founded, and a preliminary committee for the founding of an independent association is created that, in the following year, will become the Anthroposophical Society. Important lecture cycles include *Occult Physiology* (CW 128); *Wonders of the World* (CW 129); *From Jesus to Christ* (CW 131). Other themes: esoteric Christianity; Christian Rosenkreutz; the spiritual guidance of humanity; the sense world and the world of the spirit.

1912: Despite the ongoing, now increasing crisis in the Theosophical Society, much is accomplished: *Calendar 1912/1913* is published; eurythmy is created; both the third mystery drama, *The Guardian of the Threshold* (CW 14) and *A Way of Self-Knowledge* (CW 16) are written. New (or renewed) themes included life between death and rebirth and karma and reincarnation. Other lecture cycles: *Spiritual Beings in the Heavenly Bodies and the Kingdoms of Nature* (CW 136); *The Human Being in the Light of Occultism, Theosophy, and Philosophy* (CW 137); *The Gospel of St. Mark* (CW 139); and *The Bhagavad Gita and the Epistles of Paul* (CW 142). On May 8, Rudolf Steiner celebrates White Lotus Day, H.P. Blavatsky's death day, which he had faithfully observed for the past decade, for the last time. In August, Rudolf Steiner suggests the "independent association" be called the "Anthroposophical Society." In September, the first eurythmy course takes place. In October, Rudolf Steiner declines recognition of a Theosophical Society lodge dedicated to the Star of the East and decides to expel all Theosophical Society members belonging to the order. Also, with Marie von Sivers, he first visits Dornach, near Basel, Switzerland, and they stand on the hill where the Goetheanum will be. In November, a Theosophical Society lodge is opened by direct mandate from Adyar (Annie Besant). In December, a meeting of the German section occurs at which it is decided that belonging to the Order of the Star of the East is incompatible with membership in the Theosophical Society. December 28: informal founding of the Anthroposophical Society in Berlin.

1913: Expulsion of the German section from the Theosophical Society. February 2-3: Foundation meeting of the Anthroposophical Society. Board members include: Marie von Sivers, Michael Bauer, and Carl Unger. September 20: Laying of the foundation stone for the *Johannes Bau* (Goetheanum) in Dornach. Building begins immediately. The third mystery drama, *The Soul's Awakening* (CW 14), is completed.

Also: *The Threshold of the Spiritual World* (CW 147). Lecture cycles include: *The Bhagavad Gita and the Epistles of Paul* and *The Esoteric Meaning of the Bhagavad Gita* (CW 146), which the Russian philosopher Nikolai Berdyaev attends; *The Mysteries of the East and of Christianity* (CW 144); *The Effects of Esoteric Development* (CW 145); and *The Fifth Gospel* (CW 148). In May, Rudolf Steiner is in London and Paris, where anthroposophical work continues.

1914: Building continues on the *Johannes Bau* (Goetheanum) in Dornach, with artists and coworkers from seventeen nations. The general assembly of the Anthroposophical Society takes place. In May, Rudolf Steiner visits Paris, as well as Chartres Cathedral. June 28: assassination in Sarajevo ("Now the catastrophe has happened!"). August 1: War is declared. Rudolf Steiner returns to Germany from Dornach—he will travel back and forth. He writes the last chapter of *The Riddles of Philosophy*. Lecture cycles include: *Human and Cosmic Thought* (CW 151); *Inner Being of Humanity between Death and a New Birth* (CW 153); *Occult Reading and Occult Hearing* (CW 156). December 24: marriage of Rudolf Steiner and Marie von Sivers.

1915: Building continues. Life after death becomes a major theme, also art. Writes: *Thoughts during a Time of War* (CW 24). Lectures include: *The Secret of Death* (CW 159); *The Uniting of Humanity through the Christ Impulse* (CW 165).

1916: Rudolf Steiner begins work with Edith Maryon (1872-1924) on the sculpture "The Representative of Humanity" ("The Group"—Christ, Lucifer, and Ahriman). He also works with the alchemist Alexander von Bernus on the quarterly *Das Reich*. He writes *The Riddle of Humanity* (CW 20). Lectures include: *Necessity and Freedom in World History and Human Action* (CW 166); *Past and Present in the Human Spirit* (CW 167); *The Karma of Vocation* (CW 172); *The Karma of Untruthfulness* (CW 173).

1917: Russian Revolution. The U.S. enters the war. Building continues. Rudolf Steiner delineates the idea of the "threefold nature of the human being" (in a public lecture March 15) and the "threefold nature of the social organism" (hammered out in May-June with the help of Otto von Lerchenfeld and Ludwig Polzer-Hoditz in the form of two documents titled *Memoranda*, which were distributed in high places). August-September: Rudolf Steiner writes *The Riddles of the Soul* (CW 20). Also: commentary on "The Chemical Wedding of Christian Rosenkreutz" for Alexander Bernus (*Das Reich*). Lectures include: *The Karma of Materialism* (CW 176); *The Spiritual Background of the Outer World: The Fall of the Spirits of Darkness* (CW 177).

1918: March 18: peace treaty of Brest-Litovsk—"Now everything will truly enter chaos! What is needed is cultural renewal." June: Rudolf Steiner visits Karlstein (Grail) Castle outside Prague. Lecture cycle: *From Symptom to Reality in Modern History* (CW 185). In mid-November,

Emil Molt, of the Waldorf-Astoria Cigarette Company, has the idea of founding a school for his workers' children.

1919: Focus on the threefold social organism: tireless travel, countless lectures, meetings, and publications. At the same time, a new public stage of Anthroposophy emerges as cultural renewal begins. The coming years will see initiatives in pedagogy, medicine, pharmacology, and agriculture. January 27: threefold meeting: " We must first of all, with the money we have, found free schools that can bring people what they need." February: first public eurythmy performance in Zurich. Also: "Appeal to the German People" (CW 24), circulated March 6 as a newspaper insert. In April, *Toward Social Renewal* (CW 23)—"perhaps the most widely read of all books on politics appearing since the war"— appears. Rudolf Steiner is asked to undertake the "direction and leadership" of the school founded by the Waldorf-Astoria Company. Rudolf Steiner begins to talk about the "renewal" of education. May 30: a building is selected and purchased for the future Waldorf School. August-September, Rudolf Steiner gives a lecture course for Waldorf teachers, *The Foundations of Human Experience (Study of Man)* (CW 293). September 7: Opening of the first Waldorf School. December (into January): first science course, the *Light Course* (CW 320).

1920: The Waldorf School flourishes. New threefold initiatives. Founding of limited companies *Der Kommenden Tag* and *Futurum A.G.* to infuse spiritual values into the economic realm. Rudolf Steiner also focuses on the sciences. Lectures: *Introducing Anthroposophical Medicine* (CW 312); *The Warmth Course* (CW 321); *The Boundaries of Natural Science* (CW 322); *The Redemption of Thinking* (CW 74). February: Johannes Werner Klein—later a cofounder of the Christian Community—asks Rudolf Steiner about the possibility of a "religious renewal," a "Johannine church." In March, Rudolf Steiner gives the first course for doctors and medical students. In April, a divinity student asks Rudolf Steiner a second time about the possibility of religious renewal. September 27-October 16: anthroposophical "university course." December: lectures titled *The Search for the New Isis* (CW 202).

1921: Rudolf Steiner continues his intensive work on cultural renewal, including the uphill battle for the threefold social order. "University" arts, scientific, theological, and medical courses include: *The Astronomy Course* (CW 323); *Observation, Mathematics, and Scientific Experiment* (CW 324); the *Second Medical Course* (CW 313); *Color*. In June and September-October, Rudolf Steiner also gives the first two "priests' courses" (CW 342 and 343). The "youth movement" gains momentum. Magazines are founded: *Die Drei* (January), and—under the editorship of Albert Steffen (1884-1963)—the weekly, *Das Goetheanum* (August). In February-March, Rudolf Steiner takes his first trip outside Germany since the war (Holland). On April 7, Steiner receives a letter regarding "religious renewal," and May 22-23, he agrees to address the question in a practical way. In June, the Klinical-Therapeutic Institute opens in Arlesheim under the direction of Dr. Ita Wegman. In August, the Chemical-Pharmaceutical Laboratory opens in Arlesheim (Oskar Schmiedel and Ita Wegman, directors). The Clinical Therapeutic Institute is inaugurated in Stuttgart (Dr. Ludwig Noll, director); also the Research Laboratory in Dornach (Ehrenfried Pfeiffer and Gunther Wachsmuth, directors). In November-December, Rudolf Steiner visits Norway.

1922: The first half of the year involves very active public lecturing (thousands attend); in the second half, Rudolf Steiner begins to withdraw and turn toward the Society—"The Society is asleep." It is "too weak" to do what is asked of it. The businesses—*Die Kommenden Tag* and *Futura A.G.*—fail. In January, with the help of an agent, Steiner undertakes a twelve-city German tour, accompanied by eurythmy performances. In two weeks he speaks to more than 2,000 people. In April, he gives a "university course" in The Hague. He also visits England. In June, he is in Vienna for the East-West Congress. In August-September, he is back in England for the Oxford Conference on Education. Returning to Dornach, he gives the lectures *Philosophy, Cosmology, and Religion* (CW 215), and gives the third priest's course (CW 344). On September 16, The Christian Community is founded. In October-November, Steiner is in Holland and England. He also speaks to the youth: *The Youth Course* (CW 217). In December, Steiner gives lectures titled *The Origins of Natural Science* (CW 326), and *Humanity and the World of Stars: The Spiritual Communion of Humanity* (CW 219). December 31: Fire at the Goetheanum, which is destroyed.

1923: Despite the fire, Rudolf Steiner continues his work unabated. A very hard year. Internal dispersion, dissension, and apathy abound. There is conflict—between old and new visions—within the society. A wake-up call is needed, and Rudolf Steiner responds with renewed lecturing vitality. His focus: the spiritual context of human life; initiation science; the course of the year; and community building. As a foundation for an artistic school, he creates a series of pastel sketches. Lecture cycles: *The Anthroposophical Movement; Initiation Science* (CW 227) (in England at the Penmaenmawr Summer School); *The Four Seasons and the Archangels* (CW 229); *Harmony of the Creative Word* (CW 230); *The Supersensible Human* (CW 231), given in Holland for the founding of the Dutch society. On November 10, in response to the failed Hitler-Ludendorf putsch in Munich, Steiner closes his Berlin residence and moves the *Philosophisch-Anthroposophisch Verlag* (Press) to Dornach. On December 9, Steiner begins the serialization of his *Autobiography: The Course of My Life* (CW 28) in *Das Goetheanum*. It will continue to appear weekly, without a break, until his death. Late December-early January: Rudolf Steiner refounds the Anthroposophical Society (about 12,000 members internationally) and takes over its leadership. The new board members are: Marie Steiner, Ita Wegman, Albert Steffen, Elizabeth Vreede, and Guenther Wachsmuth. (See *The Christmas Meeting for the Founding of the General Anthro-posophical Society* (CW 260). Accompanying lectures: *Mystery Knowledge and Mystery Centers* (CW 232); *World History in the Light of Anthroposophy* (CW 233). December 25: the Foundation Stone is laid (in the hearts of members) in the form of the "Foundation Stone Meditation."

1924: January 1: having founded the Anthroposophical Society and taken over its leadership, Rudolf Steiner has the task of "reforming" it. The process begins with a weekly newssheet ("What's Happening in the Anthroposophical Society") in which Rudolf Steiner's "Letters to Members" and "Anthroposophical Leading Thoughts" appear (CW 26). The next step is the creation of a new esoteric class, the "first class" of the "University of Spiritual Science" (which was to have been followed, had Rudolf Steiner lived longer, by two more advanced classes). Then comes a new language for Anthroposophy—practical, phenomenological, and direct; and Rudolf Steiner creates the model for the second Goetheanum. He begins the series of extensive "karma" lectures (CW 235-40); and finally, responding to needs, he creates two new initiatives: biodynamic agriculture and curative education. After the middle of the year, rumors begin to circulate regarding Steiner's health. Lectures: January-February, *Anthroposophy* (CW 234); February: *Tone Eurythmy* (CW 278); June: *The Agriculture Course* (CW 327); June-July: Speech [?] Eurythmy (CW 279); *Curative Education* (CW 317); August: (England, "Second International Summer School"), *Initiation Consciousness: True and False Paths in Spiritual Investigation* (CW 243); September: *Pastoral Medicine* (CW 318). On September 26, for the first time, Rudolf Steiner cancels a lecture. On September 28, he gives his last lecture. On September 29, he withdraws to his studio in the carpenter's shop; now he is definitively ill. Cared for by Ita Wegman, he continues working, however, and writing the weekly installments of his *Autobiography* and *Letters to the Members/Leading Thoughts* (CW 26).

1925: Rudolf Steiner, while continuing to work, continues to weaken. He finishes *Extending Practical Medicine* (CW 27) with Ita Wegman.

On March 30, around ten in the morning, Rudolf Steiner dies.

RUDOLF STEINER'S COLLECTED WORKS

The German Edition of Rudolf Steiner's Collected Works (the Gesamtausgabe [GA] published by Rudolf Steiner Verlag, Dornach, Switzerland) presently runs to over 354 titles, organized either by type of work (written or spoken), chronology, audience (public or other), or subject (education, art, etc.). For ease of comparison, the Collected Works in English [CW] follows the German organization exactly. A complete listing of the CWs follows with literal translations of the German titles. Other than in the case of the books published in his lifetime, titles were rarely given by Rudolf Steiner himself, and were often provided by the editors of the German editions. The titles in English are therefore not necessarily the same as the German; and, indeed, over the past seventy-five years have frequently been different, with the same book sometimes appearing under different titles.

For ease of identification and to avoid confusion, we suggest that readers looking for a title should do so by CW number. Because the work of creating the Collected Works of Rudolf Steiner is an ongoing process, with new titles being published every year, we have not indicated in this listing which books are presently available. To find out what titles in the Collected Works are currently in print, please check our website at www.steinerbooks.org, or write to SteinerBooks 610 Main Street, Great Barrington, MA 01230:

Written Work

CW 1	Goethe: Natural-Scientific Writings, Introduction, with Footnotes and Explanations in the text by Rudolf Steiner
CW 2	Outlines of an Epistemology of the Goethean World View, with Special Consideration of Schiller
CW 3	Truth and Science
CW 4	The Philosophy of Freedom
CW 4a	Documents to "The Philosophy of Freedom"
CW 5	Friedrich Nietzsche, A Fighter against His Own Time
CW 6	Goethe's Worldview
CW 6a	Now in CW 30
CW 7	Mysticism at the Dawn of Modern Spiritual Life and Its Relationship with Modern Worldviews
CW 8	Christianity as Mystical Fact and the Mysteries of Antiquity
CW 9	Theosophy: An Introduction into Supersensible World Knowledge and Human Purpose
CW 10	How Does One Attain Knowledge of Higher Worlds?
CW 11	From the Akasha-Chronicle
CW 12	Levels of Higher Knowledge

CW 13	Occult Science in Outline
CW 14	Four Mystery Dramas
CW 15	The Spiritual Guidance of the Individual and Humanity
CW 16	A Way to Human Self-Knowledge: Eight Meditations
CW 17	The Threshold of the Spiritual World. Aphoristic Comments
CW 18	The Riddles of Philosophy in Their History, Presented as an Outline
CW 19	Contained in CW 24
CW 20	The Riddles of the Human Being: Articulated and Unarticulated in the Thinking, Views and Opinions of a Series of German and Austrian Personalities
CW 21	The Riddles of the Soul
CW 22	Goethe's Spiritual Nature And Its Revelation In "Faust" and through the "Fairy Tale of the Snake and the Lily"
CW 23	The Central Points of the Social Question in the Necessities of Life in the Present and the Future
CW 24	Essays Concerning the Threefold Division of the Social Organism and the Period 1915-1921
CW 25	Cosmology, Religion and Philosophy
CW 26	Anthroposophical Leading Thoughts
CW 27	Fundamentals for Expansion of the Art of Healing according to Spiritual-Scientific Insights
CW 28	The Course of My Life
CW 29	Collected Essays on Dramaturgy, 1889-1900
CW 30	Methodical Foundations of Anthroposophy: Collected Essays on Philosophy, Natural Science, Aesthetics and Psychology, 1884-1901
CW 31	Collected Essays on Culture and Current Events, 1887-1901
CW 32	Collected Essays on Literature, 1884-1902
CW 33	Biographies and Biographical Sketches, 1894-1905
CW 34	Lucifer-Gnosis: Foundational Essays on Anthroposophy and Reports from the Periodicals "Lucifer" and "Lucifer-Gnosis," 1903-1908
CW 35	Philosophy and Anthroposophy: Collected Essays, 1904-1923
CW 36	The Goetheanum-Idea in the Middle of the Cultural Crisis of the Present: Collected Essays from the Periodical "Das Goetheanum," 1921-1925
CW 37	Now in CWs 260a and 251
CW 38	Letters, Vol. 1: 1881-1890
CW 39	Letters, Vol. 2: 1890-1925
CW 40	Truth-Wrought Words
CW 40a	Sayings, Poems and Mantras; Supplementary Volume
CW 42	Now in CWs 264-266

Lectures to the Members of the Anthroposophical Society

CW 267   Soul-Exercises: Vol. 1: Exercises with Word and Image
          Meditations for the Methodological Development of Higher
          Powers of Knowledge, 1904-1924
CW 268   Soul-Exercises: Vol. 2: Mantric Verses, 1903-1925
CW 269   Ritual Texts for the Celebration of the Free Christian Religious
          Instruction. The Collected Verses for Teachers and Students of
          the Waldorf School
CW 270   Esoteric Instructions for the First Class of the School for Spiritual
          Science at the Goetheanum 1924, 4 Volumes
CW 271   Art and Knowledge of Art. Foundations of a New Aesthetic
CW 272   Spiritual-Scientific Commentary on Goethe's "Faust" in Two
          Volumes. Vol. 1: Faust, the Striving Human Being
CW 273   Spiritual-Scientific Commentary on Goethe's "Faust" in Two
          Volumes. Vol. 2: The Faust-Problem
CW 274   Addresses for the Christmas Plays from the Old Folk Traditions
CW 275   Art in the Light of Mystery-Wisdom
CW 276   The Artistic in Its Mission in the World. The Genius of
          Language. The World of the Self-Revealing Radiant Appearances
          – Anthroposophy and Art. Anthroposophy and Poetry
CW 277   Eurythmy. The Revelation of the Speaking Soul
CW 277a   The Origin and Development of Eurythmy
CW 278   Eurythmy as Visible Song
CW 279   Eurythmy as Visible Speech
CW 280   The Method and Nature of Speech Formation
CW 281   The Art of Recitation and Declamation
CW 282   Speech Formation and Dramatic Art
CW 283   The Nature of Things Musical and the Experience of Tone in the
          Human Being
CW284/285 Images of Occult Seals and Pillars. The Munich Congress of
          Whitsun 1907 and Its Consequences
CW 286   Paths to a New Style of Architecture. "And the Building Becomes
          Human"
CW 287   The Building at Dornach as a Symbol of Historical Becoming
          and an Artistic Transformation Impulse
CW 288   Style-Forms in the Living Organic
CW 289   The Building-Idea of the Goetheanum: Lectures with Slides from
          the Years 1920-1921
CW 290   The Building-Idea of the Goetheanum: Lectures with Slides from
          the Years 1920-1921
CW 291   The Nature of Colors
CW 291a   Knowledge of Colors. Supplementary Volume to "The Nature of
          Colors"
CW 292   Art History as Image of Inner Spiritual Impulses

INDEX

academic theologians, 39
Aeschylus, 34
Ahasuerus, 14, 15, 27, 28
Ahriman, 74–79, 81, 134, 143, 146
ahrimanic forces, 81, 125, 132, 134,
   135, 141–43, 146, 147
Anaxagoras, 127, 128
angels, 4, 22, 24, 26, 47
animals, astral and physical body of, 9,
   10; beings in, 146; chemistry of,
   152–53; subhuman consciousness
   of, 85–86; world of, 48;
   anthroposophical movement, 135,
   137–40, 145, 147–49;
Anthroposophy, adaptation of
   initiation science by, 97; assessment
   of, 11–12, 138; initiation offered
   by, 128; judgments about, 40, 45;
   concerning Mystery of Golgotha,
   94, 95; natural science relationship
   with, 98; as new wisdom, 50;
   purpose of, 124, 133, 153; for
   religious purposes, 109–10
   significance of, 22, 39, 58, 77,
   104–5, 136; taught to children,
   113; testimony of, 135; theoretical,
   112
Apollo, 53, 54
Apropos, 151
Aristotle, 55, 56, 128
Artemis, 53
Asian civilization, 125–26
astral body, 2–5, 9–11, 19, 51–53,
   55–58. *See also* etheric bodies; "I"
Athenian philosophers, 128
aum, 64, 68

baby. See infants
Barbarossa, Frederick, 25
beings, divine-spiritual, 150;
   elemental, 146, 147; soul-spiritual,
   2, 30, 31, 34, 148; spiritual, 6, 7,
   16, 24, 26, 29, 37, 108, 116, 121,
   122, 126–31, 143–46, 150–51,
   153; supersensible, 5

Bible, 39, 47, 93. *See also* Gospels;
   New Testament; Old Testament
birth. *See also* infants; prebirth
   experiences; rebirth
   death and, 6, 8, 10, 85, 86, 88, 89,
   91; earliest humans view of, 73, 85,
   86; hierarchies knowledge of, 91;
   mystery of, 89, 121, 122, 130;
   Mystery of Golgotha influence
   concerning, 88; physical body at,
   115; transformations of, 72
Bodhisattva, 87
brains, 63, 66, 68, 74, 91, 92, 103, 134
breath, 11, 64, 65, 69. *See also*
   respiration
breathing, 40–45, 50, 63, 67. *See also*
   exercises; yoga
Buddhists, 48, 49

catharsis, 56, 57
Catholic Church, 93, 145, 147
Charlemagne, 25
childhood, 32, 101
Christ. See also Jesus Christ; Mystery
   of Golgotha; resurrection
   appearance in physical world, 28;
   being descends as, 129, 132;
   coming of, 95; death of, 14, 76, 82,
   96, 120; on Earth, 25, 26;
   imbuement of, 50, 153, 154
   knowledge given to disciples by, 90,
   92, 93, 94, 152; light of, within
   people, 39; lost concept of, 150
   people's knowledge of, 48; sent to
   Earth by gods, 123; struggle of,
   against Ahriman, 77
Christ Event. See Mystery of Golgotha
Christ Being, 71, 150
Christianity. *See also* esoteric
   Christianity, appreciation of, 110;
   Cardinal Newman regarding, 134;
   in Central Europe, 25; in context of
   Roman civilization, 128, 132; early
   era of, 79, 120, 133; followers of,
   92, 119, 122, 129; inner, 82; new